INTERNATIONAL BIBLIOGRAPHY OF COMPARATIVE EDUCATION

*The Praeger Special Studies
Series in Comparative Education*

*Published in Cooperation with the Comparative
Education Center, State University of New York, Buffalo*

General Editor: **Philip G. Altbach**

With an Introductory Essay by:
  Gail P. Kelly and Philip G. Altbach

With the Assistance of:
  Tereffe Asrat
  Saraswati Balasubramaniam
  Robert Dischner
  Cindy Geer
  S. Gopinathan
  Y. G. M. Lulat
  Dennis Mbuyi
  Marcelle McVorran
  Chuka Okonkwo
  John Stephens

INTERNATIONAL BIBLIOGRAPHY OF COMPARATIVE EDUCATION

Philip G. Altbach,
Gail P. Kelly,
David H. Kelly

PRAEGER

PRAEGER SPECIAL STUDIES • PRAEGER SCIENTIFIC

191691

016.37
A 465

R

Library of Congress Cataloging in Publication Data

Altbach, Philip G.
  International bibliography of comparative education.

  (Praeger special studies series in comparative
education)
  Includes index.
  1. Comparative education--Bibliography. I. Title.
II. Series.
Z5814.C76A46   [LA132]   016.37019'5   81-962
ISBN 0-03-056881-1   AACR2

Published in 1981 by Praeger Publishers
CBS Educational and Professional Publishing
A Division of CBS, Inc.
521 Fifth Avenue, New York, New York 10175 U.S.A.

© 1981 by Praeger Publishers

123456789   145   987654321

Printed in the United States of America

The Praeger Special Studies Series in
Comparative Education
General Editor: **Philip G. Altbach**

ACKNOWLEDGMENTS

This volume is, in many ways, a collaborative effort of many scholars in the field of comparative education. We have relied on more than 60 colleagues who have supplied us with bibliographic materials, guidance, and suggestions. Those colleagues who specifically responded to our inquiries are listed below. We hope that this volume will be useful to them. We also relied on the help of a number of graduate students in the comparative education program in the Faculty of Educational Studies, State University of New York at Buffalo. Their names are listed on the title page of this book.

Major funding for the research was provided by the Exxon Educational Foundation. Additional funding for a preliminary bibliography was provided by the Graduate School, State University of New York at Buffalo. The Comparative Education Center, SUNY at Buffalo, assisted the project through the provision of a graduate assistant for much of the research period. This volume is published as part of the activities of the Comparative Education Center.

We are particularly indebted to Erwin Epstein, John van de Graaff, Lois Weis, Peter Seybolt, and Joseph DiBona, who were kind enough to comment on sections of our essay or on the bibliography. Eileen Raines, Chris Bogan, and Carol Breitenbach typed a very complex manuscript with skill and good humor.

The following individuals provided us with data during the course of our work on the bibliography: Don Adams, University of Pittsburgh; Chiam Adler, Hebrew University of Jerusalem, Israel; Orlando Albornoz, Universidad Central, Caracas, Venezuela; Robert Arnove, Indiana University; Ezri Atzmon, Jersey City State College; Chong Keun Bae, Dongguk University, South Korea; Munir Bashshur, American University of Beirut, Lebanon; Edward Beauchamp, University of Hawaii; George Z. F. Bereday, Teacher's College, Columbia University; Edward Berman, University of Louisville; Raymond Boudin, University of Paris, France; William Brickman, University of Pennsylvania; Martin Carnoy, Stanford University; Ngoni Chedeya, University of Zimbabwe; Robert Cowen, Institute of Education, University of London; Richard Cummings, University of Wisconsin-Milwaukee; John Davies, University of Canterbury, New Zealand; Joseph DiBona, Duke University; Thomas Eisemon, McGill University; Mechthild Engert, Max Planck Institut für Bildungsforschung, West Berlin; Erwin Epstein, University of Missouri-Rolla; Joseph Farrell, Ontario Institute for Studies in Education; Douglas Foley, University of Texas at Austin; John Georgeoff, Purdue University; Dietrich Goldschmidt, Max Planck Institut für Bildungsforschung, West Berlin; S. Gopinathan, Institute of Education, Singapore; Nigel Grant, University of Glasgow; Ann Hamori, World Council of Comparative Education Societies; Grant Harman, University of Melbourne, Australia; John Hawkins, University of California at Los Angeles; Alf Heggoy, University of Georgia; Torsten Husén,

University of Stockholm, Sweden; Edmund King, King's College, University of London; Kazayuki Kitamura, Hiroshima University, Japan; Robert Klitgaard, Harvard University; Erich Leitner, Universität für Bildungswissenschaften, Klagenfurt, Austria; Vandra Masemann, University of Toronto; Noel McGinn, Harvard University; Kathleen Howard Merriam, Bowling Green State University; D. G. Mulcahy, University College, Cork, Ireland; Harold Noah, Teachers College, Columbia University; Veronica S. Pantelidis, Greenville, North Carolina; Rolland Paulston, University of Pittsburgh; R. F. Price, LaTrobe University, Australia; Peggy Sabatier, Sacramento, California; Bikas Sanyal, International Institute for Educational Planning, Paris; Hans Dieter Schaefer, Humboldt University, East Berlin; Michael Schatzberg, Virginia Polytechnic Institute and State University; James R. Sheffield, Teachers College, Columbia University; James Shields, Jr., City College of the City University of New York; Nobuo Shimahara, Rutgers University; Susan Shirk, University of California at San Diego; Mobin Shorish, University of Illinois-Urbana Champaign; Robert Stamp, University of Calgary, Alberta, Canada; Beatrice Szekely, Ithaca, New York; R. Murray Thomas, University of California at Santa Barbara; H. van Daele, Comparative Education Society in Europe; John van de Graaff, Yale University; Bea Lin Wang, Wheaton College; Francis H. K. Wong, University of Sydney, Australia; Lois Weis, State University of New York at Buffalo; Dorothy Woodson, State University of New York at Buffalo; Mathew Zachariah, University of Calgary.

INTRODUCTION

This volume has two basic aims: to provide a highly selective initial source of bibliographical information concerning the countries of the world, and to present a more comprehensive bibliography on the field of comparative education. There is a need for more systematic information in the field of comparative education and this bibliography is an effort to provide a basic tool. While bibliographies of varying usefulness exist for many countries and regions, and the work of agencies like UNESCO and OECD have helped to provide an accessible data base for material about education, there is as yet no general bibliographic source for the field. We are also including an essay that provides a general introduction to comparative education and its literature. The essay is not intended as an evaluation of what is by now a fairly extensive literature, but is rather an overview of a field of study that has emerged in the past 20 years. We do not attempt a formal definition of the field, and include a broad range of educational phenomena as part of comparative education. We consider not only studies of educational systems of individual nations but also such new developments as nonformal education and distance learning. Cross-cultural studies of educational issues are, of course, a key part of the literature of the field. We have not considered the United States specifically in the bibliography since the literature on education is so vast.

Comparative education is a difficult field to cover adequately in a selective bibliography or essay. It has many national origins and encompasses research on education in many languages and styles. This volume is intended as a contribution to the development of a field of study. It supplements the efforts in recent years of key journals—the *Comparative Education Review*,[1] *Comparative Education*,[2] and the *International Review of Education*[3] —to survey the field.

The Essay.   The essay that follows this introduction covers the definition of the field of comparative education, its historical development and current status, and some of the key issues that have been of importance to scholars. It reflects to some degree the scope of the literature, which without question deserves codification. This volume, with its extensive bibliographies, attempts to provide a sense of the field that has emerged.

The Bibliographies.   A published bibliography, by definition, is out of date as soon as it is set in type. Furthermore, while comparative education has emerged as an identifiable field of study in recent years, the body of literature is by now too large to include in one volume. The field is international and material has appeared in many languages all over the world, making the problem of retrieval of such a scattered literature quite serious. As a result, our efforts in this book are necessarily incomplete. We stress material in English, in part because a large proportion of the literature has been published in English and the major journals in the field appear in that language, but also because our own resources did not permit a full-scale search for materials in other languages. We have tried to cover key literature in French, Spanish, and German to some degree, but have left out virtually all other languages. Furthermore, the bulk of the materials in this bibliography are from generally accessible sources, particularly from journals and books. We have excluded the very significant literature available in doctoral dissertations and theses because these are not readily available, particularly outside of the United States. We have also excluded most government documents and other more ephemeral publications. Our aim is to provide bibliographical sources that will be available to the researcher, to graduate students, and to policy makers. Our research strategy included a careful search of the relevant journals and books, coverage of appropriate bibliographical materials, and similar efforts. In addition, we relied on a large number of colleagues around the world to help us find materials and then to select what was considered to be most important.

Bibliography on Comparative Education. The first bibliographical section is an effort to provide a comprehensive guide to the literature on comparative education. We have tried to list all writings on comparative education as a field of study. We have omitted some materials that seemed of very limited relevance, but in general we have included a large proportion of the references we located. We have also included a more limited listing of materials from other social science disciplines that relate to the comparative study of education. Our basic concern here is with providing a benchmark in the study of comparative education. Again, our stress has been on material in English, but we have tried to provide a sampling of the more important material from other languages.

Selected National Bibliographies on Education. These bibliographies have a goal very different from that of the first section. We try here to provide a highly selective introductory series of listings on education in most of the world's nations, which is intended as a teaching and beginning research tool. It is a place to start for information about education and is by no means a complete guide to the literature. We have, in general, limited each country to 20 listings. For large countries on which there is a large body of literature we have been highly selective, and have, with the assistance of experts on the country, included mainly the recognized "classics" on education. We have, for such nations, included more than 20 references. For countries of the Third World and Eastern Europe, where the literature in Western languages is limited, we have included a substantial portion of the available literature. Thus, the selectivity differs according to the amount of material available to us. It is very important to keep in mind that these listings are intended as a beginning source, and we have included other bibliographies on education as a source of more detailed data.

Thus, this volume serves several different purposes. It is, overall, intended as a basic bibliographical source for the field of comparative education, which will be of use not only to the experienced scholar in the field but also to students and others seeking basic reference material. It is our hope that the bibliography will not only serve a field that has developed an impressive body of literature over the past 20 years, but also reflect our progress as an emerging interdisciplinary field of study.

Philip G. Altbach
Gail P. Kelly
David H. Kelly

NOTES

1. "The State of the Art," *Comparative Education Review* 21 (June and October 1977): 151-416.
2. "Comparative Education: Its Present State and Future Prospects," *Comparative Education* 13 (June 1977): 75-152.
3. "Contemporary Educational Theory: An Analysis and Assessment," *International Review of Education* 25, no. 2-3 (1979): 301-476.

CONTENTS

COMPARATIVE EDUCATION:
A FIELD IN TRANSITION

Gail P. Kelly and
Philip G. Altbach

Comparative education has developed as a field devoted broadly to the study of education in other countries. Excellent histories of comparative education are available, reflecting the scholarship and methodological debates.[1] This essay traces the development of comparative education over the past two decades. It highlights the methodological debates, the paradigms guiding research, and the type of knowledge that has been generated, and discusses the evolution of the field.

While comparative education has intellectual roots going back to the nineteenth century, it is new to academe. In university settings its legitimacy was established only after World War II. The field since that time, as this essay shows, has sought to delineate itself as a distinct area of inquiry with roots in educational studies but reaching beyond education for paradigms and methodological rigor. Unlike other fields such as history, sociology, economics, and psychology, whose subject matter and methodologies have been well defined, comparative education has been eclectic and has never developed one single, widely accepted method of inquiry; nor has it established a unitary body of knowledge. Rather, comparative education remains a field characterized by methodological debates and diversity of opinion as to what constitutes its subject matter and orientation.

Prior to the 1950s comparative education had a long tradition as an applied field that assisted in educational reform domestically and internationally. The demands of internal reform and of foreign policy—and the patterns of funding research to these ends—have unquestionably shaped the field. In the United States, patterns of funding as well as the dominant paradigms in the social sciences in the post-World War II period have been key factors. Modernization theory has undergirded much of the research, and comparative education has often been tied to foreign assistance programs and the intellectual and ideological orientations of the aid-giving agencies.[2] The American approach is by no means the only one. In Britain, for example, research focused on problems related to Britain's efforts to reform its own educational system. Distinct French

The authors are indebted to Lois Weis and Erwin Epstein for their detailed comments on an earlier draft of this essay.

and German orientations are also evident. Despite national differences in foreign and domestic policy interests, academic orientations, and other factors, however, the methodological orientations of Anglo-American scholars have tended to dominate the field.

This essay will sketch the development of comparative education over the past decades as well as posit several explanations of the reasons for the course the field has followed. The fact that a consensus over the parameters, method, and content of the field has yet to emerge should not be construed to imply that it has yet to achieve legitimacy. On the contrary, comparative education is well established in many countries. The continuing debates and the fluidity of the field—and its wide diversity—indicate a basic vitality as the field enters the 1980s.

THE CLIENTELE OF COMPARATIVE EDUCATION

Comparative education has a broad clientele that includes educational policy makers, administrators of international and domestic programs, officials of international agencies like UNESCO and the World Bank, and academicians both in educational studies and in the social sciences.

One of the significant accomplishments in the past 30 years has been the development of an institutional and intellectual community that supports comparative education, provides visibility, and helps to ensure its continuity. Indeed, comparative education has developed in a way similar to many of the now established social science disciplines. Beginning with a small group of scholars in a few countries, working largely on a national basis, the field has entrenched itself into several international agencies such as UNESCO, has developed national societies in nearly a dozen countries, and has spawned at least eight journals.[3] Several publishers, such as Praeger in the United States, Pergamon in Britain, and Elsevier in Holland, regularly publish books on comparative education. Academic departments and programs have built up specialties in the field and attract a significant number of students, mostly at the graduate level.

Particularly impressive has been the growth of journals in the field. The two oldest in the field, the *Comparative Education Review* (United States) and the *International Review of Education* (published in Hamburg, West Germany, for UNESCO) have a 25-year history. More recently, *Comparative Education* (Britain) has established itself as a key journal. *Compare*, the journal of the European Comparative Education Society, and the *European Journal of Education* (published in Paris for the Institute of Education of the European Cultural Foundation) have both entered the field more recently. The East German journal, *Vergleichende Pädagogik*, provides detailed coverage of the Socialist countries and is increasingly useful. *Canadian and International Education*, with a smaller circulation than the other journals, has established itself as a major publication.

Education Comparée, the publication of the French Comparative Education Society, appears infrequently. The *Newsletter* of the Comparative and International Education Society and the *Bulletin* of the World Council of Comparative Education Societies provide further information.

A number of journals dealing with national and regional education concerns have become important in comparative education. *Western European Education, Soviet Education,* and *Chinese Education,* all published by M. E. Sharpe in the United States, are translation journals and are valuable sources of data. *Slavic and European Education* focuses on Eastern Europe. The *West African Journal of Education*, the *Bulletin of the UNESCO Regional Office for Education in Asia*, the *Revista Latinoamericana de Educación*, and several other journals are also major periodicals in the field.

UNESCO's contributions to comparative education include not only the *International Review of Education* but also *Prospects*, a newer but highly informative publication issued in three languages. In addition, the publications of UNESCO, the International Institute of Educational Planning, the Institute of Education in Hamburg, and the International Bureau of Education in Geneva are all of major importance. Regional agencies, most notably the Council of Europe and the Organization for Economic Cooperation and Development, publish additional information and analysis.

These publications provide a constant flow of studies, interpretation, data, and reports on educational developments. The *Comparative Education Review*'s new bibliography is an ongoing guide to current periodical literature on comparative education. In addition to these journals specifically devoted to the field, relevant articles are regularly published in social science and area study journals. The development of these journals and publication sources in the past 30 years is an impressive accomplishment and one that helps to ensure the survival of the field in a period of general financial and other difficulties.

Comparative education has been dominated by English-language sources and to a considerable extent by scholars in the United States, Britain, and Canada. The major journals such as the *International Review of Education* and *Canadian and International Education*, which publish in more than one language, only occasionally print articles in languages other than English. There are a number of reasons for this. The domination of English reflects in part the international role of the English language in scholarship. It also is an artifact of the modern development of the field in North America and Britain and the fact that many of the Third World nations that have utilized comparative education in their development plans have been in the English-speaking orbit. Finally, most of the funding agencies have been located in the United States or Britain and have relied on English-speaking scholars. A limited exception to this trend has been the literature written in French and German by scholars in those linguistic orbits. As comparative education has grown to encompass scholars in other countries, books have appeared in other languages and journals have been established in such languages as Spanish, Japanese, Russian, and others, but despite these trends, the field remains dominated by English and will probably remain so for some time.

It is worthwhile to note some of the major centers of activity in comparative education in order to provide an indication of the scope of the field. While there have been some changes in the major centers of study in North America, with the domination of institutions like the University of Chicago, the University of Michigan, Stanford University, Teacher's College at Columbia University, the University of Wisconsin, and a few others challenged by newer institutions and programs—such as programs at the University of Pittsburgh, Florida State University, University of Illinois, UCLA, the University of Calgary, the State University of New York at Buffalo, and a few others—the field has remained fairly stable in the United States. The emergence of a major center at LaTrobe University in Australia is a new development. In addition, the Institut für Hochschulbildung at the Humboldt University in East Berlin has a large comparative education component and is responsible for *Vergleichende Pädagogik*, a new journal in the field. Concern with comparative education is evident at the University of Kyoto in Japan, the Jawaharlal Nehru University in India, the Universidad de Monterrey in Mexico, the University of Hamburg and the University of Kassel in West Germany, and at other institutions throughout the world. While it would be misleading to indicate that the field is developing very rapidly, it has nonetheless moved beyond its traditional base in North America and Britain.

In addition to these academic centers, a number of nonuniversity institutions exhibit major interest in comparative education and produce research, scholarship, and data. These institutions do not train students but are nevertheless of special importance to the field. The International Institute for Educational Planning in Paris sponsors a large number of publications of direct relevance for comparative education, and it has utilized scholars in the field for much of its work. The UNESCO Institute for Education in Hamburg, West Germany, sponsors research, and the International Bureau of Education in Geneva, Switzerland, issues valuable bibliographies and other publications. The World Bank has taken an active interest in education, and its publications are relevant to comparative educators. In Europe, the Organization for Economic Cooperation and Development and the Council of Europe have taken an active interest, as have national agencies in a number of countries. The Centro de Estudios Educativos in Mexico, the Max Planck Institute for Educational Research in West Germany, the National Institute for Educational Research in Japan, and the National Board of Universities and Colleges in Sweden have all supported comparative studies and publicized comparative research. While this listing is by no means complete, it will provide an indication of the kinds of agencies that help to produce and disseminate information, that employ comparative educators, and that participate in the intellectual community of the field.

Comparative education depends on several constituencies for its long-term survival and has served these groups in the past. In the United States the most numerous group of comparative educators are found in colleges and universities, largely in schools and colleges of education. A small proportion of these individuals are full-time specialists, teaching graduate-level courses. A larger group teaches comparative education on a part-time basis and is involved in other aspects of teaching and research in the field of education. A small group of scholars in the social sciences has also taken an interest in comparative education.

The constituency of students is also important. Most crucial for the development of the field are the small number of graduate students at about 30 universities in the United States, Canada, and Britain, who specialize in comparative education as a doctoral field. These individuals constitute the next generation of scholars in the field. They are also major consumers of knowledge, purchasing textbooks and specialized studies and subscribing to journals. With the decline in the market for Ph.Ds in the field in recent years, there are fewer advanced-level students, causing problems for established graduate programs. Increasingly, the doctoral-level academic programs have been serving students with more practical interests, including many overseas students who will return to nonacademic positions. These factors pose long-term challenges.

Comparative education also serves educational planners, policy makers, and others involved with the practical aspects of educational policy making. Much of the data base in the field has been developed with the practical interests of such groups in mind. As indicated earlier, comparative education has been a means of providing information on alternatives for planning aspects of educational systems, for educational reform, and has served as a benchmark to compare the effectiveness of educational practice. The community of planners and administrators who utilize comparative knowledge is in ministries of education, international agencies, aid organizations, and to some extent in school systems. While relatively few of these individuals are producers of comparative knowledge, they are nevertheless quite important in utilizing research, sponsoring studies, and determining the shape of the field through their funding of research.

A final constituency is more difficult to identify. This is the broader community, based mainly in universities, of individuals who may from time to time utilize material in comparative education or who may occasionally participate in the field. For example, many social scientists during the 1960s were interested in the phenomenon of student political activism, and a few undertook research on its comparative aspects or used knowledge on this topic.[4] Their participation in comparative education was limited to that topic and their involvement ended with the completion of their research. Similarly, specialists in such areas as educational psychology or curriculum may from time to time take an interest in comparative insights as a part of their own work. While this fairly large group of individuals contributes little to the overall development of the field, it is nevertheless important.

The intellectual community of the field can be seen in concentric circles in terms of involvement and contributions. At the center are full-time scholars and researchers in universities and in agencies like the World Bank or UNESCO, who contribute most directly to the knowledge base of the field. This group generally expresses itself in English and is located in English-speaking nations. These individuals are responsible for the university-based training programs and tend to be most active in the national and international organizations in the field. A second circle of participants includes scholars and researchers in education and to some extent in the social sciences, who utilize research in comparative education. These individuals are found in universities as well as in government ministries and international agencies. They are crucial to the field not only because they provide funding for research and training programs, but because they utilize the research that is provided. A final peripheral constituency for comparative education is a wider circle of researchers and scholars who make occasional use of data. This group is helpful to the field in that it provides wider visibility and ensures that the journals and books are used and therefore of relevance to academic libraries and institutions.

DISCIPLINARY AND METHODOLOGICAL ORIENTATIONS

From the foregoing discussion of the development and current status of comparative education, it is possible to move to a consideration of the intellectual and methodological orientations of the field. It is, in a sense, ironic that at the time the field won international legitimacy in universities, and in planning and other agencies, it has been plunged into a series of intellectual crises that have not been fully resolved. These crises have centered on the definition and parameters of the field. The situation can be summed up in a single question: What is comparative education?

Before the 1960s scholars had little difficulty in answering this question, for the response seemed self-evident: to compare national systems of education for a multitude of purposes—for international understanding, educational improvement, or reform, either in one's own country or abroad, and/or for explanation of national variance. It was a definition based on method rather than on the content of study.

The debates to the mid-1960s centered on the proper method for comparison and essentially begged the issue of the content of study. Isaac Kandel, for example, saw comparison necessarily based on underlying forces and factors shaping educational systems and dwelt at length on the construct of national character as well as concrete realities of school organization, curriculum, administration, finance, and the like. Nicholas Hans, departing from Kandel's historicism, defined the field in terms of tracing the ways in which education functioned to maintain the state, urging comparison of national school systems, despite varying historical and cultural antecedents. Hans himself attempted comparison more than did Kandel, for Kandel in his book *Comparative Education* organized his chapters as primary, secondary, and teacher education, but in reality provided lengthy descriptions of each nation's schools; he rarely compared them.[5]

Hans, while using many of Kandel's analytic categories, focused less on descriptions of school systems and more on how, regardless of the variation in historical forces and factors and the ways in which schools were organized, schools everywhere contributed to cultural continuity and the maintenance of the nation-state.[6] With Hans, functional analysis of school/society relations became established in the field.

The 1960s witnessed a major rethinking of comparative education. The field had previously simply borrowed methodologies from the social sciences for specific research endeavors and did not, in general, try to build up a self-conscious methodology of its own. A number of scholars, such as Andreas Kazamias,[7] and particularly Harold Noah and Max Eckstein in their important volume, *Toward a Science of Comparative Education,*[8] began to question the data base of the field and to argue for the establishment of articulate set of norms on which to base research. They argued that much of the previous research was based on fragmentary data, on eye-witness accounts, and that studies could not be replicated. Little care had been taken, they maintained, to develop common categories for data collection or for analysis. The thrust of these arguments was that comparative education had to move beyond both its impressionistic past and its more recent reliance on the paradigms of the established social sciences. It was time to build a self-conscious discipline.

In the 1960s, in short, scholars began to demand a science of comparative education. It was not only academics working in American universities who did so. British scholars such as Brian Holmes, for example, tried to provide a systematic basis for comparison in this work, *The Problem Approach to Comparative Education.*[9] He, like Edmund King,[10] was perhaps not overtly critical of past scholarship. Nonetheless, both attempted to develop systematic scientific bases for the field. Like many American colleagues, Holmes was heavily influenced by Karl Popper in his work. These scholars demanded objectivity, the development of solid categories for comparison, rigorous methods of data collection, stringent analyses, and replicable results.

The field was united only in the matter of attempting to develop new and more rigorous methodologies. This search raised new debates centered on five sets of questions. First, is there one methodology of comparative education that defines the field, or is the field one that is definable solely through the content of study? Second, if the field is definable by the content of study, then what should that content consist of? Should the field persist in the Sadlerian tradition of assuming that "things outside the school are more important than things within the school" and focus solely on school/society relationships? Or should it be more concerned with within-school phenomena such as educational administration, learning efficiency, and instructional methods? Third, if the field is to focus solely on school/society relationships, how can it be differentiated from sister disciplines that study similar phenomena both within and outside schools, institutes, and faculties of education? Is comparative education really a distinct field of inquiry? Related to these questions, what in school/society relations constitutes the proper study of the field? Can one framework or methodology be developed for studying these phenomena? Fourth, if comparative education were to focus on school phenomena divorced from social contexts, then how could the field be distinguished from educational psychology, educational administration, curriculum and instruction, and so on? Even if the field defines itself in terms of the academic discipline of education, the issue of identity still arises, as does that of method. Finally, does the field, if there is one, have a distinct contribution to make to the scholarly community, to policy formation and implementation, and to teacher education?

These five sets of questions are related. In addition, they are all facets of an identity crisis that derived in large measure from a critical evaluation of earlier research. The methodological debates will be discussed in some detail, as well as the issue of method versus content as the defining characteristic of comparative education. It should be clear, at the outset, that these debates did not develop abstractly, but rather arose from the kinds of scholarship that were carried out in the 1960s and 1970s concerning educational issues throughout the world. The methodological debate will be considered divorced from the empirical studies, although it is recognized, and will be shown later in this essay how empirical research gave rise to many of the methodological controversies.

COMPARATIVE EDUCATION:
A METHOD OR A CONTENT?

The 1960s was a decade in which several alternative methodologies for the field were put forth in an attempt to delineate it. Noah and Eckstein's *Toward a Science of Comparative Education,*[11] George Bereday's *Comparative Method in Education,*[12] Holmes's *Problems in Education: A Comparative Approach,*[13] and King's *Comparative Studies and Educational Decision Making*[14] all broke from past scholarship in the sense that they focused almost exclusively on the methodology of conducting research. The attempt to define the field by method rather than by content unifies these works; the methodologies posed, however, differ—in some cases radically—as do their focus and purpose.

Bereday's *Comparative Method in Education*, one of the earlier attempts to define the field by method, while begging the issue of content, was a plea for systematic data collection and comparison. He also attempted to blend emerging area studies with the field; he urged scholars to be well grounded in the languages and in the cultural, social, and historical backgrounds of the nations whose education they were seeking to compare.

The methodology Bereday devised consisted of systematic collection of precise, similar data from each nation studied; systematization of data; careful juxtaposition; generation of hypotheses from the data; and finally comparison, which could be either "illustrative" or "balanced." The examples Bereday used in his book implied that the phenomena to be compared were those concerning school/society relationships; he provided no examples of within-school phenomena. Far clearer was Bereday's definition of the field by its methods—which were comparative. Those methods could be either quantitative or qualitative. Both, as far as he was concerned, were scientific and rigorous. Bereday also saw the prime purpose of the field as theory construction about school/society relations. Once this was done, its contribution to educational policy, educational innovations, borrowing, and decision making would become self-evident.

This view was shared by Noah and Eckstein, who saw the field as identifying laws governing the relation between schools and society. Unlike Bereday, however, they had little tolerance for qualitative research. Science for them implied testable hypotheses bolstered by quantitative data. They also departed from Bereday in other ways; they believed hypothesis formation should precede data collection, not be a consequence of it. Bereday's concern for area studies and linguistic proficiency and knowledge of cultural and historical background were not shared by them; rather, they believed quantification would essentially control their impact.

In the United States in the 1960s many comparativists were concerned with systematizing scholarship in the field and developing a science that would yield laws and make prediction possible. For the most part, American scholars focused on the social, economic, and political outcomes of schooling, and were relatively unconcerned with the internal workings of the school or the details of educational decision making. British scholars, in attempting to define the field, departed from their American peers in several respects. They, like scholars in the United States, sought to delineate the field by developing a comparative method. But they were skeptical of American claims that through comparison one would identify laws governing school/society relations and develop an exact science of prediction. Their claims were more modest.

Holmes's *Problems in Education: A Comparative Approach*, published in mid-decade, envisioned the field as eminently practical in nature, providing the basis for solutions to educational problems, internal both to school functioning and the relation of school to society. For him comparative education exists to reform schools; Holmes basically spells out a means for finding possible solutions for a problem that has been identified, and predicting the greatest likelihood, given cultural, political, social, and school-related constraints, of a particular reform bringing about desired results. Holmes's work systematizes borrowing; the analytic framework he employs does not begin with the nation-state, or the society, but rather with the identification of an educational problem within a given school system and national context. He also attempts to develop a means for distinguishing those things that are imbedded within a national context, those that are unchangeable (or immutable), and those that can be changed under given conditions.

King, while not sharing Holmes's approach, also defined the field as practical and school-oriented in nature, as an aid to decision making and policy formation. Like Holmes, he was skeptical about the possibilities of developing an exact science that would allow prediction. Rather, comparative education could be defined as the systematic collection of data about educational systems and their contexts, and nothing more. This would allow policy makers to make informed decisions about school reform.

Not all scholars accepted a definition of the field by its method. Rather, some argued that this was folly, for comparative education was intrinsically a multidisciplinary undertaking that focused on school/society relations from varying perspectives. No one method was appropriate for such a task. C. Arnold Anderson was one of the major proponents of this position.[15] He saw the field as studying both within- and out-of-school phenomena, focusing on the complex patterns of interrelations between instructional and social outcomes of schooling. The goal, he stated, was to build theories of school/society relations. Like Bereday, he believed that once these theories were developed and tested, general laws governing school/society relations could be established that would provide a basis for policy and reform. The field, thus, could be defined in terms of its content—school/society relations—which could be studied using methodologies derived from the social sciences—economics, political science, sociology, anthropology, and history. No one method could encompass the field or define it. In addition, work in comparative education did not necessarily have to be comparative; rather, in-depth studies of educational phenomena within a country were useful to identify school/society relations, which then could be verified through testing in other national contexts.

Anderson departed from previous scholars in other significant ways. The nation-state, even national school systems, were not the prime analytic unit as they had been for Kandel, King, Hans, and others; rather, analysis centered on specific school/society relations—the relation of the school system to national systems of social stratification or to specific types of economic growth. The stress was on relating elements of schooling to aspects of social and economic life, and not the totality of the school system to all parts of a nation's life.

While Anderson perhaps articulated this viewpoint most clearly, he was not the only one to subscribe to it. It is surprising that of all the writings on the methodology of comparative education and attempted definitions of the field, there are relatively few articles and books articulating this perspective, and yet most of the scholarship produced in comparative education and published in the major journals in the field tacitly accepts this perspective.[17]

The clearest admission that it has become the mainstream of the field in the United States is the retrospective "State of the Art" issue of the *Comparative Education Review* published in 1977.[16] Much of the volume was organized around disciplinary perspectives used in the field. Articles were entitled "Anthropology and Comparative Education," "Comparative Education and Economics: When Will the Two Meet?" and the like. One contribution analyzed research according to the social science methodology employed. The "State of the Art" issue also reviewed the knowledge gained in specific school/society relations—in social stratification, ethnicity, development, the correlates of student achievement, political socialization, and so forth.

The special issue of the *Comparative Education Review* was not an aberration; rather, it accurately reflected the direction the field had taken in the United States since the 1960s. These trends have included the abandonment of cross-national comparison as the defining parameter of the field, as well as the search for a single methodology of study. As of the late 1970s, content—the study of schooling and its outcomes and their relationship to society—was the thread that held the field together. In the United States the orientation was to build general laws, recognizing that only one method would not suffice.

The "State of the Art" issue also reflected another orientation that had emerged clearly in the 1960s, but that had always existed in the field. The content of comparative education was traditionally defined as the study of school/society relations, with stress on the noncognitive outcomes of schooling. Most North American scholars treated instructional practices and the knowledge transmitted in the classroom as seemingly irrelevant. The school was, for all intents and purposes, treated as the proverbial "black box" and scholars concentrated on outcomes that, with the exception of the International Study of Educational Achievement, were not educational in the narrow sense, but rather societal. This meant that the field increasingly divorced itself from the concerns of educational faculties and teacher trainers. It became somewhat isolated within schools of education or shifted entirely to social science departments.

Professional scholars were well aware of these trends, for in the 1960s a substantial literature was published in an attempt to convince scholars in comparative education and in other specialties of education that the field had relevance. There were articles that argued that comparative education had a distinct role in teacher education, in educational psychology, in school administration, and in curriculum planning. This concern was also articulated in Kazamias's article published in 1972, "Comparative Pedagogy," but in a different way.[18] He argued that few claims could be made about the impact of schools on the outcomes of schooling without attention to what occurs in the classroom. His was a plea that the field take as its starting point the school and not the society, and that the field define itself more in terms of studying education in its fullest sense rather than just focus on the inputs and outcomes of the school system as it affects society.

In contrast to the mainstream of scholarship in North America during much of the 1960s and early 1970s, which stressed school/society relations and the effort to develop scientific laws to govern the field, British scholarship continued in a more traditional vein. British academics such as Holmes and King were skeptical about the development of a science of comparative education, although they were interested in more systematic modes of research. They stressed the importance of improving the means of data collection in order to provide a better base for determining educational policy. Many of the graduates of the influential comparative education program at the Institute of Education at the University of London reflect this approach.

If there is anything Holmes and King (in addition to being in the forefront of the field in Great Britain) have in common, it is an orientation toward comparative education as an instrument of school reform in Britain. Their work has focused less on school/society relations than on specific reforms in the school system of their own country. Because of this, the scholarship produced in Great Britain over the past two decades has been more action-oriented than directed at building a theory of school/society relationships. It has tended to treat issues like curriculum design, school organization, student achievement, learning theory, and teacher education more than have scholars of comparative education in the United States. Like the field elsewhere, however, the British have abandoned the quest for one method to define the field, but unlike American scholars have taken education quite seriously as to its content—borrowing methods as much from the disciplines within education as from the social sciences.

This trend probably is best exemplified by the special tenth anniversary issue of the British journal *Comparative Education*, published[19] in the same year the U.S.-based *Comparative Education Review* published its own "State of the Art" issue. *Comparative Education* did not organize the field according to social sciences disciplines, nor did it focus on issues like political socialization or development. Rather, it chose to look at comparative education's contribution to school organization, curricular reform, and the like. Most of the articles, like those published in regular issues of the journal, were less oriented to theory construction and more to the diffusion of knowledge about schools outside of Britain.

NEW APPROACHES

While the methodological debates in comparative education have led the field away from definitions according to a single methodology and to a reconsideration of the content of the field, new debates concerning the scope and analytic categories of scholarship have emerged since the mid-1970s. A number of factors have contributed to new orientations. The dominant structural-functional theoretical approach of sociology in North America has been questioned and alternative theoretical modes, such as conflict theory, Marxism, and others, have been recognized as legitimate forms of inquiry. In this respect North American social science has moved closer to its Western European counterparts. Within the field of educational studies, the concept of the "hidden curriculum" and other approaches have had an impact on comparative education.[20] Finally, the modernization paradigm, discussed later in this essay, has been questioned. As a result of this ferment, comparative education is in the process of developing new approaches to understanding educational realities. At present, this new scholarship is in a constructive tension with more traditional orientations to the field, making for a lively, if sometimes confusing, debate. It is fair to say that comparative education is just as far from a consensus as it ever was. This section will highlight some recent analytic trends in the field. It is by no means complete, but will provide an indication of current developments.

Expansion of schooling has been one of the major trends of the past 30 years in almost every nation. John Meyer and Michael T. Hannan have examined the causes and consequences of this expansion in their work on the "world educational revolution."[21] Concepts such as neocolonialism, world-systems analysis, dependency theory, and others have been applied directly to education in order to argue that educational systems are directly affected by international currents. Another trend in the field is the application of qualitative analysis to educational issues in an effort to relate the detail of classroom practice, curriculum development, and the like to broader questions of educational policy and development. Anthropologists and others have become involved in this general direction.[22]

Philip G. Altbach and others have argued that neocolonialism plays a key role in the educational development of the Third World and that education is linked to an international system of dependency that leaves Third World nations at a disadvantage.[23] The situation is in part due to the direct policies of the industrialized nations, but also to the peripherality of the Third World in terms of this international system. Matthew Zachariah has articulated these basic concepts and applied them directly to comparative education.[24] Arnove, taking Wallerstein's world-systems theory as his starting point, further argues that educational systems are part of a world system of inequality in which the industrialized nations dominate.[25]

A number of scholars, particularly in Latin America, have argued that the international structure of capitalism has placed the Third World in a situation of dependency and that this affects all aspects of society, including education. These various modes of analysis have a number of common threads. They assume that educational policy and practice are determined by forces beyond the nation-state, that Third World educational realities are shaped in part by the heritage of colonialism, in part by the impact of neocolonial policies, and in part by the inevitable relations between central and peripheral world forces. These trends of analysis, as applied specifically to education, are in their early stages of data collection, so the body of empirical literature is not as yet very large.

Another challenge to the nation-state as the primary context of study has been from two directions, both of which are microanalytical. One urges regional, local analysis, arguing that variation in educational practices and school/society relations is greater within nation-states than between nation-states. The other takes the position that school/society relations and instructional practices cannot be understood solely on the basis of outcomes of schooling or analysis of policy. Rather, study should focus on the internal dynamics of the school as they relate to social organization. In this case, individual classrooms, social structures, and transactions between them become the basic ingredients of comparative research.[26]

In brief, the new methodological perspectives in comparative education have rejected national school systems or the relations between school and the nation as the basic framework for study. World-systems analysis proposes study of how international power relations affect educational processes and outcomes; some micro perspectives also reject national entities as the significant framework for study, while others propose a merger of macro and micro orientations.

While much space has been devoted to the methodological and analytic trends in comparative education over the past 20 years, the mass of scholarship in the field does not dwell on methodology, or on definitions of the field, or on analytic perspectives. Rather, as the bibliography that follows shows, while many have speculated on the nature of the field, its method and content, most scholarship in comparative education has simply been devoted to studying education in its fullest sense, both inside and outside institutions called schools, either in comparative or one-nation perspective. The bibliography understates the number of empirical studies, for the lists are selective; an attempt has been made, on the other hand, to provide a comprehensive listing of the literature on the history, rationale, method, and contribution of the field.

Comparative education over time has subdivided into specialties according to either area studies or social science disciplines. The topics studied have been diverse, and reflect in large measure concerns of national governments either in reforming their own school systems or in pursuing their foreign policy. In some respects, also, many of the empirical studies undertaken in comparative education are in response to social movements in individual scholars' own countries. These shifts in emphasis over time will be discussed in the pages that follow. It also should be noted that the actual kinds of studies scholars engaged in have affected the debates about the methodology of the field. For example, studies of neocolonialism and education and of Third World educational systems often led to formulation of the world-systems analysis perspective; similarly, the studies of the school's role in social stratification and ethnic- and gender-based inequalities were key factors in developing the micro-analytic perspectives of the late 1970s. Methodological debates do not exist in a vacuum, but rather are self-conscious reflections derived from empirical work carried out in the field.

MODERNIZATION: THE DOMINANT FRAMEWORK FOR RESEARCH

Without question, the major theoretical paradigm informing research in comparative education during the 1960s and 1970s has been that of modernization. While the modernization paradigm has been particularly influential in studying education in the Third World, it has also affected research on Western schools. The modernization framework has the advantage of being applicable to research using a range of social science disciplines, such as history, economics, sociology, and anthropology. It is, in a sense, a means of unifying a range of approaches to the field. Moreover, the paradigm coincided with the concerns of the international and national assistance agencies, which were interested in developing stable educational institutions to contribute to the gradual social and economic evolution of the Third World. Modernization as a theory to guide research also satisfied the desire for an overarching orientation to the study of school/society relations. The use of modernization theory heralded an era of educational "lending," rather than "borrowing," in comparative education.

In disciplines like sociology, political science, and economics, specialties in development or modernization arose that sought to define the processes and develop ways of measuring whether development was occurring. Most believed—like T. W. Schultz (an economist), Edward Shils (a sociologist), S. N. Eisenstadt (a sociologist), and Cyril Black (a historian)—that education contributed to modernization.[27]

Scholars in comparative education by the mid-1960s began to devote much energy to research on the relation of education to development. Much of that research sought to determine what levels of education should be expanded and what types of education maximized education's contribution.[28] Many of these works were correlational in nature, and had conflicting findings. The literature viewed education as an individual and/or social investment that would, in the long run, yield returns higher than investments in heavy industry or roads.[29] It computed either the increments in individual earnings as a result of schooling or increases in the GNP that coexisted with the expansion of education. Comparisons were cross-temporal—comparing GNP and educational stocks or levels in one country at one time in the past with those of another time—or cross-national, where the goal was to determine whether countries having the highest GNP or highest rates of increases in GNP also had greater diffusion of schooling at various levels. Industrialized countries were compared with nonindustrialized countries, and nonindustrialized nations with varying levels of GNP per capita and educational levels were compared with one another. Many studies were not comparative; rather, they tended to focus on individual countries, mostly in Africa, Asia, and Latin America, and to a lesser extent the Soviet Union, Britain, and Japan.

The field moved rapidly from a focus on modernization as a whole to a focus on social, attitudinal, political, or economic modernization and their relation to education, paralleling developments in the social science disciplines.[30] By the late 1960s, disillusionment with education as a key ingredient in modernization pervaded the literature. National governments and international agencies had based policy on early correlational studies and had allocated resources to expanding schools at every level. Yet economic and social indicators showed that such allocations had not had the desired results, and that increases in education seemed related mostly to increases in political instability and social unrest, often to economic regression.[31]

In comparative education two trends emerged. One was to rethink the relationship, as did Aran, Adler, and Eisenstadt, as well as Adams, Foster, and a host of other scholars.[32] They argued that education's contribution was neither unidimensional nor one that derived from simple diffusion of any kind of schooling. In addition, they maintained that education, not formal schooling, might have a strong relation to development. This line of thinking generated a host of studies on vocational education, "basic needs education," and nonformal educational programs not necessarily tied to literacy skills, aimed at rural and educationally disadvantaged populations like women. In the early 1970s nonformal education became a major research focus in comparative education.[33]

A second trend was a rejection of modernization as it was developed in the earlier literature and also, in some cases, the educational models associated with it. Scholars, many using a Marxian framework of analysis, developed critiques of the modernization paradigm and began to look for other explanatory variables. Many of these critiques argued that it is necessary to look beyond the national framework to understand educational realities in the Third World. Dependency theory, world-systems analysis, and similar approaches exemplify this approach.[34]

The domination of the modernization paradigm in research in comparative education is not apparent in the way this bibliography has been organized. The section on modernization is fairly small. Close to half of all research conducted in the field, however, uses modernization theory as a framework. This becomes apparent when one considers the large number of studies listed in this bibliography on African, Asian, and Latin American nations and much of the work on Japan, the USSR, and Britain. In addition, many of the studies written in the 1960s and early 1970s on the politics of education, students, elites, nonformal education, economics of education, and the like depend on modernization theory. If one were to look at the field in terms of the underlying theoretical framework employed in research, one would without question find that much of the scholarship generated in the past two decades relies on the framework of modernization, regardless of the country or topical focus of each individual study.

After 1975 modernization, at least as an overt framework for scholarly work in the field, had come under criticism for a variety of reasons. Within the social science disciplines that had, especially in the United States, become the major referent for comparative education, criticism of the theory had become quite harsh. This was particularly the case in sociology and political science, where Dean Tibbs, among others, argued that basic work within established disciplines, along traditional lines—for example, growth economics, political theory, and so on—would yield more information than that based on an over-arching, and what he called "ideologically biased" construct like moderniza-tion.[35] In addition, research funds for such studies had dried up. Scholarship that had been generated had led to mixed results on the role of education, and policy that had been predicated on one or another set of findings simply had failed to yield the desired results. Economic constraints and new sets of priori-ties for foreign policy removed the stimulus for research of this sort.

In comparative education this fomented a crisis, which was discussed in part earlier in this essay and which involved redefining the scope of the field and its potential contribution. The field in the United States, which had stressed its identification with disciplines outside of education and its reliance on moderni-zation-based studies, sought its roots in education. More attention began to be paid to educational problems within the national framework, and comparativists were asked to enlighten national policy makers on solutions to domestic prob-lems. In the Third World context, questions were raised about the utility of formal schooling, the ties between the educational system and the class structure, and similar issues.

THE IMPACT OF THE MODERNIZATION PARADIGM ON THE KNOWLEDGE BASE IN COMPARATIVE EDUCATION

The preoccupation with modernization studies in the 1960s and early 1970s had significance in terms of the knowledge accumulated during the decade and a half. It resulted in a severe imbalance in what was known about education in various parts of the world. Research on English-speaking East and West Africa, major recipients of U.S. and British foreign aid, proliferated; yet little research was conducted on central African nations and nations that had been former French colonies—Senegal, Dahomey, Togo—or the Cameroons or South Africa. In Asia, studies of Indian education abounded, but there were relatively few on Burma, Indonesia, or Thailand. In Latin America, similar imbalances occurred.

While modernization studies led to the uneven development of knowledge within the Third World, it also led to a relative neglect of studies on West Euro-pean school systems. More research was conducted by scholars in comparative education on Nigeria than on France, Spain, or Italy, despite the fact that education in those countries was rapidly expanding and changing. It is true that in these Western European countries educational scholars generated much research, but that research was not placed in the context of comparative studies or incorporated into the field. Similarly, while the studies of East European educational systems flourished when Sputnik sent shock waves through the West, they were eclipsed and declined in the late 1960s and early 1970s, with the rise of modernization studies focusing on the Third World.

The dominance of modernization also meant that the knowledge gained about schools in nations that received scholarly attention was limited. The focus of research was solely on social and economic outcomes of education; it was not on what was taught and learned in schools. Thus, very little hard data were generated about educational achievement in the Third World, school curriculum and its impact, teaching methods, or classroom interaction. Rather, the knowledge gained focused solely on whether those schooled were employed, made more money than those with lesser amounts of education, represented new strata within the society, had attitudes supportive of modernization, had been socialized to accept emergent nation-states, whether the school system had modern attributes, or whether increases in education were functional or dysfunctional to modernization.

No systematic knowledge was developed about what was taught in classrooms or learned by students, nor was there any full understanding of the uses individuals made of education. Finally, research, while it acknowledged regional and ethnic variation, generally ignored that of gender. That was partly because modernization theory had assumed that schooling could and would function in a given way and that way could best be ascertained by studying those schooled, not by studying educational processes. Additionally, since the theory devolved on national entities, seen holistically, divisiveness borne of class, gender, or ethnicity was underemphasized. Ironically, it was those most involved in area studies, impelled by studies based on the modernization framework, who began to investigate ethnic and regional disparities.

While the modernization framework dominated comparative education in the mid-1960s and early 1970s and shaped the knowledge generated by the field, it would be a mistake to assume that it was the only genre of research. As this bibliography demonstrates, while the bulk of scholarly work followed the modernization framework, other types of research were carried out, reflecting less the foreign-policy-related concerns of the industrialized countries and more the concerns of those striving to reform both schools and society in their own countries. The research so generated was a smaller but significant part of the field and in some ways represented an attempt to make comparative education relevant in a way that would depend less on government priorities and policies.

ACTION RESEARCH

A strong element in comparative education has always been borrowing (as opposed to lending, which the period of the domination of the modernization paradigm represented). As Noah and Eckstein's succinct history of the field pointed out, Horace Mann was an early comparative educator—he studied the Prussian school system, not to improve Prussian schools but to improve the schools of Massachusetts over which he had some control.[36] His interest was educational efficiency, pure and simple. If Mann and others like him are to be criticized, it is on the grounds of lack of a systematic basis for deciding what could and could not be transplanted from one educational system to another. Few have questioned the spirit of his endeavor.

In the 1960s the field saw the first systematic, cross-national efforts to assess the efficiency of educational systems on cognitive outcomes, notably the International Educational Attainment Studies (IEA).[37] The IEA undertook to identify what national school systems taught certain subject matter best, in the hope of generating data that would provide the basis for pedagogical reforms. The studies were sponsored by national governments and generated a wealth of knowledge about student achievement in mathematics, science, foreign languages, reading, and civics education, and the relation of school, teacher, and student background characteristics to them. This information allowed assessments of learning efficacy of national school systems and showed to some extent that in different countries student social class predicted cognitive outcomes less strongly than would have been expected.

The IEA studies had limitations that derived from their reliance on quantifiable inputs to schooling as well as measurement through standardized tests. Another limitation arose from the fact that initial participants were confined to highly industrialized nations of Western Europe and to North America, Israel, Japan, Australia, and New Zealand. In some studies, several Third World countries participated—Thailand, India, and Chile. Few Eastern European countries provided data. Because of this, the studies could not relate levels of achievement to variations in economic development or in political systems. As Inkeles has pointed out, however, the data produced by IEA, despite their limitations, provide a basis for generating hypotheses for further study on a host of issues, ranging from improving instructional practices to testing propositions about the circumstances in which schools do not reproduce social inequalities.[38]

The IEA studies, which were carried out in the 1960s without reliance on development as a framework, may not have generated as great a volume of literature is comparative education as that based on the modernization framework, but they did relate the field to schooling and disciplines within education and provide a rationale for the continued existence of the field despite fluctuations in foreign policy.

THE DEVELOPMENT OF THE FIELD:
CAUSES AND EFFECTS

This essay has described the development of comparative education over the past two decades, underscoring the methodological debates, the knowledge generated in the field, and the paradigms guiding research. The reasons for the development of the field are complex and beyond the scope of this essay. Nevertheless, it is important to point out some of the factors that have contributed to the growth of comparative education.

There are several ways in which one can explain the field's course in the past decade. On the one hand, one can seek to explain that development in terms of trends in the academic world that have stressed methodological rigor and have led to transformations in other disciplines. Certainly the attempt to build a science of comparative education, which the field witnessed in the 1960s, parallels similar concerns in economics, sociology, political science, history, and other disciplines. Furthermore, comparative education emerged at a time when comparative specialties in other disciplines, such as comparative politics and comparative history, also took shape and gained academic respectability.

There are a series of macro factors that have helped to shape the field, as well as some micro factors that are unique to comparative education. We shall indicate the broader factors briefly, and then concentrate on some of the detailed issues. Comparative education was a part of the development of specialized interdisciplinary fields that emerged with the expansion of graduate education in North America after World War II. Journals like *Comparative Studies in Society and History* and *Comparative Politics* were established about the same time as the *Comparative Education Review*. These fields of study emerged at a time when the United States was assuming world-power status and felt a need to understand other countries. In addition, as will be discussed in this section, the foreign and economic policy needs of the United States dictated involvement with many aspects of foreign nations, including educational affairs. It is significant that the period of greatest growth in the numbers of students pursuing studies in comparative education coincided with the apogee of the Peace Corps. Many young Americans returned from working in Third World nations with an interest in foreign cultures and with a conviction that education was an important aspect of those societies. Careers in agencies like the Peace Corps seemed to be available to individuals with knowledge of educational systems and issues. Teaching positions, in the United States and in other countries, were relatively plentiful.

American higher education was expanding its international horizons. International studies were added to many curricula and many universities became involved in study-abroad programs for their students. Foreign assistance projects became commonplace, and it was not unusual to find a significant number of professors working overseas on various assignments. All of this went along with the general direction of American foreign policy, which was at the time very much concerned with overseas developments. In the pre-Vietnam era a certain humanitarianism accompanied the political necessities of foreign policy, and discussions of neocolonialism and dependency were limited to a handful of Marxists.

It was out of this general milieu that comparative education grew rapidly and developed its orientation. It was a context in which, as Philip Coombs has pointed out, education was a "fourth lever" of American foreign policy.[39] A key element in the development of the field was the interest of government agencies and private foundations, which provided substantial funding, directly and indirectly, to comparative education. A few examples of the impact of funding patterns on the field will suffice in the context of this essay.

Most of the major comparative education graduate centers in the United States were established with the funding of agencies like the Ford Foundation and Carnegie Corporation. In many instances funds were provided to train individuals, both Americans and foreign nationals, with specific skills. In addition to this general support, contract programs were awarded to carry out specific tasks, which permitted institutions to develop an academic emphasis along with a more practical task.

North American comparative educators, especially those working in the prestigious universities that had funding from the major foundations, were often called on to advise major international research and advising efforts.

Substantial stress was placed on institution building in Third World nations. Educational institutions, and particularly universities, were a key aspect of this effort and comparative education provided both intellectual underpinnings for this effort and staff for many institution-building projects. The concept of institution building was very much linked to established paradigms of modernization.[40]

Much of the funding provided to the field, directly and indirectly, was related to the foreign policy interests of the United States and to the dominant paradigms of development at the time. For example, the National Defense Education Act provided funding for the study of Third World languages, which helped comparative education indirectly. Fellowship programs permitted doctoral students to study educational questions abroad. In many cases such financial assistance was provided on a competitive basis by foundations and government agencies, which were concerned about both the quality of applicants and their research topics. Research projects were often linked to assistance programs, and were thus tied to the orientations of the funding agencies.

The major research and development thrusts of the various periods during the 1960s and 1970s were linked to the emphases of the foundations and government agencies.[41] Institutional development, nonformal education, literacy, textbooks, and others were all directly linked to the specific goal that aid agencies had in mind as the panacea for modernization and development. As these emphases shifted, comparative educators often adjusted their own research priorities.

Many of the major research efforts of the 1960s and 1970s were related to perceived governmental concerns. For example, the growth of research on student activism stemmed from a need to understand—and deal with—campus unrest in the West as well as in the Third World. Concern with institutional building in an earlier period led to research on the nature and organization of educational institutions. Interest in nonformal education led to research programs concerning aspects of extraschool educational efforts. The pages of the major journals in the field reflected these changing research efforts.

Concern for scientific and technological development in the United States following Sputnik in 1956 led to research on science education, investment in laboratories, and a stress on science in the curriculum. These emphases were reflected somewhat later in assistance policies toward Third World nations. In addition, a sense of competition in education contributed to an interest in different levels of achievement and was a stimulus to the massive IEA research enterprise.

The development of the field has been stimulated by a number of factors. As has been pointed out in this essay, individual scholarly concern, the needs of domestic educational policy, the growth of specialized graduate education in the United States, and the concerns of foreign policy have all shaped the field. In addition, policy orientations and students from the Third World have, particularly in the very recent period, had an influence. Educational advisors were in many cases invited by Third World governments. Expatriate teachers and administrators occasionally took interest in comparative education. And Third World governments were, in general, eager to accept foreign financial and technical assistance. In short, the configurations of a field of inquiry like comparative education have complex roots and motivations. There is no attempt here to posit a single cause for the direction or growth of comparative education. The policy orientations and needs of the governments of the industrialized nations, however, and particularly the United States, have without question played a key role. The importance of research funding cannot be overstated. Without the sponsorship and financial assistance of major national and international public agencies and private foundations, large-scale research in comparative education would not be possible and overseas experience by professional scholars in the field would be more limited and the literature in the field poorer.

While external funding relating to foreign policy and development interests of the industrialized nations has been a major force in the development of comparative education, the field has also been in part an instrument for reform and has been attuned to social demands on education and has engaged in action research. In the postwar period these reforms were most obvious in comparative education in Europe and Australia, given the demise of European colonial empires and the political and social changes in postwar England, France, Germany, and Italy. It is understandable that under these conditions comparative education, especially in England, undertook studies directly related to assessing postwar school reforms domestically and similar reforms made elsewhere. Of particular interest was democraticization—whether comprehensive school reforms reduced inequalities characteristic of European societies before the war, the impact of expansion of higher education on social stratification, and the relation of education to employment and postwar reconstruction. Such changes are also evident in the United States today, where multicultural and gender issues have emerged as an emphasis in comparative education.

It is clear that comparative education emerged from a variety of concerns and stimuli and that external factors, notably the research and development priorities of governments, have had a major if not a determining influence. With a decline in interest in education as a lever for social change in recent years and a turning away from concern with foreign cultures in the United States, comparative education faces a considerable challenge. If the field is to be able to develop constructively in the future, it must understand its past and examine carefully and dispassionately the forces that have shaped its development.

CONCLUSIONS

Comparative education has developed as a field from a variety of influences, in different countries at divergent historical periods. As this essay has indicated, it is difficult to trace the parameters of the field because of its multiplicity of origins. It is clear that comparative education, throughout most of its history, has been directly linked to broader social trends in education and in society, and the issues that have loomed as important to the field have, in general, been those issues that have been of concern to the society. At varying periods such questions as educational reform, student activism, the relationships among social class, schooling, and society, the effects of classroom activities, the problems of ethnic groups within societies, problems of literacy development, nonschool forms of educational activities, and many other issues have received attention.

While some of these trends have been of importance in many countries at the same time, such as student activism, other questions have been of mainly national importance. Yet the interplay between national comparative education communities has at times been significant. In this regard, the influence of the major journals in the field has been important in disseminating knowledge and in developing a sense of what is important to study.

A thorough sociology of knowledge of the field of comparative education is beyond the scope of this essay, but is a task that is quite important. It is important that we understand in detail the intellectual and other currents that have shaped the field of comparative education during the past 50 years of quite rapid and by and large impressive growth. Such a sociological and historical analysis will not be an easy task, since comparative education is composed of a number of national currents that at various time intersect one another. Furthermore, it will be difficult to determine the varying influences of funding agencies, the journals, key intellectual leaders, governmental authorities, and the international education and cultural agencies, such as UNESCO and others. Yet all of these elements and others have helped to determine the growth and development of a dynamic interdisciplinary field of study.

What, then, of the future? If this bibliography is any indication, it is clear that comparative education has built up an impressive range of scholarship and that a useful data base exists for many nations and on many topics. The field has become, in a sense, institutionalized through its journals, its national, regional, and international associations, and through the "invisible college" of scholars in the field in many countries.

The field has encountered problems in defining itself and these problems remain. Some have argued that comparative education is, or should be, a scholarly discipline in its own right. Others have argued that comparative education is a subfield of one of the established social science disciplines, usually either sociology or economics, which seem to have attracted the widest interest. Still others have attempted in recent years to orient comparative education to the academic field of educational studies with the intention of integrating comparative education with teacher education, curricular studies, and the like. These pressures have buffeted the field in one direction or another and as a result no widely accepted set of definitions has emerged. Perhaps as a result of this confusion, comparative education is a field continually in search of itself.

As comparative education enters the 1980s, it is faced with a series of problems and challenges. Some are long-standing—such as a continuing search for definitions, methodologies, and directions. In a way it is healthy to be in a state of constant questioning, since it helps to generate new knowledge. On the other hand, scholars in the field have no established canons of scholarship to which to refer. In addition, a series of new challenges have arisen, not only in North America but in many of the countries where comparative education has established itself. The financial difficulties of universities in many nations and the relative paucity of research funding presents problems. Since most comparative educators are located within faculties of education, and the situation for training and research in education is particularly serious, the field is in difficult straits. Nevertheless, the field has been growing, both in size and sophistication, in the Third World.

In the United States, the impetus provided by the recent *Report of the President's Commission on Foreign Languages and International Studies* may improve the funding and interest in comparative education.[42] The report argues, from the viewpoint of American national interests, that the nation has fallen seriously behind in knowledge of the rest of the world. In addition, the growing number of foreign students, some of whom gravitate to comparative education, is a hopeful sign. In a sense, the absence of external research funds, while hampering the growth of the literature in comparative education, may permit the field to develop more independently by permitting scholars to select research interests free from concern about governmental funding priorities.

Without question, comparative education has established itself as a viable field of inquiry. It has developed all of the infrastructures of scholarly inquiry—journals, book publishing enterprises, academic departments and centers, and an international community of specialists in and out of the universities. It is hoped that this essay and the bibliography that follows will be a step in the further codification of this field.

NOTES

1. William Brickman, "C.I.E.S.: An Historical Analysis," *Comparative Education Review* 21 (June-October 1977): 396-404; C. Arnold Anderson, "Comparative Education Over a Quarter Century: Maturity and New Challenges," *Comparative Education Review* 21 (June-October 1977): 406-16; and Andreas M. Kazamias and Karl Schwartz, "Intellectual and Ideological Perspectives in Comparative Education: An Interpretation," *Comparative Education Review* 21 (June-October 1977): 153-76.

2. This theme is developed at length in Robert Arnove, ed., *Philanthropy and Cultural Imperialism: The Foundations at Home and Abroad* (Boston: G. K. Hall, 1980). See also Edward Berman, "Foundations, United States Foreign Policy and African Education, 1945-1975," *Harvard Educational Review* 49 (May 1979): 145-79.

3. At present, comparative education organizations exist in Japan, South Korea, India, Britain, France, West Germany, the United States, Canada, and the Benelux countries. The beginnings of a Latin American group have been developed. There is also an international and several regional comparative education groups.

4. It is significant that of the 23 contributors to one of the key comparative studies of student activism, S. M. Lipset and P. G. Altbach's *Students in Revolt* (Boston: Beacon, 1968), only one is a comparative educator. The rest come from such disciplines as sociology, political science, history, and others.

5. Isaac L. Kandel, *Comparative Education* (Boston: Houghton Mifflin, 1933).

6. Nicholas Hans, *Comparative Education* (London: Routledge and Kegan Paul, 1949); and "Functionalism in Comparative Education," *International Review of Education* 10, no. 1 (1964): 94-97.

7. Andreas M. Kazamias, "Woozles and Wizzles in the Methodology of Comparative Education," *Comparative Education Review* 14 (October 1970): 255-61; and "Some Old and New Approaches to Methodology in Comparative Education," *Comparative Education Review* 5 (October 1961): 90-96.

8. Harold Noah and Max Eckstein, *Toward a Science of Comparative Education* (New York: Macmillan, 1969).

9. Brian Holmes, *Problems in Education: A Comparative Approach* (London: Routledge and Kegan Paul, 1965).

10. Edmund J. King, *Comparative Studies and Educational Decision Making* (London: Methuen, 1968).

11. Noah and Eckstein, op. cit.

12. George Z. F. Bereday, *Comparative Method in Education* (New York: Holt, Rinehart and Winston, 1964).

13. Holmes, op. cit.

14. King, op. cit.

15. C. Arnold Anderson, "Methodology of Comparative Education," *International Review of Education* 7, no. 1 (1961): 1-23; and "Three Methodological Challenges or New Approaches in Comparative Education," in *Relevant Methods in Comparative Education*, ed. R. Edwards, B. Holmes, and J. van de Graaff (Paris: UNESCO Institute for Education, 1973), pp. 175-86.

16. "The State of the Art: Twenty Years of Comparative Education," *Comparative Education Review* 21 (June-October 1977): 151-420.

17. See, for example, Patricia Broadfoot, "The Comparative Contribution—Research Perspective," *Comparative Education* 13 (June 1977): 133-38; Reginald Edwards, "Comparative Education and the Psychology of Learning," *Comparative Education Review* 10 (February 1966): 21-29; Wolfgang Mitter, "The Policy-Oriented Task of Comparative Education," *Comparative Education* 13 (June 1977): 95-100; and Edmund J. King, "Comparative Studies in the Education of Teachers," *Canadian and International Education* 2 (December 1973): 12-22.

18. A. M. Kazamias, "Comparative Pedagogy," *Comparative Education Review* 16 (October 1972): 406-11.

19. "Comparative Education: Its Present State and Future Prospects," *Comparative Education* 13 (June 1977): 75-152.

20. Michael Apple, *Ideology and Curriculum* (London: Routledge and Kegan Paul, 1979).

21. John W. Meyer and Michael T. Hannan, eds., *National Development and the World System: Educational, Economic and Political Change, 1950-1970* (Chicago: University of Chicago Press, 1979).

22. See, for example, Joan I. Roberts and Sherrie K. Akinsanya, eds., *Schooling in the Cultural Context: Anthropological Studies of Education* (New York: McKay, 1976); and Douglas Foley, "Anthropological Studies of Schooling in Developing Countries: Some Current Findings," *Comparative Education Review* 21 (June-October 1977): 311-28.

23. Philip G. Altbach, "Servitude of the Mind?: Education, Dependency and Neocolonialism," *Teachers College Record* 79 (December 1977): 187-204.

24. Mathew Zachariah, "Comparative Educators and International Development Policy," *Comparative Education Review* 23 (October 1979): 341-54.

25. Robert Arnove, "Comparative Education and World Systems Analysis," *Comparative Education Review* 24 (February 1980): 48-62.

26. Richard Heyneman, "A Theoretical Look at Knowledge, Schools and Social Change," *Comparative Education Review* 18 (October 1974): 411-28.

27. Cyril Black, *The Dynamics of Modernization* (New York: Harper and Row, 1966); S. N. Eisenstadt, *Modernization, Protest and Change* (New York: Prentice-Hall, 1966); Edward Shils, "Political Development in the New States," *Comparative Studies in Society and History* 2 (1959-60): 265-92.

28. See, for example, Don Adams and Robert Bjork, *Education In Developing Areas* (New York: McKay, 1971); C. E. Beeby, *The Quality of Education in Developing Countries* (Cambridge, Mass.: Harvard University Press, 1966); John W. Hanson and Cole S. Brembeck, eds., *Education and The Development of Nations* (New York: Holt, Rinehart and Winston, 1966). A fine review article is Donald K. Adams, "Development Education," *Comparative Education Review* 21 (June-October 1977): 296-310.

29. See Philip J. Foster, "Dilemmas of Educational Development: What We Might Learn from the Past," *Comparative Education Review* 19 (October 1975): 375-92; and

Irvin Sobel, "The Human Capital Revolution in Economic Development: Its Current History and Status," *Comparative Education Review* 22 (June 1978): 278–308.

30. See, for example, Don Adams, "The Study of Education and Social Development," *Comparative Education Review* 9 (October 1965): 258–69; Philip J. Foster, "Education and Social Differentiation in Less Developed Countries," *Comparative Education Review* 21 (June-October 1977): 211–29; Adam Curle, "Education, Politics and Development," *Comparative Education Review* 7 (February 1964): 226–45; Bert Hoselitz, "Investment in Education and Its Political Impact," in *Education and Political Development*, ed. J. S. Coleman (Princeton: Princeton University Press, 1964), pp. 541–65; and A. Inkeles and D. Smith, *Becoming Modern: Individual Change in Six Developing Countries* (Cambridge, Mass.: Harvard University Press, 1974).

31. See Martin Carnoy, *Education as Cultural Imperialism* (New York: McKay, 1974).

32. Philip J. Foster, "The Vocational School Fallacy in Development Planning," in *Education and Economic Development*, ed. C. Arnold Anderson and Mary Jean Bowman (London: Cass, 1965), pp. 142–66; and "Dilemmas of Educational Development: What We Might Learn from the Past," *Comparative Education Review* 19 (October 1972): 375–92; L. Aran, S. N. Eisenstadt, and C. Adler, "The Effectiveness of Educational Systems in the Process of Modernization," *Comparative Education Review* 16 (February 1972): 30–43; Nicholas Georgescu-Roegen, "Economics and Educational Development," *Journal of Educational Finance* 2 (Summer 1976): 1–15; and Donald K. Adams, "Development Education," *Comparative Education Review* 21 (June-October 1977): 296–310.

33. See, for example, Thomas J. LaBelle, ed., *Educational Alternatives in Latin America* (Los Angeles, Calif.: UCLA Latin American Center, 1975).

34. See, for example, Robert Arnove, "Comparative Education and World Systems Analysis," op. cit.; Philip G. Altbach, "Neocolonialism and Education," *Teachers College Record* 72 (May 1971): 543–58; Martin Carnoy, op. cit.; and Philip G. Altbach and Gail P. Kelly, eds., *Education and Colonialism* (New York: Longmans, 1978).

35. Dean C. Tipps, "Modernization Theory and the Study of National Societies: A Critical Perspective," *Comparative Studies in Society and History* 15 (1973): 199–226.

36. Noah and Eckstein, op. cit., pp. 14–33.

37. L. C. Comber and John Keever, *Science Education in Nineteen Countries: An Empirical Study, International Studies in Evaluation 1* (New York: Wiley, 1973); Torsten Husén, *International Study of Achievement in Mathematics: A Comparison of Twelve Countries* (New York: Wiley, 1967); A. Harry Passow, H. J. Noah, M. A. Eckstein, and J. R. Mallea, *The National Case Study: An Empirical Comparative Study of Twenty-One Educational Studies* (New York: Wiley, 1976); Alan C. Purves, *Literature Education in Ten Countries: An Empirical Study* (New York: Wiley, 1973); Robert L. Thorndike, *Reading Comprehension Education in Fifteen Countries: An Empirical Study* (New York: Wiley, 1973); Judith Torney, A. N. Oppenheim, and Russel Farnen, *Civic Education in Ten Countries: An Empirical Study* (New York: Wiley, 1975).

38. Alex Inkeles, "National Differences in Scholastic Performance," *Comparative Education Review* 23 (October 1979): 386–407.

39. Philip Coombs, *The Fourth Dimension of Foreign Policy: Education and Cultural Affairs* (New York: Harper and Row, 1964).

40. See Edward Berman, op. cit., for a detailed discussion of this topic in the African context.

41. For a discussion of changing priorities of funding agencies in the area of higher education, see Kenneth Thompson et al., *Higher Education and Social Change* (New York: Praeger, 1976).

42. *Strength Through Wisdom: A Report to the President from the President's Commission on Foreign Language and International Studies* (Washington, D.C.: U.S. Government Printing Office, 1979).

BIBLIOGRAPHY
ON COMPARATIVE EDUCATION

COMPARATIVE EDUCATION AS A FIELD OF INQUIRY

General Definitions of the Field

1 Bereday, George Z. F. "Comparative Education and Ethnocentrism." *International Review of Education* 7, no. 1 (1961): 24-34.

2 Brodbelt, Samuel S. "Educational Ideals and Practice in Comparative Perspective." *International Review of Education* 11 (1965): 144-50.

3 Butts, R. Freeman. "New Futures for Comparative Education." *Comparative Education Review* 17 (October 1973): 289-94.

4 Debesse, Maurice. "Qu'est-ce que l'éducation comparée?" *Bulletin de la Societé Française de Pédagogie* 125 (July 1958): 43-64.

5 Eckstein, Max. "Defining Comparative Education: Operations." In *Relevant Methods in Comparative Education*, edited by R. Edwards, B. Holmes, and J. van de Graff, pp. 161-74. Hamburg: UNESCO Institute for Education, 1973.

6 Fuentealba, L. "The Concept of Comparative Education." *International Review of Education* 8, no. 3-4 (1963): 363-83.

7 Halls, W. D. "Comparative Education: Explorations." *Comparative Education* 3 (June 1967): 189-94.

8 Heath, Kathryn G. "Is Comparative Education a Discipline?" *Comparative Education Review* 2 (October 1958): 31-32.

9 Hernandez, Leonardo F. "Le concept d'éducation comparée." *International Review of Education* 8, no. 3-4 (1963): 363-82.

10 Hilker, F. "What Can the Comparative Method Contribute to Education?" *Comparative Education Review* 7 (February 1964): 223-25.

11 Hopkins, Richard L. "Prescriptions for Cultural Revolutions: A Reassessment of the Limits of Comparative Education Research." *Comparative Education Review* 17 (October 1973): 299-301.

12 Kandel, I. L. "Problems of Comparative Education." *International Review of Education* 2, no. 1 (1956): 1-15.

13 Kneller, G. F. "Comparative Education." In *Encyclopedia of Educational Research*, edited by C. W. Harris, pp. 316-22. New York: Macmillan, 1960.

14 Kneller, G. F. "The Prospects of Comparative Education." *International Review of Education* 9, no. 4 (1963-64): 396-406.

15 Laska, John A. "The Future of Comparative Education: Three Basic Questions." *Comparative Education Review* 17 (October 1973): 295-98.

16 Noah, Harold J. "Defining Comparative Education: Conceptions." In *Relevant Methods in Comparative Education*, edited by R. Edwards, B. Holmes, and J. van de Graaff, pp. 109-18. Paris: UNESCO Institute for Education, 1973.

17 Rapacz, Richard V., and Albert S. Kahn. "Comparative Education." *Review of Educational Research* 31 (February 1961): 57-69.

18 Ruscoe, Gordon C., and Thomas W. Nelson. "Prolegomena to a Definition of Comparative Education." *International Review of Education* 10, no. 4 (1965): 385-92.

19 Ulich, Robert. "The Challenge of Definitions in Comparative Education." *Comparative Education Review* 1 (October 1957): 3-4.

20 Wagsobal, Harry. "Radical Criticism and Its Implications for Comparative Education." *Comparative Education Review* 18 (October 1974): 354-58.

History of Comparative Education

Books

21 Brewer, Walter V. *Victor Cousin as a Comparative Educator*. New York: Teacher's College Press, 1971.

22 Fraser, S., ed. *Jullien's Plan for Comparative Education, 1816-1817*. New York: Teacher's College, Columbia University, 1964.

23 Fraser, Stewart E., and William W. Brickman. *A History of International and Comparative Education*. Glenview, Ill.: Scott, Foresman, 1968.

24 Scanlon, David G., ed. *International Education: A Documentary History*. New York: Bureau of Publications, Teacher's College, Columbia University, 1960.

Articles

25 Anderson, C. Arnold. "Comparative Education Over a Quarter Century: Maturity and New Challenges." *Comparative Education Review* 21 (June-October 1977): 405-16.

26 Benjamin, H. R. W. "Growth in Comparative Education." *Phi Delta Kappan* 37 (January 1956): 141-44.

27 Bereday, George Z. F. "Memorial to Isaac Kandel 1881-1965." *Comparative Education* 2 (June 1966): 147-51.

28 Brickman, William W. "A Historical Introduction to Comparative Education." *Comparative Education Review* 3 (February 1960): 6-12.

29 Brickman, William W. "C.I.E.S.: An Historical Analysis." *Comparative Education Review* 2 (June-October 1977): 396-404.

30 Brickman, William W. "Prehistory of Comparative Education to the End of the Eighteenth Century." *Comparative Education Review* 10 (February 1966): 30-47.

31 Brickman, William W. "Ten Years of the Comparative Education Society." *Comparative Education Review* 10 (February 1966): 4-15.

32 Brickman, William W. "The Meeting of East and West in Educational History." *Comparative Education Review* 5 (October 1961): 82-89.

33 Brickman, William W. "Works of Historical Interest in Comparative Education." *Comparative Education Review* 7 (February 1964): 324-26.

34 Halls, W. D. "Comparative Studies in Education, 1964-1977: A Personal View." *Comparative Education* 13 (March 1977): 81-86.

35 Hans, Nicholas. "English Pioneers of Comparative Education." *British Journal of Educational Studies* 1 (November 1952): 56-59.

36 Hans, Nicholas. "K. D. Ushinsky—Russian Pioneer of Comparative Education." *Comparative Education Review* 5 (February 1962): 162-66.

37 Hausmann, G. "A Century of Comparative Education, 1785-1885." *Comparative Education Review* 11 (February 1967): 1-21.

38 Higginson, J. H. "The Centenary of an English Pioneer in Comparative Education, Sir Michael Sadler (1861-1943)." *International Review of Education* 7, no. 4 (1962): 286-98.

39 Johnson, William H. E. "The Comparative Education Society." *Comparative Education Review* 1 (June 1957): 16.

40 O'Brien, John James. "The International Educational Interests of Robert Boyle." *Comparative Education Review* 9 (June 1965): 195-200.

41 Read, Gerald H. "Constitution of the Comparative Education Society." *Comparative Education Review* 3 (October 1959): 37-40.

42 Röhrs, Hermann. "The Realm of Education in the Thought of Kurt Hahn." *Comparative Education* 3 (October 1959): 37-40.

43 Siffin, William J. "Comparative Studies and the Rise of the Social Sciences." In *International Dimensions in the Social Studies, 38th Yearbook, National Council for the Social Studies*, edited by Mames Becker and Howard Mehlinger, pp. 237-54. Washington, D.C.: National Education Association, 1968.

44 Spolton, Lewis. "Kay-Shuttleworth: Quantitative Comparative Educator." *Comparative Education Review* 12 (February 1968): 84-86.

45 Templeton, Robert G. "The Study of Comparative Education in the United States." *Harvard Educational Review* 24 (Summer 1954): 141-58.

46 Travers, Paul D. "G. Stanley Hall: Pioneer in Comparative Education." *Educational Forum* 33 (March 1969): 301-5.

Overviews of the Field

Books

47 Aggarwal, J. C. *Introduction to World Education*. New Delhi, Arya, 1965.

48 Aggarwal, J. C. *Recent Educational Developments in the World*. New Delhi: Arya, 1971.

49 Archer, Margaret Scotford. *Social Origins of Educational Systems*. Beverly Hills, Calif.: Sage, 1979.

50 Berger, Walter. *Schulentwicklungen in Vergleichender Sicht*. Munich: Jugend und Volk, 1978.

51 Brickman, William, ed. *Comparative Education: Concept, Research and Application*. Norwood, Pa.: Norwood Editions, 1973.

52 Bristow, T., and B. Holmes. *Comparative Education Through the Literature*. London: Butterworths, 1963.

53 Chaube, S. P. *Comparative Education*. Agra, India: Ram Prasad, 1965.

54 Coombs, Philip. *The World Educational Crisis: A Systems Analysis*. New York: Oxford University Press, 1968.

55 Cramer, John F., and George S. Brown. *Comparative Education*. New York: Harcourt, Brace and World, 1960.

56 Czycholl, Reinhard. *Vergleichende Wirtschaft Pädagogik*. Trier: Spree, 1971.

57 Faure, Edgar, et al. *Learning to Be: The World of Education Today and Tomorrow*. Paris: UNESCO Press, 1972.

58 Freire, Paulo. *Pedagogy of the Oppressed*. New York: Herder and Herder, 1970.

59 Gloton, R. *L'art à l'école*. Paris: Presses Universitaires de France, 1965.

60 Hans, N. *Comparative Education*. London: Routledge and Kegan Paul, 1949.

61 Havelock, R. G., and A. M. Huberman. *Solving Educational Problems*. New York: Praeger, 1978.

62 Holmes, Brian, ed. *Diversity and Unity in Education*. London: Allen and Unwin, 1980.

63 Hughes, Emmet John, ed. *Education in World Perspective*. New York: Harper and Row, 1962.

64 Husén, Torsten. *The Learning Society*. London: Methuen, 1975.

65 Kandel, Isaac L. *Comparative Education*. Boston: Houghton Mifflin, 1933.

66 Kandel, I. L. *The New Era in Education: A Comparative Study*. Boston: Houghton Mifflin, 1955.

67 Kazamias, A. M., and B. G. Massialas. *Tradition and Change in Education: A Comparative Study*. Englewood Cliffs, N.J.: Prentice-Hall, 1965.

68 King, E. J. *Comparative Studies and Educational Decision*. London: Methuen, 1968.

69 King, E. J. *Education and Social Change*. Oxford: Pergamon Press, 1966.

70 King, E. J. *Other Schools and Ours*. New York: Holt, Rinehart and Winston, 1979.

71 King, E. J. *World Perspectives in Education*. London: Methuen, 1965.

72 Ley, K. T. *Comparative Study of Educational Systems*. Taipei: Taiwan Book Company, 1967.

73 Lourenco Filho, M. B. *Educação Comparada*. São Paulo, Brazil: Melhoramentos, 1961.

74 Mallinson, V. *An Introduction to the Study of Comparative Education*. London: Heinemann, 1975.

75 Moehlman, Arthur H. *Comparative Educational Systems*. New York: Center for Applied Research, 1964.

76 Monroe, Paul. *Essays in Comparative Education*. New York: Bureau of Publications, Teacher's College, Columbia University, 1932.

77 Mori, Takao. *Comparative Educational Systems*. Tokyo: Fukumura, 1968. (in Japanese)

78 Mukherjee, K. K. *A Comparative Study of Some Educational Problems.* Bombay: Lalvani, 1971.

79 Mukherjee, L. *Comparative Education.* Allahabad, India: Kitab Mahal, 1964.

80 Niskier, A., and M. Carvalho. *Educação Comparada Moderna.* Pôrto Alegre, Brazil: Tabajara, 1973.

81 Orata, Pedro T. *Comparative Education in Action: How to Profit Most from Foreign Experience.* Quezon City, Philippines: Alemar, 1973.

82 Paulston, R. G. *Conflicting Theories of Social and Educational Change.* Washington, D.C.: The World Bank, 1975.

83 Schneider, F. *Vergleichende Erziehungswissenschaft.* Heidelberg, West Germany: Quelle and Meyer, 1961.

84 Thomas, Jean. *World Problems in Education: A Brief Analytical Survey.* Paris: UNESCO Press, 1975.

85 Thut, I. N., and Don Adams. *Educational Patterns in Contemporary Societies.* New York: McGraw-Hill, 1964.

86 Tretheway, J. *Comparative Education.* Elmsford, N.Y.: Pergamon Press, 1976.

87 Ulich, R. *The Education of Nations: A Comparison in Historical Perspective.* Cambridge, Mass.: Harvard University Press, 1961.

88 UNESCO. *Comparative Education.* Hamburg: UNESCO Institute for Education, 1955.

Contributions of Comparative Education

Articles

89 Broadfoot, Tricia. "The Comparative Contribution-Research Perspective." *Comparative Education* 13 (June 1977): 133-38.

90 Cormack, Margaret L. "Is Comparative Education Serving Cultural Revolution?" *Comparative Education Review* 17 (October 1973): 302-6.

91 Bereday, George Z. F. "Sir Michael Sadler's Study of Foreign Systems of Education." *Comparative Education Review* 7 (February 1964): 307-14.

92 Cowen, Robert. "A Query Concerning Developments within and the Responsibilities of Comparative Education." *Canadian and International Education* 2 (June 1973): 15-29.

93 Edwards, Reginald. "Comparative Education and the Psychology of Learning." *Comparative Education Review* 10 (February 1966): 21-29.

94 Entwistle, Harold. "Comparative Studies in the Education of Teachers: Some Pedagogical Problems." *Canadian and International Education* 2 (December 1973): 23-29.

95 Grant, Nigel. "Educational Policy and Cultural Pluralism: A Task for Comparative Education." *Comparative Education* 13 (June 1977): 139-50.

96 Kandel, Isaac L. "Comparative Education and Underdeveloped Countries: A New Dimension." *Comparative Education Review* 4 (February 1961): 130-35.

97 King, Edmund. "Comparative Studies: An Evolving Commitment, a Fresh Realism." *Comparative Education* 13 (June 1977): 101-8.

98 King, Edmund. "Comparative Studies and Policy Decisions." *Comparative Education* 4 (November 1967): 51-64.

99 King, Edmund. "Comparative Studies in the Education of Teachers." *Canadian and International Education* 2 (December 1973): 12-22.

100 King, Edmund. "Students, Teachers, and Researchers in Comparative Education." *Comparative Education Review* 3 (June 1959): 33-36.

101 King, Edmund J. "The Purpose of Comparative Education." *Comparative Education* 1 (June 1965): 147-59.

102 Lawson, Robert L. "Thoughts on Cultural Revolution and Comparative Studies." *Comparative Education* 9 (October 1973): 119-26.

103 Mitter, Wolfgang. "The Policy-oriented Task of Comparative Education." *Comparative Education* 13 (June 1977): 95-100.

104 Parkyn, G. W. "Comparative Education Research and Development Education." *Comparative Education* 13 (March 1977): 87-94.

105 Schneider, Friedrich. "The Immanent Evolution of Education: A Neglected

Aspect of Comparative Education." *Comparative Education Review* 4 (February 1961): 136-39.

106 Seidenfaden, F. "Some Thoughts on the Function of Comparative Education in the Context of Educational Research." *Comparative Education* 8 (April 1972): 31-42.

Methodology of Comparative Education

Books

107 Bereday, George Z. F. *Comparative Method in Education.* New York: Holt, Rinehart and Winston, 1964.

108 Edwards, Reginald, Brian Holmes, and John Van de Graaff, eds. *Relevant Methods in Comparative Education.* Hamburg: UNESCO Institute for Education, 1974.

109 Holmes, Brian. *Problems in Education: A Comparative Approach.* London: Routledge and Kegan Paul, 1965.

110 Holmes, Brian, and S. B. Robinsohn, eds. *Relevant Data in Comparative Education: Report on an Expert Meeting, March 11-13, 1963.* Hamburg: UNESCO Institute for Education, 1963.

111 Jones, Philip E. *Comparative Education: Purpose and Method.* St. Lucia, Australia: University of Queensland Press, 1971.

112 Kobayashi, Tetsuya. *Survey on Current Trends in Comparative Education.* Paris: UNESCO, 1971.

113 Marquez, Angel Diego. *Educación Comparada: Teoría y Metodología.* Buenos Aires: Editorial "El Alteneo," 1972.

114 Noah, Harold, and Max Eckstein. *Toward a Science of Comparative Education.* New York: Macmillan, 1969.

115 Rosselló, Pedro. *La Teoría de las Corrientes Educativas: Sillo de Educación Comparada Dinámica.* Barcelona: Editorial Promoción Cultural, 1974.

116 Tusquets, Juan. *Teoría y Práctica de la Pedagogia Comparada.* Madrid: Editorial Magisterio Español, 1969.

117 Vexliard, A. *La pédagogie comparée: méthodes et problèmes.* Paris: Presses Universitaires de France, 1967.

118 Villalpando, J. M. *Pedagogia Comparada: Teoría y Técnica.* Mexico: Editorial Porrúa, 1966.

Articles

119 Anderson, C. A. "Methodology of Comparative Education." *International Review of Education* 7, no. 1 (1961): 1-23.

120 Anderson, C. Arnold. "Three Methological Challenges for New Approaches in Comparative Education." In *Relevant Methods in Comparative Education,* edited by R. Edwards, B. Holmes, and J. Van de Graaff, pp. 175-86. Hamburg: UNESCO Institute of Education, 1973.

121 Anderson, C. A. "The Utility of Societal Typologies in Comparative Education." *Comparative Education Review* 3 (June 1959): 20-22.

122 Barber, Benjamin. "Science, Salience and Comparative Education: Some Reflections on Social Scientific Inquiry." *Comparative Education Review* 16 (October 1972): 424-36.

123 Bereday, George Z. F. "Comparative Analysis in Education." *Prospects* 7, no. 48 (1977): 424-36.

124 Bereday, George Z. F. "Reflections on Comparative Methodology in Education 1964-1966." *Comparative Education* 3 (June 1967): 169-87.

125 Bereday, George Z. F. "Some Discussions of Methods in Comparative Education." *Comparative Education Review* 1 (June 1957): 13-15.

126 Berstecher, Dieter, and Bernard Dieckmann. "On the Role of Comparisons in Educational Research." *Comparative Education Review* 13 (February 1969): 96-104.

127 Bone, Louis W. "Sociological Framework for Comparative Study of Educational Systems." *Comparative Education Review* 4 (October 1960): 121-26.

128 Brickman, W. W. "Theoretical Foundations of Comparative Education." *Journal of Educational Sociology* 30 (November 1956): 116-25.

129 Carey, Robert D. "Conceptual Tools for Research in Comparative Education." *Comparative Education Review* 10 (October 1966): 418-25.

130 Cirigliano, Gustavo F. J. "Stages of Analysis in Comparative Education." *Comparative Education Review* 10 (February 1966): 18-20.

131 Clark, Burton. "The Study of Educational Systems." In *International Encyclopedia of the Social Sciences*, Vol. 4, pp. 509-16. New York: Free Press, 1968.

132 Clayton, A. S. "Valuation in Comparative Education." *Comparative Education Review* 16 (October 1972): 412-23.

133 Edwards, Reginald. "Between the Micrometer and the Divining Rod: Methodologies in Comparative Education." In *Relevant Methods in Comparative Education*, edited by R. Edwards, B. Holmes, and J. van de Graaff, pp. 81-94. Hamburg: UNESCO Institute for Education, 1973.

134 Edwards, Reginald. "The Dimensions of Comparison, and of Comparative Education." *Comparative Education Review* 14 (October 1970): 239-54.

135 Elliott, A. "Comparison and Interchange: The Relevance of Cultural Relations to Comparative Education." *Comparative Education* 2 (March 1966): 63-70.

136 Farrell, J. P. "Some New Analytic Techniques for Comparative Educators: A Review." *Comparative Education Review* 14 (October 1970): 269-78.

137 Fernig, L. "The Global Approach to Comparative Education." *International Review of Education* 5, no. 3 (1959): 343-55.

138 Foshay, A. W. "The Use of Empirical Methods in Comparative Education." *International Review of Education* 9 (1963-64): 257-68.

139 Foster, Philip. "Comparative Methodology and Study of African Education." *Comparative Education Review* 4 (October 1960): 110-18.

140 Galtung, Johan. "The Dialectics of Education." *Convergence* 8, no. 3 (1975): 64-77.

141 Hans, Nicholas. "Functionalism in Comparative Education." *International Review of Education* 10, no. 1 (1964): 94-97.

142 Hans, Nicholas. "The Historical Approach to Comparative Education." *International Review of Education* 5, no. 3 (1959): 299-310.

143 Henry, Michael M. "Methodology in Comparative Education: An Annotated Bibliography." *Comparative Education Review* 17 (June 1973): 231-44.

144 Heyman, Richard D. "A Theoretical Look at Knowledge, Schools and Social Change." *Comparative Education Review* 18 (October 1974): 411-18.

145 Higson, J. M. "The Methodology of Comparative Analysis of Education." *Comparative Education Review* 12 (October 1968): 338-49.

146 Holmes, Brian. "Conceptual Analysis and Empirical Inquiry." In *Relevant Methods in Comparative Education*, edited by R. Edwards, B. Holmes, and J. van de Graaff, pp. 41-56. Hamburg: UNESCO Institute for Education, 1973.

147 Holmes, Brian. "Rational Constructs in Comparative Education." *International Review of Education* 12, no. 4 (1965): 466-78.

148 Holmes, Brian. "The Positivist Debate in Comparative Education—an Anglo Saxon Perspective." *Comparative Education* 13 (June 1977): 115-32.

149 Holmes, Brian. "The Problem Approach in Comparative Education: Some Methodological Considerations." *Comparative Education Review* 2 (June 1977): 115-32.

150 Holmes, Brian, and Saul Robinsohn. "Relevant Data in Comparative Education." *International Review of Education* 9, no. 2 (1963-64): 135-57.

151 Idenburg, Philip J. "Statistics in the Service of Comparative Education." *International Review of Education* 11, no. 4 (1965): 434-52.

152 Irving, J. A. "The Comparative Method and the Nature of Human Nature." *Philosophy and Phenomenological Research* 9 (March 1949): 545-56.

153 Johnstone, James N. "The Dimensions of Educational Systems." *Comparative Education Review* 21 (February 1977): 51-68.

154 Kandel, I. L. "The Methodology of Comparative Education." *International Review of Education* 5, no. 2 (1959): 270-80.

155 Kandel, I. L. "The Study of Comparative Education." *Educational Forum* 20 (November 1955): 5-15.

156 Kazamias, A. M. "Comparative Pedagogy." *Comparative Education Review* 16 (October 1972): 406-11.

157 Kazamias, A. M. "History, Science and Comparative Education: A Study in Methodology." *International Review of Education* 8, no. 3-4 (1963): 383-98.

158 Kazamias, A. M. "Some Old and New Approaches to Methodology in Comparative Education." *Comparative Education Review* 5 (October 1961): 90-96.

159 Kazamias, A. M. "Woozles and Wizzles in the Methodology of Comparative Education." *Comparative Education Review* 14 (October 1970): 255-61.

160 Kazamias, A. M., and Karl Schwartz. "Intellectual and Ideological Perspectives in Comparative Education: An Interpretation." *Comparative Education Review* 21 (June-October 1977): 153-76.

161 Kidd, J. R. "Developing a Methodology for Comparative Studies in Adult Education." *Convergence* 3, no. 3 (1970): 12-27.

162 Kienitz, W. "On the Marxist Approach to Comparative Education in the German Democratic Republic." *Comparative Education* 7 (August 1971): 21-32.

163 King, Edmund. "Analytical Frameworks in Comparative Studies of Education." *Comparative Education* 11 (March 1975): 85-105.

164 Koehl, Robert. "The Comparative Study of Education: Prescription and Practice." *Comparative Education Review* 21 (June-October 1977): 177-94.

165 Koehl, R. "Towards a Comparative History of Education." *Comparative Education Review* 18 (February 1974): 6-9.

166 Kuz'mina, E. N., and M. A. Sokolova. "Research in Comparative Education." *Soviet Education* 8 (November 1970): 82-97.

167 Laska, John. "A Typology of School Systems." *Compare* 9, no. 2 (1979): 97-117.

168 Laska, John. "The Use of Educational Pyramid in Comparative Education." *International Review of Education* 11, no. 4 (1965): 485-88.

169 Lauwerys, J. A. "The Philosophical Approach to Comparative Education." *International Review of Education* 5, no. 2 (1959): 281-98.

170 Mallinson, Vernon. "Literary Studies in the Service of Comparative Education." *Comparative Education* 4 (June 1968): 177-81.

171 Moore, Jill. "Comparative Education and Sociolinguistics." *Comparative Education* 8 (September 1972): 57-62.

172 Parkyn, G. W. "The Particular and the General: Towards a Synthesis." *Compare* 5 (May 1976): 20-26.

173 Perkinson, H. J. "The Comparison of Educational Programs—A Methodological Proposal." *School Review* 70 (Autumn 1963): 314-21.

174 Petty, Michael F. "Comment on Barber's 'Science, Salience and Comparative Education.'" *Comparative Education Review* 17 (October 1973): 389-92.

175 Rosselló, Pedro. "Concerning the Structure of Comparative Education." *Comparative Education Review* 7 (October 1963): 103-7.

176 Rosselló, Pedro. "Difficultés inherentes aux recherches d'éducation comparée dynamique." *International Review of Education* 7, no. 2 (1963-64): 203-14.

177 Rosselló, Pedro. "Les principaux courants éducatifs en 1958-1959: Essai d'éducation comparée dynamique." *International Review of Education* 6, no. 4 (1960): 385-98.

178 Samonte, Quirico S. "Some Problems of Comparison and the Development of Theoretical Models in Education." *Comparative Education Review* 6 (February 1963): 177-81.

179 Schneider, Friedrich. "Toward Substantive Research in Comparative Education." *Comparative Education Review* 10 (February 1966): 16-17.

180 Siffin, W. J. "The Social Sciences, Comparative Education, and the Future and All That." *Comparative Education Review* 13 (October 1969): 252-59.

181 Spolton, Lewis. "Methodology of Comparative Education." *Comparative Education* 4 (March 1968): 109-15.

182 Sucholdolski, Bogdan. "Egalité et éducation: problèmes, méthodes et difficultés des recherches comparées." *International Review of Education* 9, no. 2 (1963-64): 182-95.

183 Templeton, Robert G. "Some Reflections on the Theory of Comparative Education." *Comparative Education Review* 2 (October 1958): 27-30.

184 Wilson, John. "Comparative Aims in Moral Education: Problems in Methodology." *Comparative Education* 4 (March 1968): 117-24.

Comparative Education and the Academic Disciplines

SOCIAL SCIENCES

Books

185 Musgrave, P. W. *Sociology, History and Education: A Reader*. London: Methuen, 1970.

Articles

186 Anderson, C. A. "Sociology of Education in a Comparative Perspective." *International Review of Education* 16, no. 2 (1970): 147-60.

187 Anderson, C. A. "Sociology in the Service of Comparative Education." *International Review of Education* 5 (1959): 310-19.

188 Epperson, D. C., and R. A. Schmuck. "The Uses of Social Psychology in Comparative Education." *Comparative Education Review* 6 (February 1963): 182-90.

189 Butts, R. Freeman. "Civilization as Historical Process: Meeting Ground for Comparative and International Education." *Comparative Education* 3 (June 1967): 155-68.

190 Halsey, A. H. "Authority, Bureaucracy and the Education Debate." *Oxford Review of Education* 3 (October 1977): 217-34.

191 Langeveld, M. J. "Education and Sociology." *International Review of Education* 4, no. 2 (1958): 129-38.

PHILOSOPHY OF EDUCATION

Books

192 Bereday, George Z. F., and Joseph A. Lauwerys, eds. *Education and Philosophy*. New York: World Book Company, 1957.

Articles

193 Agoston, G. "L'idéal humain de la pédagogie socialiste." *International Review of Education* 16, no. 3 (1970): 260-70.

194 Brodbelt, Samuel S. "Educational Ideals and Practice in Comparative Perspective." *International Review of Education* 11, no. 2 (1965): 144-50.

195 Grace, Harry A. "Comparative Theories of Education." *Comparative Education Review* 5 (February 1962): 189-98.

196 Ivie, Stanley D. "A Comparison in Educational Philosophy: Jose Vasconcelos and John Dewey." *Comparative Education Review* 10, no. 3 (1966): 404-16.

197 McClellan, James E. "An Educational Philosopher Looks at Comparative Education." *Comparative Education Review* 1 (June 1957): 8-9.

198 Phenix, Philip H. "Comparative Study in Religion and Education." *Comparative Education Review* 1 (October 1957): 7-10.

199 Ulich, Robert. "Education and the Concept of Mankind." *Comparative Education Review* 3 (February 1960): 2-6.

ANTHROPOLOGY

Books

200 Kimball, Solon T. *Culture and the Educative Process: An Anthropological Perspective*. New York: Teacher's College Press, 1974.

201 Lindquist, Harry M., ed. *Education: Readings in the Process of Cultural Transmission*. Boston: Houghton Mifflin, 1970.

202 Roberts, Joan I., and Sherrie K. Akinsanya, eds. *Schooling in the Cultural Context: Anthropological Studies of Education*. New York: McKay, 1976.

Articles

203 de Landsheere, Gilbert. "Anthropologie Culturelle et Education Comparée." *International Review of Education* 12, no. 1 (1966): 61-72.

204 Foley, Douglas E. "Anthropological Studies of Schooling in Developing Countries: Some Recent Findings and Trends." *Comparative Education Review* 21 (June-October 1977): 311-28.

205 Halls, W. D. "Culture and Education: The Culturalist Approach to Comparative Studies." In *Relevant Methods in Comparative Education*, edited by R. Edwards, B. Holmes, and J. van de Graaff, pp. 119-36. Hamburg: UNESCO Institute for Education, 1973.

206 Masemann, Vandra. "Anthropological Approaches to Comparative Education." *Comparative Education Review* 20 (October 1976): 368-80.

207 Roberts, Joan I. "Social Environmental Influences on Individuals in Sub-Cultural and Cross-Cultural Perspective." *Comparative Education Review* 14 (October 1970): 301-11.

208 Taba, Hilda. "Cultural Orientation in Comparative Education." *Comparative Education Review* 6 (February 1963): 171-76.

Readers

Books

209 Bereday, George Z. F., ed. *Essays on World Education: The Crisis of Supply and Demand*. New York: Oxford University Press, 1969.

210 Bereday, G. Z. F., ed. *Liberal Traditions in Education: Essays in Honor of Robert Ulich*. Cambridge, Mass.: Harvard Graduate School of Education, 1958.

211 Bereday, George, and Joseph A. Lauwerys, eds. *The Education Explosion*. New York: Harcourt, Brace and World, 1965.

212 Brembeck, Cole S. *Social Foundations of Education–A Cross Cultural Approach*. New York: Wiley, 1966.

213 Brickman, W. W., ed. *Comparative Education: Concept, Research and Application*. Norwood, Pa.: Norwood Editions, 1973.

214 Eckstein, Max, and Harold Noah, eds. *Scientific Investigations in Comparative Education*. New York: Macmillan, 1969.

215 Espe, Hans, ed. *Die Bedeutung der Vergleichenden Erziehungswissenschaft für Lehrerschaft und Schule*. Berlin: Orbis, 1956.

216 Fischer, J., ed. *The Social Sciences and the Comparative Study of Educational Systems*. Scranton, Pa.: International Textbook, 1970.

217 Fishman, Sterling, A. M. Kazamias, and H. M. Klaibard, eds. *Teachers, Students and Society: Perspectives on Education*. Boston: Little, Brown, 1974.

218 Fraser, Stewart, ed. *American Education in Foreign Perspectives: Twentieth Century Essays*. New York: Wiley, 1969.

219 Fraser, Stewart E., ed. *Sex, School, and Society: International Perspectives*. Nashville, Tenn.: Aurora Press, 1971.

220 Gezi, Kalil I., ed. *Education in Comparative and International Perspective*. New York: Holt, Rinehart and Winston, 1971.

221 Halsey, A. H., et al. *Education, Economy and Society*. Glencoe, Ill.: Free Press, 1965.

222 Karabel, Jerome, and A. H. Halsey, eds. *Power and Ideology in Education*. New York: Oxford University Press, 1977.

223 Kazamias, A. M., and E. H. Epstein, eds. *Schools in Transition*. Boston: Allyn and Bacon, 1970.

224 King, Edmund, ed. *Education for Uncertainty*. Beverly Hills, Calif.: Sage, 1979.

225 Lauwerys, J. A. *Essays in Comparative Education*. London: Evans, 1969.

226 Lauwerys, Joseph, and Graham Tayar, eds. *Education at Home and Abroad*. London: Routledge and Kegan Paul, 1973.

227 Moehlman, Arthur H., and Joseph S. Roucek, eds. *Comparative Education*. New York: Dryden Press, 1952.

228 Reller, T. L., and E. L. Morphet, eds. *Comparative Educational Administration*. Englewood Cliffs, N.J.: Prentice-Hall, 1962.

229 Verma, G. K., and C. Bagley, eds. *Race and Education Across Cultures*. London: Heinemann, 1975.

Surveys and Guides

Books

230 Holmes, Brian. *International Guide to Education Systems*. Paris: UNESCO, 1979.

231 International Bureau of Education. *Educational Trends in 1970: An International Survey*. Paris: UNESCO, 1970.

232 Organization for Economic Cooperation and Development. *Beyond Compulsory Schooling: Options and Changes in Upper Secondary Education*. Paris: OECD, 1977.

233 Organization for Economic Cooperation and Development. *Educational Statistics Handbook, Vol. I: International Tables, Vol. II: Country Tables, Vol. III*. Paris: OECD, 1974-75.

Articles

234 Anderson, C. Arnold. "World Patterns of Education." *Comparative Education Review* 4 (October 1960): 68-70.

235 Bereday, George Z. F. "School Systems and the Enrollment Crisis: A Comparative Overview." *Comparative Education Review* 12 (June 1968): 126-38.

236 Brickman, W. W. "Church, State and School in International Perspective." In *Religion, Government and Education*, edited by W. W. Brickman and Stanley Lehrer, pp. 144-247. New York: Society for the Advancement of Education, 1961.

237 Fernig, L. "The Collection of Educational Data." *International Review of Education* 9 (1963-64): 213-25.

238 Kandel, I. L. "Current Issues on Expanding Secondary Education." *International Review of Education* 5, no. 2 (1959): 155-65.

239 King, Edmund. "The 15-20 Age Group: A Comparative Survey." *Comparative Education* 6 (November 1970): 161-78.

240 Kleinberger, Sharon F. "A Comparative Analysis of Compulsory Education Laws." *Comparative Education* 11 (October 1975): 219-30.

241 Meyer, John W. "Economic and Political Effects on National Education Enrollment Patterns." *Comparative Education Review* 15 (February 1971): 28-43.

Teaching Comparative Education

Books

242 Holmes, B., and T. H. Bristow, eds. *Teaching Comparative Education: A Bibliographical Guide*. Paris: UNESCO, 1964.

Articles

243 Adejunmobi, S. A. "The Problems of Teaching Comparative Education in Nigeria." *Comparative Education* 8 (November 1972): 147-53.

244 Anderson, C. Arnold. "A New Swedish Textbook in Comparative Education." *Comparative Education Review* 4 (October 1960): 127-28.

245 Belding, Robert E. "Teaching by Case Method in Comparative Education." *Comparative Education Review* 2 (June 1958): 31-32.

246 Bereday, G. Z. F. "A Note on Textbooks in Comparative Education." *Comparative Education Review* 1 (June 1957): 3-4.

247 Bereday, G. Z. F. "Some Methods of Teaching Comparative Education." *Comparative Education Review* 1 (February 1958): 4-9.

248 Dottrens, R. "Pédagogie expérimentale, pédagogie comparée et plans d'études." *International Review of Education* 5, no. 3 (1959): 320-28.

249 Eckstein, Max. "On Teaching a 'Scientific' Comparative Education." *Comparative Education Review* 14 (October 1970): 279-82.

250 Noah, H. J., and Max Eckstein. "A Design for Teaching 'Comparative Education.'" *Comparative Education Review* 10 (October 1966): 511-13.

251 Scarangello, Anthony. "The Use of Motion Pictures in Comparative Education." *Comparative Education Review* 3 (October 1959): 24-27.

PROGRAMS AND CENTERS

Articles

252 Anderson, C. Arnold. "The Program of the Comparative Education Center, University of Chicago." In *Governmental Policy and International Education*, edited by S. Fraser, pp. 73-88. New York: Wiley, 1965.

253 Bereday, G. Z. F. "Comparative Education at Columbia University." *Comparative Education Review* 4 (June 1960): 15-17.

254 Bristow, Thelma. "The University of London Research Library for Comparative Education." *Comparative Education Review* 9 (June 1965): 213-18.

255 Coombs, Philip H. "The International Institute for Educational Planning." *International Review of Education* 12, no. 3 (1966): 333-45.

256 Hilker, Franz. "Comparative Education in the Documentation and Information Center in Bonn." *Comparative Education Review* 3 (February 1960): 13-15.

257 Lauwerys, Joseph A. "Comparative Education at the University of London." *Comparative Education Review* 3 (October 1959): 3-5.

258 Noah, Harold J. "Two Contemporary Projects in Comparative Education." *Comparative Education Review* 14 (October 1970): 262-68.

259 Peterson, A. O. C. "Applied Comparative Education: The International Baccalaureate." *Comparative Education* 13 (March 1977): 77-80.

260 Priscott, Linda. "The UNESCO Institute for Education, Hamburg: 25 Years in the Service of Educational Research." *International Review of Education* 22 (1976): 311-17.

261 Robinsohn, Saul B. "The Newly Founded Institute for Educational Research (Institut für Bildungsforschung) within the Max-Planck-Gesellschaft." *Comparative Education* 2 (November 1965): 31-36.

262 Veikshan, V. A. "The Moscow Center in Comparative Education." *Comparative Education Review* 3 (June 1959): 4-5.

263 Von Klemperer, Lily. "The Institute of International Education." *Comparative Education* 3 (November 1966): 49-53.

International Education

Books

264 Bereday, George, and Joseph A. Lauwerys, eds. *Education and International Life*. New York: Evan Brothers and Harcourt, Brace and World, 1964.

265 Fraser, Stewart, ed. *Governmental Policy and International Education*. New York: Wiley, 1965.

266 Leach, Robert J. *International Schools and Their Role in the Field of International Education*. Elmsford, N.Y.: Pergamon Press, 1969.

267 Paulsen, F. Robert, ed. *Changing Dimensions in International Education*. Tucson: University of Arizona Press, 1969.

268 Peterson, A. D. C. *The International Baccalaureate: An Experiment in International Education*. London: Harrap, 1972.

269 Phillips, H. M. *Educational Cooperation between Developed and Developing Countries*. New York: Praeger, 1976.

270 Scanlon, David, ed. *International Education: A Documentary History*. New York: Teacher's College, 1960.

271 Scanlon, David G., and James J. Shields, Jr. *Problems and Prospects in International Education*. New York: Teacher's College Press, 1968.

Articles

272 Anderson, C. A. "Challenges and Pitfalls in International Education." *National Society for the Study of Education Yearbook* 68 (1969): 66-85.

273 Anweiler, Oscar. "Comparative Education and the Internationalization of Education." *Comparative Education* 13 (June 1977): 109-14.

274 Humphrey, R. D. "International Education and Public Priority." *International Education and Cultural Exchange* 5 (Spring 1970): 12–23.

275 Kandel, I. L. "Education and Statesmanship." *International Review of Education* 4, no. 1 (1958): 1–16.

276 Kandel, I. L. "National and International Aspects of Education." *International Review of Education* 1, no. 1 (1955): 5–16.

277 Noll, Victor H. "International Cooperation in Educational Research." *International Review of Education* 4, no. 1 (1958): 77–87.

278 Quattlbanin, C. A. "Government Programs in International Education." *Educational Record* 40 (July 1959): 249–55.

279 Rohrs, Hermann. "Responsibilities and Problems of International Education." *Comparative Education* 6 (June 1970): 125–36.

280 Sasnett, Martena. "World-wide Exchange of Information on Education." *Comparative Education Review* 10, no. 3 (1966): 508–10.

Comparative Education: National Developments

Books

281 Elizalde, Elena. *Pedagogos Comparativistas Españoles*. Madrid: Fundación Universitaria Española, 1980.

282 Ikeda, Susunu. *Studies in Comparative Education*. Tokyo: Fukuwura Shuppan, 1969. (in Japanese)

283 Katz, J., et al. *The Comparative and International Education Society of Canada. Founding Proceedings: 1967*. Toronto: University of Toronto Press, 1968.

Articles

284 Bristow, Thelma. "A Survey of Education Libraries and Documentation Centres in Europe." *Comparative Education* 11 (June 1975): 113–27.

285 Cowen, Robert. "Comparative Education in Europe: A Note." *Comparative Education Review* 24 (February 1980): 98–108.

286 Hans, N. "The Soviet Approach to Comparative Education." *Comparative Education Review* 8 (June 1964): 90-93.

287 Kallen, D. "The Present Status of Comparative Education in Europe." *Comparative Education Review* 7 (October 1963): 108-12.

288 Katz, Joseph. "Comparative Education and External Aid Programs in Canada." *Comparative Education Review* 6 (June 1962): 12-15.

289 Lauwerys, J. A. "Comparative Education in Moscow." *International Review of Education* 11, no. 2 (1965): 218-19.

290 Ray, Douglas. "Comparative and International Education in Canada, 1973." *Canadian and International Education* 3 (June 1974): 1-3.

291 Wiloch, Tadeusz J. "The Development of Comparative Education in the Soviet Union." *Comparative Education Review* 20 (February 1976): 94-100.

TOPICAL COMPARATIVE STUDIES

Educational Policy

Books

292 Comparative Education Society in Europe. *Comparative Education Research and the Determinants of Educational Policy*. Amsterdam: European Cultural Foundation, 1963.

293 Kogan, M. *Educational Policies in Perspective: An Appraisal*. Paris: Organization for Economic Cooperation and Development, 1979.

294 Organization for Economic Cooperation and Development. *Educational Policies for the 1970s*. Paris: OECD, 1971.

295 Organization for Economic Cooperation and Development. *The Educational Situation in OECD Countries. A Review of Trends and Priority Issues for Policy*. Paris: OECD, 1974.

296 Purves, Alan C., and Daniel U. Levine, eds. *Educational Policy and International Assessment*. Berkeley, Calif.: McCutcheon, 1975.

Articles

297 Bereday, George Z. F. "The Law and Exclusion from Schools in Comparative Perspective." *Comparative Education Review* 24 (June 1980): 192–205.

298 Husén, Torsten. "Educational Research and Policy-Making." *Western European Education* 1 (Winter 1969–70): 8–22.

299 Kleinberger, Aharon F. "A Comparative Analysis of Compulsory Education Laws." *Comparative Education* 11 (October 1975): 219–31.

300 Stenhouse, Lawrence A. "Educational Decisions as Units of Study in an Exploratory Comparative Education." *International Review of Education* 7, no. 4 (1962): 412–19.

301 Thompson, A. R. "How Far Free? International Networks of Constraint upon National Education Policy in the Third World." *Comparative Education* 13 (October 1977): 155–68.

Educational Planning

Books

302 Adams, Don, ed. *Educational Planning*. Syracuse, N.Y.: Syracuse University Press, 1964.

303 Adams, Raymond S., ed. *Educational Planning: Towards a Qualitative Perspective*. Paris: UNESCO, 1978.

304 Anderson, C. Arnold. *The Social Context of Educational Planning*. Paris: International Institute for Educational Planning, 1977.

305 Beeby, C. E., ed. *Qualitative Aspects of Educational Planning*. Paris: UNESCO, International Institute for Educational Planning, 1969.

306 Bereday, George, and Joseph A. Lauwerys, eds. *Educational Planning*. New York: Harcourt, Brace and World, 1967.

307 Chau, Tâ Ngoc. *Demographic Aspects of Educational Planning*. Paris: UNESCO, 1969.

308 Chesswas, J. D. *Methodologies for Educational Planning for Developing Countries*. Paris: International Institute for Educational Planning, 1969.

309 Coombs, Philip H. *What Is Educational Planning?* Paris: International Institute for Educational Planning, 1970.

310 Correa, H. *Quantitative Methods of Educational Planning*. Scranton, Pa.: International Textbook, 1969.

311 Curle, Adam. *The Professional Identity of the Educational Planner*. Paris: International Institute for Educational Planning, 1969.

312 Da Nóbrega, V. L. *Ensino Planificudo e Edução Comparada*. Rio de Janeiro: Freitas Bastos, 1974.

313 Evans, David R. *Responsive Educational Planning: Myth or Reality*. Paris: UNESCO, 1977.

314 Hon-Chan, Chai. *Planning Education for a Plural Society*. Paris: UNESCO, 1971.

315 International Institute for Educational Planning. *Educational Planning: A Bibliography*. Paris: International Institute for Educational Planning, 1964.

316 International Institute for Educational Planning. *Manpower Aspects of Educational Planning: Problems for the Future*. Paris: International Institute for Educational Planning, 1968.

317 International Institute for Educational Planning. *New Educational Media in Action: Case Studies for Planners*, 3 vols. Paris: International Institute for Educational Planning, 1967.

318 Jamison, Dean T. *Cost Factors in Planning Educational Technology Systems*. Paris: UNESCO, 1977.

319 Lewy, Arieh. *Planning the School Curriculum*. Paris: UNESCO, 1977.

320 Lyons, Raymond, ed. *Administrative Aspects of Educational Planning*. Paris: International Institute for Educational Planning, 1970.

321 Montgomery, John D. *Alternatives and Decisions in Educational Planning*. Paris: UNESCO, 1976.

322 Onushkin, Victor G., ed. *Planning the Development of Universities*, 4 vols. Paris: UNESCO Press, 1975.

323 Organization for Economic and Cultural Development. *Long Range Policy Planning in Education*. Paris: OECD, 1974.

324 Organization for Economic and Cultural Development. *Participatory Planning in Education*. Paris: OECD, 1974.

325 Platt, William J. *Research for Educational Planning: Notes on Emergent Needs*. Paris: UNESCO, 1970.

326 Ramanathan, G. *Educational Planning and National Integration*. New York: Asia Publishing House, 1965.

327 Rosselló, Pedro. L'éducation comparée au service de la planification. Neuchâtel and Paris: Delachaux et Niestlé, 1952.

328 Rowley, C. D. *The Politics of Educational Planning in Developing Countries*. Paris: International Institute for Educational Planning, 1971.

329 Ruscoe, G. C. *The Conditions for Success in Educational Planning*. Paris: International Institute for Educational Planning, 1969.

330 Tibi, Claude. *Changing Needs for Training in Educational Planning and Administration*. Paris: UNESCO, 1977.

331 UNESCO. *Manpower Aspects of Educational Planning: Problems for the Future*. Paris: International Institute for Educational Planning, 1968.

332 Williams, Peter. *Planning Teacher Demand and Supply*. Paris: UNESCO, 1979.

333 Wilson, M. J. *A Systems Approach to the Planning of Educational Projects*. Dakar: UNESCO, Regional Office for Education in Africa, 1971.

334 Woodhall, Maureen. *Cost-Benefit Analysis in Educational Planning*. Paris: International Institute of Educational Planning, 1970.

Articles

335 Adams, Don. "A Model for a Cross-National Study of the Educational Planning Process." *International Education* 2 (Spring 1973): 33-51.

336 Anderson, C. Arnold. "Some Heretical Views on Educational Planning." *Comparative Education Review* 13 (October 1969): 260-75.

337 Balogh, Thomas. "The Economics of Educational Planning: Sense and Non-sense." *Comparative Education* 1 (October 1964): 5-18.

338 Bowman, Mary Jean. "An Economist's Approach to Education." *International Review of Education* 16, no. 2 (1970): 160-78.

339 Curle, Adam. "Some Aspects of Educational Planning in Underdeveloped Areas." *Harvard Educational Review* 32 (Summer 1962): 292-300.

340 Dalin, Per. "Planning for Change in Education: Qualitative Aspects of Educational Planning." *International Review of Education* 16, no. 4 (1970): 436-51.

341 Evans, David R. "The Use of Graphical Analysis in Educational Planning." *Comparative Education Review* 12 (June 1968): 139-48.

342 Ewers, C. D. "Educational Planning Within the Framework of Economic Planning." *International Review of Education* 10, no. 2 (1964): 129-40.

343 Garms, Walter I., Jr. "A Multivariate Analysis of the Correlates of Educational Effort by Nations." *Comparative Education Review* 12 (October 1968): 281-99.

344 Halls, W. D. "Educational Planning in an Industrial Society: The French Experience." *Comparative Education* 1 (October 1964): 19-28.

345 Hochleitner, R. Diez. "Utilización de la Educación Comparada en el Planeamiento Integral de la Educación." *International Review of Education* 5 (1959): 356-66.

346 Jacobs, Robert. "The Interdisciplinary Approach to Educational Planning." *Comparative Education Review* 8 (June 1964): 17-27.

347 Kelly, Michael. "Educational Planning from a Teacher's Point of View." *Comparative Education* 8 (September 1972): 85-92.

348 Kluchnikov, Boris K. "Reflections on the Concept and Practice of Educational Planning." *Prospects* 10, no. 1 (1980): 27-42.

349 Lave, Roy E., Jr., and Donald W. Kyle. "The Application of Systems Analysis to Educational Planning." *Comparative Education Review* 12 (February 1968): 39-56.

350 Olivier, R., and Y. Sabolo. "Simultaneous Planning of Employment, Production and Education." *International Labour Review* 107 (April 1973): 359-72.

351 Platt, William J. "Conflicts in Educational Planning." In *Education and Political Development*, edited by J. S. Coleman, pp. 566-84. Princeton: Princeton University Press, 1964.

352 Psacharapoulos, George. "Educational Planning: Past and Present." *Prospects* 8, no. 2 (1978): 135-42.

353 Psacharopoulos, George, and Gareth Williams. "Public Sector Earnings and Educational Planning." *International Labour Review* 108 (July 1973): 43-58.

354 Rosselló, Pedro. "Comparative Education as an Instrument of Planning." *Comparative Education Review* 4 (June 1960): 3-12.

355 Sen, Amartya K. "Models of Educational Planning and Their Applications." *Journal of Development Planning*, no. 2 (1970): 1-30.

356 Spaulding, Seth. "Educational Planning: Who Does What to Whom and With What Effect?" *Comparative Education* 13 (March 1977): 55-68.

357 Spitzberg, Irving J., Jr. "Educational Planning: Politics, Ideology, and Development." *African Studies Review* 21 (December 1978): 101-10.

358 Weiler, Hans N. "Towards a Political Economy of Educational Planning." *Prospects* 8, no. 3 (1978): 247-67.

359 Winn, Ira J. "Educational Planning and 'The System': Myth and Reality." *Comparative Education Review* 13 (October 1969): 343-50.

Development and Education: General

Books

360 Adams, Don, ed. *Education in National Development*. New York: McKay, 1971.

361 Adams, Don, and Robert Bjork. *Education in Developing Areas*. New York: McKay, 1971.

362 Adiseshian, M. S. *Education and Development: Restless Nations*. New York: Meade and Company, 1962.

363 Ahmed, Manzoor, and Philip H. Coombs. *The Assault on World Poverty: Problems of Rural Development, Education and Health*. Baltimore: Johns Hopkins University Press, 1975.

364 Beeby, C. E. *The Quality of Education in Developing Countries*. Cambridge, Mass.: Harvard University Press, 1966.

365 Brode, John. *The Process of Modernization: An Annotated Bibliography on the Sociocultural Aspects of Development*. Cambridge, Mass.: Harvard University Press, 1969.

366 Carnoy, Martin. *The Economics of Schooling and International Development*. Cuernavaca, Mexico: Centro Intercultural de Documentacion, 1971.

367 Castel, R., and J. C. Passeron. *Education, Développement et Démocratie*. Paris: Mouton, 1967.

368 Castle, E. B. *Education for Self-Help: New Strategies for Developing Countries*. New York: Oxford University Press, 1972.

369 Center for the Study of Education in Changing Societies. *Educational Problems in Developing Countries*. Groningen: Wolters-Noordhoff, 1969.

370 Cerych, Ladislav. *Problems of Aid to Education in Developing Countries*. New York: Praeger, 1965.

371 Chenery, Hollis, and Moisas Sygnin. *Patterns of Development 1950-1970*. New York: Oxford University Press, 1975.

372 Curle, Adam. *Educational Problems of Developing Societies, with Case Studies of Ghana, Pakistan, and Nigeria*. New York: Praeger, 1973.

373 Curle, Adam. *The Role of Education in Developing Societies*. Legon: Ghana University Press, 1961.

374 Dore, R. P. *The Diploma Disease: Education, Qualification and Development*. Berkeley: University of California Press, 1976.

375 *Education in Developing Countries of the Commonwealth. Reports of Research in Education*. London: Commonwealth Secretariat, 1973.

376 Elliot, William Jandell, ed. *Education and Training in the Developing Countries: The Role of U.S. Foreign Aid*. New York: Praeger, 1966.

377 Foster, P., and J. R. Sheffield, eds. *Education and Rural Development*. London: Evans, 1973.

378 Gillon, Phillip, and Hadassah Gillon, eds. *Science and Education in Developing States: Proceedings of the Fifth Rehovot Conference*. New York: Praeger, 1971.

379 Haddad, Wadi, et al. *Education: Sector Policy Paper*. Washington, D.C.: The World Bank, 1980.

380 Hanson, John W., and Cole S. Brembeck, eds. *Education and the Development of Nations*. New York: Holt, Rinehart and Winston, 1966.

381 Harbison, F. H. *Human Resources as the Wealth of Nations*. New York: Oxford University Press, 1973.

382 Jones, Graham. *The Role of Science and Technology in Developing Countries*. London: Oxford University Press, 1971.

383 Nader, Claire, and A. B. Zahlan. *Science and Technology in Developing Countries*. London: Cambridge University Press, 1969.

384 Organization for Economic Cooperation and Development. *Education and Regional Development*, 2 vols. Paris: OECD, 1979.

385 Organization for Economic Cooperation and Development. *Education in OECD Developing Countries, Trends and Perspectives*. Paris: OECD, 1974.

386 Panitchpakdi, S. *Educational Growth in Developing Countries: An Empirical Analysis*. Rotterdam: Rotterdam University Press, 1974.

387 Parkinson, Nancy. *Educational Aid and National Development*. London: Macmillan, 1976.

388 Shields, James J., Jr. *Education in Community Development; Its Function in Technical Assistance*. New York: Praeger, 1967.

389 Shipman, M. D. *Education and Modernization*. London: Faber and Faber, 1971.

390 Tugan, M. I. *Education and Development in Underdeveloped Countries*. The Hague: Centre for the Study of Education in Changing Societies, 1975.

391 Ward, F. Champion, ed. *Education and Development Reconsidered*. New York: Praeger, 1974.

Articles

392 Adams, Donald K. "Development Education." *Comparative Education Review* 21 (June-October 1977): 296-310.

393 Adiseshiah, Malcolm. "Education and Culture in the Service of Development." *Convergence* 2, no. 1 (1969): 22-29.

394 Adwere-Boamah, J. "Intellect and Commitment: A Potential for Educational Change in the New Nations." *International Journal of Comparative Sociology* 13 (June 1972): 99-112.

395 Anderson, C. A. "The Sorcerer's Apprentice: Education in Developing Nations." *Comparative Education* 6 (March 1970): 5-18.

396 Anderson, C. Arnold, and M. J. Bowman. "Concerning the Role of Education in Development." In *Old Societies and New Societies*, edited by C. Geertz, pp. 247-79. Glencoe, Ill.: Free Press, 1963.

397 Aran, L., S. Eisenstadt, and C. Adler. "The Effectiveness of Educational Systems in the Process of Modernization." *Comparative Education Review* 16 (February 1972): 30-43.

398 Brembeck, Cole S. "Education for National Development." *Comparative Education Review* 5 (February 1962): 223-31.

399 Burton, L. "Education and Development." *British Journal of Educational Studies* 17 (June 1969): 129-46.

400 Connor, Walter. "Education and National Development in the European

Socialist States: A Model for the Third World?" *Comparative Studies in Society and History* 17 (July 1975): 326-48.

401 Dedijer, Stevan. "Underdeveloped Science in Underdeveloped Countries." *Minerva* 2 (Autumn 1963): 61-82.

402 Dore, Ronald. "The Educational Impasse in the Developing World." *Manpower Journal* 9 (April-June 1973): 42-63.

403 Foster, Philip. "The Revolt Against the Schools." *Comparative Education Review* 15 (October 1971): 267-75.

404 Jansen, Marius B., and Lawrence Stone. "Education and Modernization in Japan and England." *Comparative Studies in Society and History* 9 (January 1967): 208-32.

405 Kandel, I. L. "Comparative Education and Underdeveloped Countries: A New Dimension." *Comparative Education Review* 4 (February 1961): 130-36.

406 Moravscik, Michael J. "Technical Assistance and Fundamental Research in Underdeveloped Countries." *Minerva* 2 (Winter 1964): 197-210.

407 Park, Wook. "Modernity and Views of Education: A Comparative Survey of Three Countries." *Comparative Education Review* 24 (February 1980): 35-47.

408 Parkyn, G. W. "Comparative Education Research and Development Education." *Comparative Education* 13 (June 1977): 87-94.

409 Peaslee, Alexander L. "Education's Role in Development." *Economic Development and Cultural Change* 17 (April 1969): 293-318.

410 Smirnov, A. G. "Education in Developing Countries." *Soviet Education* 14 (August 1972): 65-70.

411 Waisanen, F. B., and Hideya Kumata. "Education, Functional Literacy, and Participation in Development." *International Journal of Comparative Sociology* 13 (March 1972): 21-35.

412 Weiler, Hans N. "Education and Development: From the Age of Innocence to the Age of Scepticism." *Comparative Education* 14 (October 1978): 179-98.

DEVELOPMENT OF EDUCATIONAL SYSTEMS:
PROBLEMS AND PERSPECTIVES

Books

413 Brembeck, Cole S., and Timothy J. Thompson. *New Strategies for Educational Development*. Lexington, Mass.: D. C. Heath, 1972.

414 Heron, Alastair. *Planning Early Childhood Care and Education in Developing Countries*. Paris: UNESCO, 1979.

415 Organization for Economic Cooperation and Development. *Development of Secondary Education: Trends and Implications*. Paris: OECD, 1975.

416 UNESCO. *Asia, Arab States, Africa: Education and Progress*. Paris: UNESCO, 1961.

Articles

417 Allen, Dwight W. "Alternative Schools and the Crisis of Education in Developed Countries." *Prospects* 5, no. 2 (1975): 187-93.

418 Anderson, C. Arnold. "The Modernization of Education." In *Modernization*, edited by M. Weiner, pp. 68-80. New York: Basic Books, 1966.

419 Beeby, C. E. "Stages in the Growth of a Primary Education System." *Comparative Education Review* 6 (June 1962): 2-11.

420 Berstecher, D. "Wastage in Primary Education: A Comparative Look at Three Developing Countries." *Comparative Education* 8 (September 1972): 75-84.

421 Chaudhry, Mahinder D. "Educational Growth in Less Developed Countries." *International Journal of Comparative Sociology* 15 (March-June 1975): 13-34.

422 Clark, Jill. "Correlates of Educational Policy Priorities in Developing Nations." *Comparative Education Review* 20 (June 1976): 129-39.

423 Coombs, Philip H. "The Need for a New Strategy of Educational Development." *Comparative Education Review* 14 (February 1970): 75-89.

424 Correa, Hector. "Quality of Education and Socio-Economic Development." *Comparative Education Review* 8 (June 1964): 11-16.

425 de Landsheere, Gilbert. "Pre-School Education in Developing Countries." *Prospects* 7, no. 4 (1977): 506-12.

426 "Educational Trends in Some Developing Countries." *International Review of Education* 17, no. 2 (1971): 131-210. (special issue)

427 Fields, G. S. "The Private Demand for Education in Relation to Labour Market Conditions in Less-Developed Countries." *Economic Journal* 84 (December 1974): 706-925.

428 Foster, Philip J. "Dilemmas of Educational Development: What We Might Learn from the Past." *Comparative Education Review* 19 (October 1975): 375-92.

429 Fredriksen, Birger. "Universal Primary Education in Developing Countries: A Statistical Review." *Prospects* 8, no. 3 (1978): 363-74.

430 Galtung, Johan. "Literacy, Education and Schooling For What?" *Convergence* 8, no. 4 (1975): 39-51.

431 Ginzberg, Eli. "Educational Realism in Less Developed Countries." *Teachers College Record* 75 (February 1974): 319-26.

432 Goody, F., and I. Watt. "The Consequences of Literacy." In *Literacy in Traditional Societies*, edited by J. Goody, pp. 27-68. Cambridge: Cambridge University Press, 1968.

433 King, Kenneth. "Minimum Learning Needs for the Third World: New Panacea or New Problems." *Prospects* 6, no. 1 (1976): 39-57.

434 Laska, John A. "The Stages of Educational Development." *Comparative Education Review* 8 (December 1964): 251-63.

435 Levy, Mildred B. "Determinants of Primary School Dropouts in Developing Countries." *Comparative Education Review* 15 (February 1971): 44-58.

436 Miller, Ralph M. "Alternatives for Educational Development: Case Studies or Practical Applications." *Canadian and International Education* 1 (December 1972): 44.

437 Newbry, Burton C., and Kenneth L. Martin. "The Educational Crisis in the Lesser Developed Countries." *Journal of Developing Areas* 6 (January 1972): 155-62.

438 Peshkin, Alan. "Education in the Developing Nations: Dimensions of Change." *Comparative Education Review* 10 (February 1966): 53-66.

439 Sanders, Donald P. "Toward a Theory of Educational Development." *Comparative Education Review* 13 (October 1969): 276-93.

440 Schuman, H., A. Imkelas, and D. H. Smith. "Some Psychological Effects and Non-Effects of Literacy in a New Nation." *Economic Development and Cultural Change* 16, no. 1 (1967): 1-14.

441 Schutz, Richard E. "The Nature of Educational Development." *Journal of Research and Development in Education* 3 (Winter 1970): 39-64.

442 Swetz, Frank J. "Educational Crisis in Developing Nations: Alternatives." *Journal of Developing Areas* 8 (January 1974): 173-80.

443 van Baal, Jan. "Education in Non-Western Countries." *International Review of Education* 10, no. 1 (1965): 1-11.

444 Versluis, Jan. "The Qualitative Mismatch in Developing Countries." *Prospects* 3 (Autumn 1973): 349-57.

445 Zymelman, Manuel. "Analog Simulation of an Elementary School System in a Developing Country—Some Policy Implications." *Comparative Education Review* 12 (June 1968): 149-58.

EDUCATION AND ECONOMIC DEVELOPMENT

Books

446 Adelman, Irma, and C. Taft Morris. *Society, Politics and Economic Development: A Quantitative Approach*. Baltimore, Md.: Johns Hopkins University Press, 1971.

447 Ahmed, Manzoor, and Philip Coombs, eds. *Education for Rural Development: Case Studies for Planners*. New York: Praeger, 1974.

448 Anderson, C. A., and M. J. Bowman, eds. *Education and Economic Development*. Chicago: Aldine, 1965.

449 Chau, T. N. *Population Growth and Costs of Education in Developing Countries*. Paris: International Institute for Educational Planning, 1972.

450 Cipolla, Carlo M. *Literacy and Economic Development in the West.* New York: Penguin, 1969.

451 Curle, Adam. *Educational Strategy for Developing Societies: A Study of Education and Social Factors in Relation to Economic Growth.* London: Tavistock, 1970.

452 Harbison, Frederick M. *Human Resources as the Wealth of Nations.* New York: Oxford University Press, 1973.

453 Harbison, Frederick, and Charles A. Myers. *Education, Manpower and Economic Growth.* New York: McGraw-Hill, 1964.

454 Machlup, Fritz. *Education and Economic Growth.* Lincoln: University of Nebraska Press, 1970.

455 Myiat, H. *Economic Theory and the Underdeveloped Countries.* New York: Oxford University Press, 1971.

456 Piper, D. C., and T. Cole, eds. *Post-Primary Education and Political and Economic Development.* London: Cambridge University Press, 1964.

Articles

457 Arnesen, Carl. "Structure économique et réforme scolaire dans les pays evoluées." *International Review of Education* 3, no. 1 (1957): 69-80.

458 Asher, William, and Joe E. Shively. "The Technique of Discriminant Analysis: A Reclassification of Harbison and Myer's Seventy-five Countries." *Comparative Education Review* 13 (June 1969): 180-86.

459 Bennett, William S., Jr. "Educational Change and Economic Development." *Sociology of Education* 40 (Spring 1967): 101-14.

460 Blaug, Mark. "Economic and Educational Planning in Developing Countries." *Prospects* 2 (Winter 1972): 431-41.

461 Bowman, Mary Jean. "The Human Investment Revolution in Economic Thought." *Sociology of Education* 39 (Spring 1966): 111-38.

462 Coombs, Philip H. "The Adjustment of the Educational Structure to the Requirements of Economic Development." *International Review of Education* 10, no. 1 (1964): 53-70.

463 Dore, R. P. "Human Capital Theory, the Diversity of Societies and the Problem of Quality in Education." *Higher Education* 5 (February 1976): 70-102.

464 Foster, Philip J. "The Vocational School Fallacy in Development Planning." In *Education and Economic Development*, edited by C. Arnold Anderson and M. J. Bowman, pp. 142-66. London: Cass, 1965.

465 Johnson, H. A. "Toward a Generalized Capital Accumulation Approach to Economic Development." In *Economics of Education*, edited by M. Blaugh, pp. 34-44. New York: Pergamon, 1970.

466 King, Anthony. "Higher Technical Education and Socio-Economic Development." *Comparative Education* 5 (December 1969): 263-82.

467 Lewis, W. A. "Education for Economic Development." *International Social Science Journal* 14, no. 4 (1962): 685-99.

468 McClelland, David C. "Does Education Accelerate Economic Growth?" *Economic Development and Cultural Change* 14 (April 1966): 257-78.

469 Miller, William L. "Education as a Source of Economic Growth." *Journal of Economic Issues* 1 (December 1967): 280-96.

470 Peaslee, Alexander L. "Primary School Enrollments and Economic Growth." *Comparative Education Review* 11 (February 1967): 57-67.

471 Rado, E. R. "Manpower, Education, and Economic Growth." *Journal of Modern African Studies* 4 (May 1966): 83-93.

472 Skorov, G. E. "The Developing Countries: Education, Employment, Economic Growth." *Soviet Education* 14 (August 1972): 5-64.

473 Sobel, Irvin. "The Human Capital Revolution in Economic Development: Its Current History and Status." *Comparative Education Review* 22 (June 1978): 278-308.

474 Steadman, Henry J. "Some Questions about National Educational Investments and Economic Development." *Journal of Developing Areas* 6 (October 1971): 51-62.

475 Vaizey, John. "Comparative Notes on Economic Growth, and Social Change in Education." *Comparative Education Review* 5 (June 1961): 7-12.

EDUCATION AND SOCIAL DEVELOPMENT

Books

476 Adams, Don, and Joseph P. Farrell, eds. *Education and Social Development*. Syracuse, N.Y.: Center for Development Education, Syracuse University, 1967.

Articles

477 Adams, Don. "Education and Social Development." *Review of Educational Research* 38 (June 1968): 243-63.

478 Adams, Don. "The Study of Education and Social Development." *Comparative Education Review* 9 (October 1965): 258-69.

479 Foster, Philip J. "Education and Social Differentiation in Less-Developed Countries." *Comparative Education Review* 21 (June-October 1977): 211-29.

EDUCATION AND POLITICAL DEVELOPMENT

Books

480 Coleman, J. S., ed. *Education and Political Development*. London: Oxford University Press, 1968.

Articles

481 Abernathy, David, and Trevor Coombe. "Education and Politics in Developing Countries." *Harvard Educational Review* 35 (Summer 1965): 287-302.

482 Adam, Roy. "Education and Politics in Developing Countries." *Teachers College Record* 70 (March 1969): 495-503.

483 Curle, Adam. "Education, Politics and Development." *Comparative Education Review* 7 (February 1964): 226-45.

484 Eisenstadt, S. N. "Education and Political Development." In *Post-primary Education and Political and Economic Development*, edited by Don C. Piper and Taylor Cole, pp. 27-47. Durham, N.C.: Duke University Press, 1964.

485 Eisenstadt, S. N. "Political Modernization: Some Comparative Notes." *International Journal of Comparative Sociology* 5 (March 1964): 3-24.

486 Eisenstadt, S. N. "The Development of Socio-Political Centers at the Second Stage of Modernization—A Comparative Analysis of Two Types." *International Journal of Comparative Sociology* 7 (March 1966): 119-38.

487 Epstein, E. H., ed. "Education and Nationality: The Sociopolitical Role of Schools." *Education and Urban Society* 10 (February 1978): 107-254.

488 Gibson, G. W. "A Revolution in Education: Some Aspects of Bureaucracies, Development and Education." *Comparative Education* 4 (March 1968): 97-108.

489 Goel, M. Lal. "The Relevance of Education for Political Participation in a Developing Society." *Comparative Political Studies* 3 (October 1970): 333-46.

490 Hanf, Theodor, et al. "Education—An Obstacle to Development? Reflections on the Political Function of Education in Asia and Africa." *Comparative Education Review* 19 (February 1975): 68-87.

491 Hoselitz, Bert. "Investment in Education and Its Political Impact." In *Education and Political Development*, edited by J. S. Coleman, pp. 541-65. Princeton, N.J.: Princeton University Press, 1964.

492 Simbulan, Danle C. "On Models and Reality: Some Notes on the Approaches to the Study of Elites in Developing Societies." *Asian Studies* 6 (December 1968): 421-30.

EDUCATION AND INDIVIDUAL MODERNITY

Books

493 Inkeles, A., and D. Smith. *Becoming Modern: Individual Change in Six Developing Countries*. Cambridge, Mass.: Harvard University Press, 1974.

494 Lerner, Daniel. *The Passing of Traditional Society*. New York: Free Press, 1958.

Articles

495 Coughenour, C. Milton, and John B. Stephenson. "Measures of Individual Modernity: Review and Commentary." *International Journal of Comparative Sociology* 3 (June 1972): 81-99.

496 Inkeles, Alex. "The School as a Context for Modernization." *International Journal of Comparative Sociology* 14 (September-December 1973): 163-80.

497 Inkeles, Alex, and Donald B. Holsinger. "Introduction. Education and Individual Modernity in Developing Countries." *International Journal of Comparative Sociology* 14 (September-December 1973): 157-63.

498 Inkeles, Alex, and David H. Smith. "The Fate of Personal Adjustment in the Process of Modernization." *International Journal of Comparative Sociology* 11 (June 1970): 81-115.

499 Kumar, Krishna, and F. B. Waisanen. "Education, Adoption of Innovations and Individual Modernity: A Study of Two Developing Societies." *International Journal of Comparative Sociology* 20 (September-December 1979): 213-24.

Colonialism and Education

Books

500 Altbach, Philip, and Gail Kelly, eds. *Education and Colonialism*. New York: Longmans, 1978.

501 Arnove, Robert F., ed. *Philanthropy and Cultural Imperialism: The Foundations at Home and Abroad*. Boston: G. K. Hall, 1980.

502 Carnoy, Martin. *Education as Cultural Imperialism*. New York: McKay, 1974.

503 Mende, Tibor. *From Aid to Recolonization: Lessons of a Failure*. New York: Pantheon, 1973.

Articles

504 Altbach, Philip G. "Neocolonialism and Education." *Teachers College Record* 72 (May 1971): 543-58.

505 Altbach, Philip G. "Servitude of the Mind?: Education, Dependency and Neocolonialism." *Teachers College Record* 79 (December 1977): 188-204.

506 Altbach, Philip G. "The Distribution of Knowledge in the Third World: A

Case Study in Neocolonialism." In *Education and Colonialism*, edited by P. Altbach and G. Kelly, pp. 301-30. New York: Longmans, 1978.

507 Arnove, Robert F. "Comparative Education and World Systems Analysis." *Comparative Education Review* 24 (February 1980): 48-62.

508 Clignet, Remi. "Damned If You Do, Damned If You Don't: The Dilemmas of Colonizer-Colonized Relations." *Comparative Education Review* 15 (October 1971): 296-312.

509 Epstein, E. H. "The Social Control Thesis and Educational Reform in Dependent Nations." *Theory and Society* 5 (March 1978): 255-76.

510 Evans, David R. "Decolonization: Does the Teacher Have a Role?" *Comparative Education Review* 15 (October 1971): 276-87.

511 Kelly, Gail P. "The Relation Between Colonial and Metropolitan Schools: A Structural Analysis." *Comparative Education* 15 (June 1979): 209-16.

512 Kelly, Gail, and Philip Altbach. "Introduction to Colonialism and Education." In *Education and Colonialism*, edited by P. G. Altbach and G. P. Kelly, pp. 1-52. New York: Longmans, 1978.

513 Zachariah, Mathew. "Educational Aid: A Bibliographic Essay and a Plea for New Lines of Enquiry." *Comparative Education* 6 (June 1970): 115-24.

Education and the Economy

Books

514 Blaug, Mark. *Introduction to the Economics of Education*. London: Penguin, 1970.

515 Blaug, Mark, ed. *Economics of Education: A Selected Annotated Bibliography*. Oxford: Pergamon, 1966.

516 Bowman, Mary Jean, ed. *Readings in the Economics of Education*. Paris: UNESCO, 1971.

517 Brimer, M. A., and L. Pauli. *Wastage in Education: A World Problem*. Paris: UNESCO, 1971.

518 Cohn, E. *The Economics of Education*. Cambridge, Mass.: Ballinger, 1979.

519 Hall, Robert King, and J. A. Lauwerys, eds. *Education and Economics*. New York: World, 1956.

520 Hufner, K., and J. Neuman, eds. *Economics of Education in Transition*. Stuttgart, West Germany: Ernest Klett Verlag, 1969.

521 Lauwerys, Joseph A. *Education and the Economy*. London: Evans, 1969.

522 Miller, Gordon W. *Success, Failure and Wastage in Higher Education: An Overview of the Problems Derived from Research and Theory*. London: Harrap, 1970.

523 Organization for Economic Cooperation and Development. *Economic Aspects of Higher Education*. Paris: OECD, 1964.

524 Organization for Economic Cooperation and Development. *Selection and Certification in Education and Employment*. Paris: OECD, 1977.

525 Rogers, Daniel C., and Hirsch S. Ruchlin. *Economics and Education: Principles and Applications*. London: Collier-Macmillan, 1971.

526 Schultz, T. W. *The Economic Value of Education*. New York: Columbia University Press, 1963.

527 Tinbergen, Jan, et al. *Econometric Models of Education: Some Applications*. Paris: Organization for Economic Cooperation and Development, 1965.

528 UNESCO. *Readings in the Economics of Education*. Paris: UNESCO, 1968.

529 UNESCO Office of Statistics. *A Statistical Study of Wastage at School*. Paris: UNESCO-International Bureau of Education, 1972.

530 Vaizey, John. *The Economics of Education*. New York: The Free Press, 1962.

531 Vaizey, John. *The Political Economy of Education*. London: Gerald Duckworth, 1972.

532 Windham, D. *Economic Dimensions of Education*. Washington, D.C.: National Academy of Education, 1979.

Articles

533 Benson, Charles. "Economics in the Making of Educational Policy." In *The Social Sciences and the Comparative Study of Educational Systems*, edited by J. Fischer, pp. 451-71. Scranton, Pa.: International Textbook, 1970.

534 Benson, Charles S., J. Ritzen, and Irene Blumenthal. "Recent Perspectives in the Economics of Education." *Social Science Quarterly* 55 (September 1974): 244-61.

535 Bowman, M. J. "Converging Concerns of Economists and Educators." *Comparative Education Review* 6 (October 1962): 111-19.

536 Bowman, M. J. "An Economist's Approach to Education." *International Review of Education* 16, no. 2 (1970): 160-77.

537 Edding, Friedrich. "The Use of Economics in Comparing Educational Systems." *International Review of Education* 11, no. 4 (1965): 453-65.

538 Foster, P. "Education, Economy, Equality." *Interchange* 2, no. 1 (1971): 51-61.

539 Hansen, W. Lee. "Economics and Comparative Education: Will They Ever Meet? And, If So, When?" *Comparative Education Review* 21 (June-October 1977): 230-46.

540 Roberts, K. "Economy and Education: Foundations of a General Theory." *Comparative Education* 7 (August 1971): 3-14.

541 Vaizey, John. "Education as Investment in Comparative Education." *Comparative Education Review* 5 (October 1961): 97-104.

542 Weisbrod, B. A. "Education and Investment in Human Capital." *Journal of Political Economy* 70 (October 1962): 106-23.

543 Windham, D. M. "Social Benefits and Subsidization of Higher Education: A Critique." *Higher Education* 5 (August 1976): 237-52.

EDUCATION AND EMPLOYMENT

Books

544 Ahamad, Bashir, and Mark Blaug. *The Practice of Manpower Forecasting: A Collection of Case Studies*. San Francisco: Jossey-Bass, 1973.

545 Blaug, Mark. *Education and the Employment Problem in Developing Countries*. Geneva: International Labour Office, 1973.

546 Callaway, Archibald. *Educational Planning and Unemployed Youth*. Paris: International Institute for Educational Planning, 1971.

547 Carnoy, Martin. *Education and Employment*. Paris: International Institute for Educational Planning, 1977.

548 Edwards, E. O., ed. *Employment in Developing Nations: Report on a Ford Foundation Study*. New York and London: Columbia University Press, 1974.

549 Heyduk, M., ed. *Education and Work: A Symposium*. New York: Institute of International Education, 1979.

550 Staley, E. *Planning Occupational Education and Training for Development*. New York: Praeger, 1971.

Articles

551 Anderson, C. A. "Technical and Vocational Education in the New Nations." In *Schools in Transition*, edited by A. Kazamias and E. Epstein, pp. 174-89. Boston: Allyn and Bacon, 1968.

552 Eedle, J. H. "The Education Spiral: Education and Employment in the Commonwealth." *Comparative Education* 9 (October 1973): 135-50.

553 Fretwell, D. H. "Industrial Education and the Career Education Concept: Implications for Developing Countries." *Man/Society/Technology* 4 (January 1976): 119-21.

554 Harbison, Frederick, and C. A. Myers. "Education and Employment in the Newly Developing Economies." *Comparative Education Review* 8 (June 1964): 5-10.

555 Husén, Torsten. "Ability, Opportunity and Career: A 26-Year Follow-up." *Educational Research* 10 (June 1968): 170-84.

556 Rado, Emil R. "The Relevance of Education for Employment." *Journal of Modern African Studies* 10 (October 1972): 459-75.

557 Roberts, K. "The Organization of Education and the Ambitions of School-Leavers: A Comparative Review." *Comparative Education* 4 (March 1968): 87-96.

EDUCATION AND INCOME

Books

558 Organization for Economic Cooperation and Development. *Education, Inequality and Life Chances*, 2 vols. Paris: OECD, 1975.

559 Psacharopoulos, George. *Earnings and Education in OECD Countries*. Paris: Organization for Economic Cooperation and Development, 1975.

560 Psacharopoulos, George, and Keith Hinchcliffe. *Returns to Education: An International Comparison*. San Francisco: Jossey-Bass, 1973.

561 Taubman, P. J. *Sources of Inequality in Earnings: Personal Skills, Random Events, Preferences Toward Risk and Other Occupational Characteristics*. New York: American Elsevier, 1975.

Articles

562 Bhagawati, J. N. "Education, Class Structure and Income Inequality." *World Development* 1 (May 1973): 21-36.

563 Blaug, Mark. "The Correlation Between Education and Earnings: What Does It Signify?" *Higher Education* 1 (February 1972): 53-76.

564 Carnoy, Martin. "Can Educational Policy Equalize Income Distribution?" *Prospects* 8, no. 1 (1978): 3-18.

565 Fields, G. S. "Higher Education and Income Distribution in a Less Developed Country." *Oxford Economic Papers* 27 (July 1975): 245-59.

566 Psacharopoulos, George. "Rates of Return to Investment in Education Around the World." *Comparative Education Review* 16 (February 1972): 54-67.

567 Woodhall, Maureen. "The Economic Returns to Investment in Women's Education." *Higher Education* 2, no. 3 (1973): 275-99.

EDUCATION AND HUMAN RESOURCE MIGRATION

Books

568 Myers, Robert G. *Education and Emigration: Study Abroad and Migration of Human Resources*. New York: McKay, 1972.

569 Staley, Eugene. *Planning Occupational Education and Training for Development*. New York: Praeger, 1971.

Articles

570 Bhagwati, Jagdish N. "International Migration of the Highly Skilled: Economics, Ethics and Taxes." *Third World Quarterly* 1 (July 1979): 17-30.

571 Watanabe, S. "The Brain Drain from Developing to Developed Countries." *International Labour Review* 99 (April 1969): 401-34.

Politics of Education and Political Socialization

Books

572 Abbot, Joan. *Student Life in a Class Society*. Oxford: Pergamon, 1971.

573 Almond, Gabriel A., and S. Verba. *The Civic Culture: Political Attitudes and Democracy in Five Nations*. Princeton, N.J.: Princeton University Press, 1963.

574 Harman, Grant. *Research in the Politics of Education, 1973-1978: An International Review and Bibliography*. Canberra, Australia: Australian National University Press, 1979.

575 Lowe, John. *Adult Education and Nation Building*. Chicago: Aldine, 1970.

576 Emmery, Louis. *Can the School Build a New Social Order?* Amsterdam: Elsevier, 1974.

577 Gerbod, Paul. *Les Enseignants et la Politique*. Paris: Presses Universitaires de France, 1976.

578 Kogan, Maurice. *The Politics of Education*. London: Penguin, 1971.

579 Massialas, Byron G. *Education and Political System*. Reading, Mass.: Addison-Wesley, 1969.

580 Nielsen, H. Dean. *Tolerating Political Dissent: The Impact of High School Social Climates in the United States and West Germany*. Stockholm: Almquist and Wiksell, 1977.

581 Oppenheim, A. N., and J. Torney. *The Measurement of Children's Civic Attitudes in Different Nations*. New York: Wiley, 1974.

Articles

582 Benoit, André. "A Note on Decision-Making Processes in the Politics of Education." *Comparative Education Review* 19 (February 1975): 155-69.

583 Bielas, Leon. "Comparison of Systems of Education in Two Countries with Common Historical Traditions and Different Social Orders." In *Relevant Methods in Comparative Education*, edited by R. Edwards, B. Holmes, and J. van de Graaff, pp. 143-52. Hamburg: UNESCO Institute for Education, 1973.

584 Bruner, Jerome S. "Culture, Politics and Pedagogy." *International Education* 2 (Fall 1972): 31-35.

585 "The Classroom Behavior of Teachers." *International Review of Education* 18, no. 4 (1972): 427-568.

586 Entwistle, Harold. "Problems of Political Education." *Canadian and International Education* 1 (June 1972): 15-28.

587 Harman, G. S. "The Politics of Education: A Bibliographical Guide." *International Review of Education* 22, no. 4 (1976): 555-60.

588 Hess, Robert D. "The Socialization of Attitudes Toward Political Authority: Some Cross-National Comparisons." *International Social Science Journal* 15, no. 4 (1963): 542-57.

589 LeVine, Robert. "Political Socialization and Cultural Change." In *Old Societies and New States*, edited by Clifford Geertz, pp. 280-303. Glencoe, Ill.: Free Press, 1963.

590 Massialas, Byron G. "Education and Political Development." *Comparative Education Review* 21 (June-October 1977): 274-95.

591 Massialas, Byron G. "Some Propositions About the Role of the School in the Formation of Political Behavior and Political Attitudes of Students: Cross-National Perspectives." *Comparative Education Review* 19 (February 1975): 169-76.

592 Merelman, Richard. "Social Stratification and Political Socialization in Mature Industrial Societies." *Comparative Education Review* 19 (February 1975): 13-30.

593 Merritt, Richard I., and Fred Coombs. "Politics and Educational Reform." *Comparative Education Review* 21 (June-October 1977): 247-73.

594 Mhaiki, P. J. "Political Education and Adult Education." *Convergence* 6, no. 1 (1973): 15-22.

595 Mwanakatwe, J. M. "Adult Education and Political and Social Change." *Convergence* 3, no. 1 (1970): 26-39.

596 Rothman, Kenneth I. "A Bibliographic Guide to Education and Political Socialization." In *Education and Political Development*, edited by J. S. Coleman, pp. 585-609. Princeton: Princeton University Press, 1964.

597 Van Egmond, Elmer. "Socialization Processes and Education." *Review of Educational Research* 31 (February 1961): 80-90.

598 Wirt, Frederick M. "Comparing Educational Politics: Theory, Units of Analysis and Research Strategies." *Comparative Education Review* 24 (June 1980): 174-91.

Schools and Social Stratification

Books

599 Boudon, Raymond. *Education, Opportunity, and Social Inequality: Changing Prospects in Western Societies*. New York: Wiley, 1974.

600 Boudon, Raymond. *Mathematical Structures of Social Mobility*. San Francisco: Jossey-Bass, 1973.

601 Burn, Barbara B., ed. *Access Systems. Youth and Employment*. New York: International Council for Educational Development, 1977.

602 Husén, Torsten. *Social Background and Educational Career*. Paris: Organization for Economic Cooperation and Development, 1972.

603 Neave, Guy. *Patterns of Equality*. Paris: Institute of Education, European Cultural Foundation, 1976.

604 Organization for Economic Cooperation and Development. *Education, Inequality and Life Chances*. Paris: OECD, 1975.

605 Organization for Economic Cooperation and Development. *Equal Educational Opportunity*. Paris: OECD, 1971.

Articles

606 Adams, Don, and Joseph P. Farrell. "Societal Differentiation and Educational Differentiation." *Comparative Education* 5 (December 1969): 249-62.

607 Anderson, C. Arnold. "Education, Class and the Nation." *Higher Education* 7 (February 1978): 95-106.

608 Anderson, C. Arnold. "Equality of Opportunity in a Pluralistic Society: A Theoretical Framework." *International Review of Education* 21, no. 3 (1975): 287-301.

609 Anderson, C. Arnold. "Expanding Educational Opportunities: Conceptualization and Measurement." *Higher Education* 4 (November 1975): 393-408.

610 Anderson, C. Arnold. "A Skeptical Note on the Relation of Vertical Mobility to Education." *American Journal of Sociology* 66 (May 1961): 560-69.

611 Bereday, George Z. F. "School Systems and the Enrollment Crisis: A Comparative Overview." *Comparative Education Review* 12 (June 1968): 126-38.

612 Bereday, George Z. F. "Social Stratification and Education in Industrial Countries." *Comparative Education Review* 21 (June-October 1977): 195-210.

613 Bowles, S. "Schooling and Inequality from Generation to Generation." In *Investment in Education*, edited by T. W. Schultz, pp. 219-51. Chicago: University of Chicago Press, 1972.

614 Corwin, Ronald G. "Education in Crisis: A Sociological Analysis of Schools and Universities in Transition." *International Review of Education* 22, no. 4 (1976): 562-63.

615 Eckstein, Max A., and Harold J. Noah. "Metropolitanism and Education: A Comparative Study of Teachers and School Success in Amsterdam, London, Paris, and New York." *Comparative Education Review* 18 (October 1974): 359-73.

616 Fox, Thomas G., and S. M. Miller. "Economic, Political and Social Determinants of Mobility: An International Cross-Sectional Analysis." *Acta Sociologica* 9 (1966): 76-93.

617 Hans, Nicholas. "Class, Caste, and Intellectual Elite in Comparative Perspective." *Comparative Education Review* 4 (February 1961): 140-46.

618 Havinghurst, Robert J. "Education and Social Mobility in Four Societies." In *Education, Economy, and Society*, edited by A. H. Halsey, J. Floud, and C. A. Anderson, pp. 105-20. New York: Free Press, 1972.

619 Havinghurst, Robert J. "Education, Social Mobility and Social Change in Four Societies: A Comparative Study." *International Review of Education* 4, no. 2 (1958): 167-85.

620 Husén, Torsten. "Academic Performance in Selective and Comprehensive Schools." In *Power and Ideology in Education*, edited by J. Karabel and A. H. Halsey, pp. 275-81. New York: Oxford University Press, 1977.

621 Kandel, I. L. "Equalizing Educational Opportunities and its Problems." *International Review of Education* 3, no. 1 (1957): 1-12.

622 Merelman, Richard M. "Social Stratification and Political Socialization in Mature Industrial Societies." *Comparative Education Review* 19 (February 1975): 13-31.

623 Nash, Paul. "Training an Elite." *History of Education Quarterly* 1 (March 1961): 14-21.

624 Neelsen, John. "Education and Social Mobility." *Comparative Education Review* 19 (February 1975): 129-44.

625 Podmore, Chris. "Private Schools—An International Comparison." *Canadian and International Education* 6 (December 1977): 8-33.

626 Stephenson, R. M. "Stratification, Education and Occupational Orientation." *British Journal of Sociology* 9 (March 1958): 42-52.

627 Treiman, Donald J., and Kermit Teller. "The Process of Status Attainment in the United States and Great Britain." *American Journal of Sociology* 81 (November 1975): 563-83.

ETHNICITY AND EDUCATION

Books

628 Chan, Chai H. *Planning Education for Plural Society*. Paris: International Institute for Educational Planning, 1971.

Articles

629 LaBelle, Thomas, and Peter White. "Education and Multiethnic Integration: An Intergroup Relations Typology." *Comparative Education Review* 24 (June 1980): 155-73.

630 Paulston, Rolland G. "Ethnicity and Educational Change: A Priority for Comparative Education." *Comparative Education Review* 20 (October 1976): 269-77.

631 Singleton, John. "Education and Ethnicity." *Comparative Education Review* 21 (June-October 1977): 329-44.

632 Watson, Keith. "Educational Policies in Multi-Cultural Societies." *Comparative Education* 15 (March 1979): 17-33.

Language and Education

Books

633 Carroll, John B. *The Teaching of French as a Second Language in Eight Countries*. New York: Wiley, 1975.

634 Fishman, Joshua, C. Ferguson, and J. Das Gupta, eds. *Language Problems of Developing Nations*. New York: Wiley, 1968.

635 Lewis, E. G. *Bilingualism and Bilingual Education: A Comparative Study*. Albuquerque: University of New Mexico Press, 1980.

636 Lewis, E. Glyn, and C. E. Massad. *The Teaching of English as a Foreign Language in Ten Countries*. New York: Wiley, 1975.

Articles

637 Illich, Ivan. "Vernacular Values and Education."*Teachers College Record* 81 (Fall 1979): 31-76.

638 Francis, Russell. "Paradise Lost and Regained: Educational Policy in Melanesia." *Comparative Education* 14 (March 1978): 49-64.

639 Kehoe, Monika. "Language and Politics in Developing Areas." *Canadian and International Education* 1 (June 1972): 51-58.

640 LaBelle, T., and P. White. "Education and Colonial Language Policies." *International Review of Education* 24, no. 3 (1978): 243-62.

641 Masemann, V. "Ethnography of the Bilingual Classroom." *International Review of Education* 24, no. 3 (1978): 295-308.

642 "Schooling in the Mother Tongue in a Multilingual Environment." *Prospects* 6, no. 3 (1976): 382-450.

643 Seif, N. S. "The Teaching of Modern Languages in Belgium, England, Holland, and Germany." *Comparative Education Review* 9 (June 1965): 163-69.

644 Stahl, Abraham. "The Cultural Antecedents of Sociolinguistic Differences." *Comparative Education* 11 (June 1975): 147-52.

WOMEN AND EDUCATION

Books

645 Boserup, Esther. *Women's Role in Economic Development*. New York: St. Martin's, 1970.

646 Chabaud, Jacqueline. *The Education and Advancement of Women*. Paris: UNESCO Press, 1970.

647 Clark, N. *Education for Development and the Rural Women*, vol. 1. Washington, D.C.: World Education, 1979.

648 Cochrane, S. H. *Education and Fertility: What Do We Know?* Baltimore, Md.: Johns Hopkins University Press, 1979.

649 Epskamp, C. *Inequality in Female Access to Education in Developing Countries, A Bibliography*. The Hague: Centre for the Study of Education in Developing Countries, 1979.

650 Fogarty, M. P., R. Rapoport, and R. N. Rapoport. *Sex, Career and Family, Including an International Review of Women's Roles*. London: George Allen and Unwin, 1971.

651 Giole, Janet Z., and Audrey C. Smock, eds. *Women and Society: In International and Comparative Perspective*. New York: Wiley-Interscience, 1976.

652 Smock, Audrey C. *Women's Education and Roles*. Chicago: University of Chicago Press, 1980.

653 UNESCO. *Comparative Study on Access of Girls and Women to Higher Education*. Paris: UNESCO, 1967.

654 UNESCO. *Women, Education, Equality: A Decade of Experiment*. Paris: UNESCO, 1975.

Articles

655 Barber, Elinor G. "Some International Perspectives on Sex Differences in Education." *Signs* 4 (Spring 1979): 584-92.

656 Biraimah, Karen Coffyn. "The Impact of Western Schools in Girls' Expectations: A Togolese Case." *Comparative Education Review* 24 (June 1980): S196-S208.

657 Bowman, Mary Jean, and C. Arnold Anderson. "The Participation of Women in the Third World." *Comparative Education Review* 24 (June 1980): S13-S31.

658 Finn, Jeremy. "Sex Differences in Educational Outcomes: A Cross-National Study." *Sex Roles* 6 (February 1980): 9-26.

659 Finn, Jeremy, Loretta Dulberg, and Janet Reis. "Sex Differences in Educational Attainment: A Cross-National Perspective." *Harvard Educational Review* 49 (November 1979): 477-503.

660 Finn, Jeremy, Janet Reis, and Loretta Dulberg. "Sex Differences in Educational Attainment: The Process." *Comparative Education Review* 24 (June 1980): S33-S52.

661 Hoffman, Lois. "The Employment of Women, Education and Fertility." *Merrill-Palmer Quarterly* 20, no. 2 (1974): 99-120.

662 Jones, Marie Thourson. "Education of Girls in Tunisia: Policy Implications of the Drive for Universal Enrollment." *Comparative Education Review* 24 (June 1980): S106-S123.

663 Johnson, Dale D. "Sex Differences in Reading Across Cultures." *Reading Research Quarterly* 9, no. 1 (1973-74): 67-86.

664 Kalia, Narendra Nath. "Images of Men and Women in Indian Textbooks." *Comparative Education Review* 24 (June 1980): S209-S223.

665 Kelly, Gail P. "Research on the Education of Women in the Third World: Problems and Perspectives." *Women's Studies: International Quarterly* 1, no. 4 (1978): 365-73.

666 Kelly, Gail P., and Younus Lulat. "Women and Schooling in the Third World: Bibliography." *Comparative Education Review* 24 (June 1980): S224-S263.

667 Kotwal, M. "Inequalities in the Distribution of Education Between Countries, Sexes, Generations, and Individuals." In *Education, Inequality and Life Chances*, vol. 1, pp. 31-109. Paris: Organization for Economic Cooperation and Development, 1975.

668 LeVine, Robert. "Influence of Women's Schooling on Maternal Behavior in the Third World." *Comparative Education Review* 24 (June 1980): S78-S105.

669 Mair, Lucille. "Adult Learning, Women and Development." *Prospects* 7, no. 2 (1977): 238-43.

670 McSweeney, B. G., and Marion Freedman. "Lack of Time as an Obstacle to Women's Education: The Case of Upper Volta." *Comparative Education Review* 24 (June 1980): S124-S139.

671 Miemi, Albert W., Jr. "Sexist Differences in Returns to Educational Investment." *Quarterly Review of Economics and Business* 15 (Spring 1975): 17-26.

672 Parker, Franklin. "Women's Education; Historical and International View." *Contemporary Education* 43 (Fall 1972): 198-201.

673 Ram, Rati. "Sex Differences in the Labor Market Outcomes of Education." *Comparative Education Review* 24 (June 1980): S53-S77.

674 Safilios-Rothschild, Constantina. "A Cross-Cultural Examination of Women's Marital, Educational and Occupational Options." *Acta Sociologica* 14 (1971): 96-113.

675 Schiefelbein, Ernesto, and Joseph Farrell. "Women, Schooling, and Work in Chile: Evidence from a Longitudinal Study." *Comparative Education Review* 24 (June 1980): S160-S179.

676 Shafer, Susanne M. "Factors Affecting the Utilization of Women in Professional and Managerial Roles." *Comparative Education* 10 (March 1974): 1-12.

677 Silver, Catherine B. "Salon, Foyer, Bureau: Women and the Professions in France." *American Journal of Sociology* 78 (January 1973): 836-51.

678 Simmons, John, and Leigh Alexander. "The Determinants of School Achievement in Developing Countries: A Review of the Research." *Economic Development and Cultural Change* 26 (January 1978): 341-57.

679 Standing, Guy. "Education and Female Participation in the Labor Force." *International Labor Review* 114 (November/December 1976): 281-97.

680 Wainerman, Catalina H. "The Impact of Education on the Female Labor Force in Argentina and Paraguay." *Comparative Education Review* 24 (June 1980): S180-S195.

681 Wang, Bee-Lan Chan. "Sex and Ethnic Differences in Educational Investment in Malaysia: The Effect of Reward Structures." *Comparative Education Review* 24 (June 1980): S140-S159.

682 Weisinger, Rita. "Economic Development and Functional Literacy for Women." *International Review of Education* 19, no. 1 (1973): 96-100.

683 Woodhall, Maureen. "Investment in Women: A Reappraisal of the Concept of Human Capital." *International Review of Education* 19, no. 1 (1973): 9-29.

Educational System Analysis

CURRICULUM

Books

684 Beauchamp, George, and Kathryn Beauchamp. *Comparative Analysis of Curriculum Systems*. Wilmette, Ill.: Kagg, 1967.

685 Bereday, George, and Joseph A. Lauwerys, eds. *The Secondary School Curriculum: The Year Book of Education*. New York: World Book Company, 1958.

686 Comparative Education Society in Europe. *Curriculum Development at the Second Level of Education*. Amsterdam: European Cultural Foundation, 1969.

687 Comparative Education Society in Europe. *General Education in a Changing World*. Berlin: Max Planck Institute for Educational Research, 1965.

688 Organization for Economic Cooperation and Development. *Handbook on Curriculum Development*. Paris: OECD, 1975.

689 Thomas, R. Murray, Dale L. Brubaker, and Lester B. Sands. *Strategies for Curriculum Change: Cases from 13 Nations*. Scranton, Pa.: International Textbook, 1968.

Articles

690 Anweiler, Oskar. "Curriculum Research from the Perspective of Comparative Education." In *Relevant Methods in Comparative Education*, edited by R. Edwards, B. Holmes, and J. van de Graaff, pp. 187-98. Hamburg: Institute for Education, 1973.

691 Gunther, Karl-Heinz. "The Planning and Organization of Curriculum Research." *Comparative Education* 5 (December 1969): 221-34.

692 Robinson, Saul B. "A Conceptual Structure of Curriculum Development." *Comparative Education* 5 (December 1969): 221-34.

693 Springer, Ursala. "Education, Curriculum and Pedagogy." *Comparative Education Review* 21 (June-October 1977): 358-69.

694 Swetz, Frank J. "Mathematics Curricular Reform in Less Developed Nations: An Issue of Concern." *Journal of Developing Areas* 10 (October 1975): 3-14.

EDUCATIONAL ACHIEVEMENT

Books

695 Bereday, George, and Joseph Lauwerys, eds. *The Gifted Child*. New York: Harcourt, Brace and World, 1962.

696 Bergling, Kurt. *The Development of Hypothetico-Deductive Thinking in Children*. New York: Wiley, 1974.

697 Clifton, Rodney. *Socioeconomic Status, Attitudes and Educational Performance: A Comparison of Students in England and New Zealand*. Stockholm: Almquist and Wiksell, 1978.

698 Comber, L. C., and John Keever. *Science Education in Nineteen Countries: An Empirical Study*. International Studies in Evaluation 1. New York: Wiley, 1973.

699 Foshay, A., et al. *Educational Achievements of Thirteen Year Olds in Other Countries*. Hamburg: UNESCO Institute for Education, 1962.

700 Gray, William S. *The Teaching of Reading: An International View*. Cambridge, Mass.: Harvard University Press, 1957.

701 Husén, Torsten, ed. *International Study of Achievement in Mathematics, A Comparison of Twelve Countries*. New York: John Wiley, 1967.

702 Husén, T. *Social Influences on Educational Attainment*. Paris: Organization for Economic Cooperation and Development, 1975.

703 Kelly, Alison. *Girls and Science: An International Study of Sex Differences in School Science Achievement*. Stockholm: Almquist and Wiksell, 1978.

704 Noonan, Richard. *School Resources, Social Class, and Student Achievement*. New York: Wiley, 1976.

705 Organization for Economic Cooperation and Development. *Selection and Certification in Education and Employment*. Paris: OECD, 1975.

706 Passow, A. Harry, H. J. Noah, M. A. Eckstein, and J. R. Mallea. *The National Case Study: An Empirical Comparative Study of Twenty-One Educational Systems*. New York: Wiley, 1976.

707 Peaker, Gilbert F. *An Empirical Study of Education in Twenty-One Countries: A Technical Report*. New York: Wiley, 1975.

708 Postlethwaite, Neville. *School Organization and Student Achievement: A Study Based on Achievement in Mathematics in Twelve Countries*. New York: Wiley, 1967.

709 Purves, Alan C. *Literature Education in Ten Countries: An Empirical Study*. New York: Wiley, 1973.

710 Saenger-Ceha, M. T. *Psychological and Social Factors in Student Drop-out*. Amsterdam: Swets and Zeitlanger, 1972.

711 Thorndike, Robert L. *Reading Comprehension Education in Fifteen Countries: An Empirical Study*. New York: Wiley, 1973.

712 Torney, Judith, A. N. Oppenheim, and Russell Farnen. *Civic Education in Ten Countries: An Empirical Study*. New York: Wiley, 1975.

713 Walker, David A. *The IEA Six Subject Survey: An Empirical Study of Education in Twenty-One Countries*. New York: Wiley, 1976.

714 Whiting, Beatrice B., ed. *Six Cultures, Studies of Child Rearing*. New York: Wiley, 1963.

Articles

715 Anderson, C. Arnold. "The International Comparative Study of Achievement in Mathematics." *Comparative Education Review* 11 (June 1967): 182-96.

716 Bonora, Denis. "Educational Aims and Curriculum in France: An IEA Survey." *Comparative Education Review* 18 (June 1977): 217-27.

717 Eckstein, Max A. "Comparative Study of Educational Achievement." *Comparative Education Review* 21 (June-October 1977): 345-57.

718 Husén, Torsten. "Productivity of Comprehensive and Selective Educational Systems." In *Education in Europe*, edited by M. A. Malthijseen and C. E. Vervoont, pp. 155-68. The Hague: Mouton, 1965.

719 Husén, Torsten. "School Structure and the Utilization of Talent." In *Essays on World Education*, edited by G. Z. Bereday, pp. 68-92. New York: Oxford University Press, 1969.

720 Lewy, Arieh. "Comparative, Cooperative and Universal Aspects of the IEA Subject Matter Surveys." *International Review of Education* 23, no. 3 (1977): 305-20.

721 Lindsey, J. K., and M. Cherkaoui. "Some Aspects of Social Class Differences in Achievement Among 13 Year Olds." *Comparative Education* 11 (October 1975): 247-62.

722 Marjoribanks, Kevin. "Psychological Environments of Learning: An International Perspective." *Comparative Education* 9 (March 1973): 28-33.

723 Noonan, Richard. "Comparative Education Methodology of the International Association for the Evaluation of Educational Achievement— (IEA)." In *Relevant Methods in Comparative Education*, edited by R. Edwards, B. Holmes, and J. van de Graaff, pp. 199-210. Paris: UNESCO Institute for Education, 1973.

724 Omari, I. M. "Cross-Cultural Studies on the Abilities of Children." *Prospects* 6, no. 3 (1976): 370-82.

725 Pidgeon, D. "Technical Problems of International Cooperative Research Projects." *International Review of Education* 25, no. 2 (1969): 247-53.

726 Postlethwaite, T. N. "International Project for the Evaluation of Educational Achievement." *International Review of Education* 12, no. 3 (1966): 356-69.

727 Postlethwaite, T. Neville. "Target Populations, Sampling Instrument Construction and Analysis Procedures." *Comparative Education Review* 18 (June 1974): 164-79.

728 Postlethwaite, T. N., and G. R. Austin. "Cognitive Results Based on Differ-

ent Ages of Entry to School: A Comparative Study." *Journal of Educational Psychology* 66 (1974): 857-63.

729 Simmons, John, and Leigh Alexander. "The Determinants of School Achievement in Developing Countries: A Review of the Research." *Economic Development and Cultural Change* 26 (January 1978): 341-58.

730 Trowbridge, Norma. "Cross-Cultural Study of Creative Ideas in Children." *Comparative Education Review* 12 (February 1968): 80-83.

731 "What Do Children Know? International Studies on Educational Achievement." *Comparative Education Review* 18 (June 1974): 155-332. (special issue)

732 Wiersma, William. "A Cross-National Comparison of the Academic Achievement of Prospective Secondary School Teachers." *Comparative Education Review* 13 (June 1969): 209-13.

TEACHER EDUCATION

Books

733 Bereday, George, and Joseph A. Lauwerys, eds. *The Education and Training of Teachers. The Year Book of Education.* New York: Harcourt, Brace and World, 1963.

734 Busch, F. W., ed. *Vergleichende Erziehungswissenschaft in der Lehrerausbildung.* Oldenburg, West Germany: Heinz Holzberg Verlag, 1978.

735 Comparative Education Society in Europe. *Teacher Education, Fifth General Meeting Stockholm 1971.* Brussels: Comparative Education Society in Europe, 1971.

736 Lauwerys, Joseph A. *Teachers and Training.* London: Evans, 1969.

737 Lynch, James, and H. Dudley Plunkett. *Teacher Education and Cultural Change: England, France, West Germany.* London: Allen and Unwin, 1973.

738 Organization for Economic Cooperation and Development. *New Patterns of Teacher Education and Tasks. General Analysis.* Paris: OECD, 1974.

739 Organization for Economic Cooperation and Development. *The Teacher and Educational Change: A New Role*, 2 vols. Paris: OECD, 1974.

740 Organization for Economic Cooperation and Development. *Teacher Policies: General Report of the Conference*. Paris: OECD, 1976.

741 Organization for Economic Cooperation and Development. *Teacher Policies in a New Context*. Paris: OECD, 1979.

742 Organization for Economic Cooperation and Development. *Teachers as Innovators*. Paris: OECD, 1977.

743 Razik, Taher. *Systems Approach to Teacher Training and Curriculum Development: The Case of Developing Countries*. Paris: International Institute for Educational Planning, 1972.

Articles

744 Correa, Hector. "Quantity Versus Quality in Teacher Education." *Comparative Education Review* 8 (October 1964): 141-45.

745 Dove, Linda A. "The Teacher and the Rural Community in Developing Countries." *Compare* 10, no. 1 (1980): 17-30.

746 King, Edmund J. "Comparative Studies in the Education of Teachers." *Canadian and International Education* 2 (1973): 12-29.

747 Lewis, L. J. "Getting Good Teachers for Developing Countries." *International Review of Education* 16, no. 4 (1970): 393-406.

748 "New Designs in Teacher Training." *Western European Education* 2 (Summer-Fall 1970): 99-255.

NONFORMAL EDUCATION

Books

749 Ahmed, Manzoor. *The Economics of Non Formal Education: Resources, Costs and Benefits*. New York: Praeger, 1975.

750 Arnove, Robert F., ed. *Educational Television: A Policy Critique and Guide for Developing Countries*. New York: Praeger, 1976.

751 Comparative Education Society in Europe. *Recurrent Education. Concepts and Policies for Lifelong Education. Sixth General Meeting*. Brussels: Comparative Education Society in Europe, 1973.

752 Coombs, Philip H., with Manzoor Ahmed. *Attacking Rural Poverty: How Non Formal Education Can Help.* Baltimore, Md.: Johns Hopkins University Press, 1974.

753 Cropley, A. J. *Lifelong Learning: A Stocktaking.* Hamburg: Institute for Education, 1979.

754 Edstrom, Lars-Olaf, Renee Erdos, and Roy Prosser, eds. *Mass Education: Studies in Adult Education and Teaching by Correspondence in Some Developing Countries.* New York: Africana Publishing, 1970.

755 Furter, Pierre. *The Planner and Lifelong Education.* Paris: UNESCO, 1977.

756 Lengrand, Paul. *An Introduction to Lifelong Education.* Paris: UNESCO, 1970.

757 Lowbeer, H., et al. *Lifelong Education and University Resources.* Paris: UNESCO, 1978.

758 Organization for Economic Cooperation and Development. *Recurrent Education: A Strategy for Lifelong Learning.* Paris: OECD, 1973.

759 Paulston, R. A. *Non-formal Education.* New York: Praeger, 1972.

Articles

760 Bock, John C. "The Institutionalization of Nonformal Education: A Response to Conflicting Needs." *Comparative Education Review* 20 (October 1976): 346-67.

761 Coombs, Philip H. "Non Formal Education: Myths, Realities, and Opportunities." *Comparative Education Review* 20 (October 1976): 281-93.

762 Cunningham, Griffiths L. "A New Approach to Adult Education in Developing Countries." *Convergence* 2, no. 1 (1969): 11-16.

763 Evans, David R. "Technology in Nonformal Education: A Critical Appraisal." *Comparative Education Review* 20 (October 1976): 305-27.

764 Grandstaff, Marvin. "Nonformal Education: Some Indications for Use." *Comparative Education Review* 20 (October 1976): 294-304.

765 Grandstaff, Marvin. "Non-Formal Education as a Concept." *Prospects* 8, no. 2 (1978): 177-82.

766 Husén, Torsten. "Some Thoughts Concerning Educational Technology." *International Review of Education* 13, no. 1 (1967): 6-13.

767 LaBelle, Thomas J. "Goals and Strategies of Non-Formal Education in Latin America." *Comparative Education Review* 20 (October 1976): 328-45.

768 Lawler, Laurence J. "Educational Television and Its Role in Developing Countries." *International Review of Education* 11, no. 3 (1965): 326-36.

769 Lowe, John. "Research Priorities in Adult Education in Developing Countries." *Convergence* 4, no. 4 (1971): 78-84.

770 Paulston, R., and G. LeRoy. "Strategies for Non-Formal Education." *Teachers College Record* 76 (May 1975): 569-96.

771 Spaulding, Seth. "Life-long Education: A Modest Model for Planning and Research." *Comparative Education* 10 (June 1974): 101-14.

772 Wilson, David N. "A Comparative Analysis of Four Models in Non-Formal Education: Denmark, Israel, Malawi and Côte d'Ivoire." *Canadian and International Education* 3 (June 1974): 34-52.

REFORM AND INNOVATION

Books

773 Heyman, Richard D., Robert F. Lawson, and Robert M. Stamp. *Studies in Educational Change*. Toronto: Holt, Rinehart and Winston, 1972.

774 Husén, Torsten, and G. Boalt. *Educational Research and Educational Change*. New York: Wiley, 1968.

775 International Bureau of Education. *Initiatives in Education: A World Profile for 1971-72*. Paris: UNESCO, 1972.

776 Paulston, R. G. *Evaluating Educational Reform: An International Case Book*. Washington, D.C.: The World Bank, 1976.

777 Röhrs, Hermann, ed. *Die Schulreform in den Industriestatten*. Frankfurt am Main: Akademische Verlagsgesellschaft, 1971.

778 Rust, Val D. *Alternatives in Education: Theoretical and Historical Perspectives*. Beverly Hills, Calif.: Sage, 1977.

Articles

779 Adisheshian, Malcolm S. "International Co-operation for Educational Reform in the 1980s." *Prospects* 8, no. 2 (1978): 143-56.

780 Duran, Graciela Ruíz. "A Conceptual Framework for the Reform of Educational Administration." *Prospects*, no. 1 (1977): 65-72.

781 Husén, Torsten. "Responsiveness and Resistance in the Educational System to Changing Needs of Society." *International Review of Education* 15, no. 4 (1969): 476-86.

782 Husén, Torsten. "The Contribution of Research to the Reform of Secondary Education." *Paedagogica Europaea* 2 (1966): 250-60.

783 Lam, Y. L. J. "A Path Analysis of Cultures, School Structures, and Educational Technology." *Canadian and International Education* 6 (June 1977): 35-52.

784 Lauwerys, Joseph A. "General Education in a Changing World." *International Review of Education* 11, no. 4 (1965): 385-403.

785 Meyer, John W., Francisco O. Ramirez, Richard Rubinson, and John Boli-Bennett. "The World Educational Revolution, 1950-1970." *Sociology of Education* 50 (October 1977): 242-58.

786 Paulston, Rolland G. "Social and Educational Change: Conceptual Frameworks." *Comparative Education Review* 21 (June-October 1977): 370-95.

787 Porter, P. "Models for Fostering Change in Educational Systems: A Comparative Perspective." *Australian Journal of Education* 3 (October 1976): 241-59.

EDUCATIONAL FINANCE

Books

788 Coombs, Philip G., and Jacques Hallak. *Educational Cost Analysis in Action: Case Studies for Planners*. Paris: International Institute for Educational Planning, 1972.

789 Coombs, Philip, and Jacques Hallak. *Managing Educational Costs*. New York: Oxford University Press, 1972.

790 Edding, F., and D. Berstecher. *International Development of Educational Expenditure, 1950-1965*. Paris: UNESCO, 1969.

791 Glenney, Lyman, ed. *Funding Higher Education: A Six Nation Analysis*. New York: Praeger, 1979.

792 Hallak, J. *The Analysis of Educational Costs and Expenditures*. Paris: International Institute of Educational Planning, 1969.

793 Hussain, K. M. *Institutional Resource Allocation Models in Higher Education*. Paris: Organization for Economic Cooperation and Development, 1976.

794 Leite, Manuela Ferreira, Patrick Lynch, Keith Norris, John Sheehan, and John Vaizey. *The Economics of Educational Costing: Inter-Country and Inter-Regional Comparisons*. Lisbon: CEF, 1969.

795 Levy-Garbova, L., et al. *Educational Expenditure in France, Japan and the United States*. Paris: Organization for Economic Cooperation and Development, 1977.

796 Organization for Economic Cooperation and Development. *Public Expenditure on Education*. Paris: OECD, 1974.

797 Vaizey, John. *The Costs of Education*. London: Faber and Faber, 1963.

798 Woodhall, Maureen. *Student Loans, A Review of Experience in Scandinavia and Elsewhere*. London: Harrap, 1970.

Articles

799 Eedle, J. H. "Financing Education in Developing Countries." *Comparative Education* 7 (November 1971): 60-67.

800 MacBeth, A. M. "Educational Finance: Some Difficulties of Comparison." *Comparative Education* 4 (March 1968): 125-34.

801 Rogers, Daniel C. "Financing Higher Education in Less Developed Countries." *Comparative Education Review* 15 (February 1971): 20-27.

802 Sheehan, John. "The Problem of International Comparisons of Unit Costs

in Education." *Comparative Education Review* 14 (June 1970): 186-98.

803 Windham, D. M. "The Efficiency/Equity Quandary and Higher Educational Finance." *Review of Educational Research* 42 (Fall 1972): 541-60.

COMPARATIVE HIGHER EDUCATION

Books

804 Altbach, Philip G. *Comparative Higher Education: Research Trends and Bibliography*. London: Mansell, 1979.

805 Altbach, Philip G., ed. *University Reform: Comparative Perspectives for the Seventies*. Cambridge, Mass.: Schenkman, 1974.

806 Altbach, Philip G. *The University's Response to Societal Demands*. New York: International Council for Educational Development, 1975.

807 Ashby, Eric, and Mary Anderson. *Universities: British, Indian, African: A Study in the Ecology of Higher Education*. Cambridge, Mass.: Harvard University Press, 1966.

808 Ben-David, J. *Centers of Learning. Britain, France, Germany, United States*. New York: McGraw-Hill, 1977.

809 Bereday, George, and Joseph A. Lauwerys, eds. *Higher Education: The Year Book of Education*. New York: World Book Company, 1959.

810 Burn, Barbara, P. G. Altbach, C. Kerr, and J. Perkins. *Higher Education in Nine Countries*. New York: McGraw-Hill, 1971.

811 Centre for Educational Research and Innovation. *University Decision Structures. Technical Report*. Paris: Organization for Economic Cooperation and Development/Centre for Educational Research and Innovation, 1971.

812 Comparative Education Society in Europe. *The University Within the Educational System*. Brussels: Ministry of Education, 1967.

813 Driver, Christopher. *The Exploding University*. Indianapolis: Bobbs Merrill, 1971.

814 Flexner, A. *Universities: American, English, German*. New York: Oxford University Press, 1930.

815 Fogel, Barbara R. *Design for Change: Higher Education in the Service of Developing Countries: A Handbook for Planners*. New York: International Council for Educational Development, 1977.

816 Hannah, H. W., and Robert R. Caughey. *The Legal Base for Universities in Developing Countries*. Urbana: University of Illinois Press, 1967.

817 Holmes, Brian, David G. Scanlon, and W. R. Niblett, eds. *Higher Education in a Changing World: The World Year Book of Education 1971-72*. London: Evans, 1971.

818 Kertesz, Stephen, ed. *The Task of the Universities in a Changing World*. South Bend, Ind.: University of Notre Dame Press, 1972.

819 Knowles, A. S. ed. *The International Encyclopedia of Higher Education*. San Francisco: Jossey-Bass, 1977.

820 Le Gall, A., et al. *Present Problems in the Democratization of Secondary and Higher Education*. Paris: UNESCO, 1973.

821 Miller, Gordon W. *Success, Failure, and Wastage in Higher Education: An Overview of the Problem Derived from Research and Theory*. London: Harrap, 1970.

822 Niblett, W. Roy, and R. Freeman Butts, eds. *Universities Facing the Future. The World Year Book of Education*. San Francisco: Jossey-Bass, 1972.

823 Nitsch, Wolfgang, and Walter Weller. *Higher Education and Universities: Part 1, Trend Report*. The Hague: Mouton, 1973.

824 Organization for Economic Cooperation and Development. *Development of Higher Education 1950-1967: Analytical Report*. Paris: OECD, 1971.

825 Organization for Economic Cooperation and Development. *Economic Aspects of Higher Education*. Paris: OECD, 1964.

826 Organization for Economic Cooperation and Development. *General Report: Policies for Higher Education*. Paris: OECD, 1973.

827 Organization for Economic Cooperation and Development. *Towards Mass Higher Education: Issues and Dilemmas*. Paris: OECD, 1974.

828 Organization for Economic Cooperation and Development. *Towards New Structures of Post-Secondary Education: Preliminary Statements of Issues*. Paris: OECD, 1971.

829 Stephens, M., and G. Roderick, eds. *Higher Education Alternatives*. London: Longmans, 1978.

830 Stephens, Michael D., and Gordon W. Roderick, eds. *Universities for a Changing World—The Role of the University in the Late Twentieth Century*. London: David and Charles, 1975.

831 Thompson, Kenneth, et al. *Higher Education and Social Change*, 2 vols. New York: Praeger, 1976.

832 UNESCO and The International Association of Universities. *The International Study of University Admissions. Access to Higher Education*. Paris: UNESCO and the International Association of Universities, 1965.

833 Waggoner, G. R., and A. Herzfeld, eds. *Metología de la Evaluación Universitaria*. Lawrence: University of Kansas, 1969.

Articles

834 Anderson, C. Arnold. "Emerging Common Problems in the World of Universities." *International Review of Education* 11, no. 1 (1965): 3-20.

835 Bowles, Frank. "Patterns of Development in Higher Education." *International Review of Education* 11, no. 1 (1965): 21-33.

836 Burn, Barbara B. "Comparative Higher Education." In *International Encyclopedia of Higher Education*, edited by A. Knowles, pp. 969-77. San Francisco: Jossey-Bass, 1977.

837 Clark, Burton R. "Development of the Sociology of Higher Education." *Sociology of Education* 46 (Winter 1973): 2-14.

838 "Implications of Mass Higher Education." *Higher Education* 2 (May 1973): 133-274. (special issue)

839 Kwapong, A. A. "Some Problems in Academic and Administrative Development in Universities in the Developing Countries." *Bulletin of the Association of African Universities* 1 (May 1974): 29-37.

840 Lauwerys, J. A. "General Education in a Changing World." *International Review of Education* 11, no. 4 (1965): 385-403.

841 Mason, Henry L. "Shared Authority, Triparity, Tripolarity: Cross-National Patterns of University Government." *Polity* 10 (Spring 1978): 308-25.

842 Meadows, Dennis, and Lewis Perelman. "Limits to Growth, a Challenge to Higher Education." *Prospects* 7, no. 1 (1977): 33-43.

843 Sadlak, Jan. "Efficiency in Higher Education—Concepts and Problems." *Higher Education* 7 (May 1978): 213-20.

844 Thompson, A. P. "Higher Education in the Colonies." *Universities Quarterly* 10 (August 1956): 359-70.

Academic Profession

Books

845 Altbach, Philip G. *Comparative Perspectives on the Academic Profession.* New York: Praeger, 1977.

846 Ben-David, J. *The Scientist's Role in Society: A Comparative Study.* Englewood Cliffs, N.J.: Prentice-Hall, 1971.

847 van de Graaff, John H., et al. *Academic Power: Patterns of Authority in Seven National Systems of Higher Education.* New York: Praeger, 1978.

848 Williams, Gareth, et al. *The Academic Labour Market: Economic and Social Aspects of a Profession.* Amsterdam: Elsevier, 1974.

Articles

849 Ashby, Eric. "Anatomy of the Academic Life." *Educational Record* 48 (Winter 1967): 45-50.

850 Blackstone, Tessa, and Oliver Fulton. "Men and Women Academics: An Anglo-American Comparison of Subject Choices and Research Activity." *Higher Education* 3 (April 1974): 119-40.

851 Lofthouse, Stephen. "Thoughts on 'Publish or Perish.'" *Higher Education* 3 (February 1974): 59-80.

852 Shimbori, Michiya. "Comparative Study of Career Patterns of College Professors." *International Review of Education* 10, no. 3 (1964): 284-96.

Students and Student Activism

Books

853 Altbach, Philip G., ed. *Student Politics: Perspectives for the 1980s*. Metuchen, N.J.: Scarecrow, 1981.

854 Altbach, Philip G., ed. *The Student Revolution: A Global Analysis*. Bombay: Lalvani, 1970.

855 Altbach, Philip G., and R. S. Laufer, eds. *The New Pilgrims*. New York: McKay, 1972.

856 Altbach, Philip G., and Norman Uphoff. *The Student Internationals*. Metuchen, N.J.: Scarecrow, 1973.

857 Archer, Margaret S., ed. *Students, University and Society; a Comparative Sociological Review*. New York: Crane, Russak, 1972.

858 Bakke, E. Wight, and Mary S. Bakke. *Campus Challenge: Student Activism in Perspective*. Hamden, Conn.: Archon, 1971.

859 Emmerson, Donald K., ed. *Students and Politics in Developing Nations*. New York: Praeger, 1968.

860 Feuer, Lewis. *The Conflict of Generations*. New York: Basic Books, 1969.

861 Lipset, S. M., ed. *Student Politics*. New York: Basic Books, 1967.

862 Lipset, S. M., and P. G. Altbach, eds. *Students in Revolt*. Boston: Beacon, 1968.

Articles

863 Altbach, Philip G. "The International Student Movement." *Comparative Education Review* 8 (October 1964): 131-37.

864 Altbach, Philip G., ed. "Student Activism." *Higher Education* 8 (November 1979): 603-707.

865 Altbach, Philip G. "Students and Politics." *Comparative Education Review* 10 (June 1966): 175-87.

866 Ben-David, Joseph, and Randall Collins. "A Comparative Study of Academic

Freedom and Student Politics." *Comparative Education Review* 10 (June 1966): 220-49.

867 Bereday, George Z. F. "Student Unrest on Four Continents: Montreal, Ibadan, Warsaw and Rangoon." *Comparative Education Review* 10 (June 1966): 188-204.

868 Eisenstadt, S. N. "Changing Patterns of Youth Protest in Different Stages of Development of Modern Society." *Youth and Society* 1 (December 1969): 133-50.

869 Hanson, Mark. "A Cross-Cultural Comparison of Student Stereotypes: Authentic Versus Imagined Beliefs." *Comparative Education* 7 (November 1971): 49-59.

870 Lipset, Seymour Martin. "University Students and Politics in Underdeveloped Countries." *Comparative Education Review* 10 (June 1966): 132-62.

871 Long, Samuel. "Sociopolitical Ideology as a Determinant of Students' Perceptions of the University." *Higher Education* 5 (November 1976): 423-36.

872 Martinelli, A., and A. Cavalli. "Towards a Conceptual Framework for the Comparative Analysis of the Student Movement." *International Social Science Journal* 24, no. 2 (1972): 301-11.

873 Pinner, Frank. "Student Trade Unionism in France, Belgium and Holland." *Sociology of Education* 37 (Spring 1964): 1-23.

874 Roucek, Joseph S. "The Political Role of Students in Underdeveloped Countries." *Comparative Education* 3 (March 1967): 115-24.

875 Soares, Glaucio A. D. "The Active Few: Student Ideology and Participation in Developing Countries." *Comparative Education Review* 10 (June 1966): 205-19.

876 Weinberg, Ian, and Kenneth Walker. "Student Politics and Political Systems: Toward a Typology." *American Journal of Sociology* 75 (July 1969): 77-96.

JOURNALS IN COMPARATIVE EDUCATION

877 *Canadian and International Education* (Canada)

878 *Comparative Education* (Britain)

879 *Comparative Education Review* (United States)

880 *Compare* (Britain)

881 *Education Comparée* (France)

882 *European Journal of Education* (France)

883 *Higher Education* (Netherlands)

884 *Interchange* (Canada)

885 *International Education* (United States)

886 *International Review of Education* (UNESCO)

887 *Minerva* (Britain)

888 *Paedagogica Historica* (Belgium)

889 *Prospects* (UNESCO)

890 *Times Educational Supplement* (Britain)

891 *Times Higher Education Supplement* (Britain)

892 *World Higher Education Communique* (United States)

893 *Vergleichende Pädagogik* (German Democratic Republic)

BIBLIOGRAPHIES

Books

894 Altbach, Philip G., ed. *Comparative Higher Education Abroad: Bibliography and Analysis.* New York: Praeger, 1976.

895 Altbach, Philip G. *Higher Education in Developing Countries: A Select Bibliography*. Cambridge, Mass.: Harvard University Center for International Affairs, 1970.

896 Altbach, Philip G., and David H. Kelly. *Higher Education in Developing Countries, 1969-1974: A Selected Bibliography*. New York: Praeger, 1974.

897 Brickman, William. *Bibliographical Essays on Comparative and International Education*. Norwood, Pa.: Norwood Editions, 1975.

898 de Grandpré, Marcel. *Analytical Index of Three Journals of Comparative Education*. Montreal: Librairie de l'Université de Montreal, 1972.

899 Fomerand, Jacques, J. van de Graaff, and Henry Wasser. *Higher Education in Western Europe and North America: A Selected and Annotated Bibliography*. New York: Council on European Studies, Columbia University, 1979.

900 Nitsch, Wolfgang, and Walter Weller. *Social Science Research on Higher Education and Universities, Part II: Annotated Bibliography*. The Hague: Mouton, 1970.

901 Ohliger, John, and David Guelette. *Media and Adult Learning: A Bibliography With Abstracts, Annotations and Quotations*. New York: Garland, 1975.

902 UNESCO. *Analytical Bibliography on Comparative Education*. Paris: UNESCO Division of Comparative Education, 1964.

903 UNESCO. *Comparative Education Bibliography*. Hamburg: UNESCO Institute for Education, 1963.

904 UNESCO. *International Guide to Educational Documentation*. Paris: UNESCO, 1971.

Articles

905 Brickman, William W. "Introductory Bibliography of Comparative Education." *Western European Education* 4 (Spring-Summer 1972): 136-53.

906 Brickman, William W. "Selected and Classified Bibliography on Comparative Higher Education." *Western European Education* 8 (Winter 1976-77): 30-46.

907 Brickman, William W. "Selected and Classified References on Comparative Pre-School Education." *Western European Education* 6 (Spring 1974): 67–76.

908 Brickman, William W. "Selected Bibliography of the History of International Relations in Higher Education." *Paedagogica Historica* 5 (1965): 164–82.

909 "International Studies in Education." *Western European Education* 4 (Spring-Summer 1972): 31–36.

910 Leitner, Erich. "Selected Bibliographies on Research into Higher Education: An International Inventory." *Higher Education* 7 (August 1978): 311–30.

911 Narang, H. L. "Bibliography of Canadian Theses on Comparative and International Education." *Canadian and International Education* 1 (June 1972): 70–86.

SELECTIVE BIBLIOGRAPHY
ON REGIONS AND COUNTRIES

AFRICA

Bibliographies

Books

912 African Bibliographic Center. *Educational Development in Africa.* Washington, D.C.: African Bibliographic Center, 1973.

913 Brembeck, Cole S., and John P. Keith. *Education in Emerging Africa: A Select and Annotated Bibliography.* East Lansing: College of Education, Michigan State University, 1962.

914 Couch, M. *Education in Africa: A Select Bibliography.* London: University of London, Institute of Education, 1962.

915 Evans, Judith L. *Children in Africa: A Review of Psychological Research.* New York: Teacher's College Press, 1970.

916 Hanson, John W., and Geoffrey W. Gibson, eds. *African Education and Development Since 1960: A Select and Annotated Bibliography.* East Lansing: Institute for International Studies in Education and African Studies Center, Michigan State University, 1968.

917 Ofori, P. E. *Education in Ghana from the Earliest Times to the Nineteen Sixties: A Bibliography.* Accra: Ghana Publishing Corporation, 1974.

918 Oshin, N. R. Olu. *Education in West Africa: A Bibliography.* Yaba, Nigeria: West African Examinations Council, Test Development and Research Office, 1969.

919 Oshin, N. R. O., and H. A. Odetoyinbo. *Education in Nigeria: A Bibliographical Guide.* Yaba, Nigeria: 1972.

920 Strowbridge, Nancy. *Education in East Africa, 1962-1968. A Selected Bibliography*. Kampala, Uganda: Makerere University College Library, 1969.

921 World Conference of Organizations of the Teaching Professions. *African Education: A Bibliography of 121 U.S.A. Doctoral Dissertations*. Washington, D.C.: World Confederation of the Teaching Professions, 1965.

Articles

922 Adelabu, Adedeji. "Education in Nigeria: A Selected and Annotated Introductory Bibliographic Survey of Current Resources." *Current Bibliography of African Affairs* 4 (March 1971): 78-87.

923 Adelabu, Adedeji. "Studies in Trends in Nigeria's Educational Development: An Essay on Sources and Resources." *African Studies Review* 14 (April 1971): 101-12.

924 Aladejana, A. "A Critique of 'Education in West Africa—A Bibliography.'" *West African Journal of Education* 14 (February 1970): 77-80.

925 Boogaerts, M. "Education in the Congo: A Provisional Systematical Bibliography." *Cahiers Economiques et Sociaux* 5 (June 1967): 237-65.

926 Gardinier, D. E. "Education in the States of Equatorial Africa: A Bibliographical Essay." *Africana Library Journal* 3, no. 3 (1972): 7-20.

927 Kay, Stafford, and Bradley Nystrom. "Education and Colonialism in Africa: An Annotated Bibliography." *Comparative Education Review* 15 (June 1971): 240-59.

928 Parker, Franklin. "African Education in Zambia (Formerly Northern Rhodesia), A Partial Bibliography of Magazine Articles, 1925-1963." *African Studies Bulletin* 10 (December 1967): 6-15.

929 Steinberg, Bernard. "Education in South Africa: A Select Annotated Bibliography of Works in English Published Locally." *Education Libraries Bulletin* 20 (Spring 1977): 32-35.

930 Yates, Barbara A. "A Bibliography on Special Problems in Education in Tropical Africa." *Comparative Education Review* 8 (December 1964): 307-19.

931 Yates, Barbara A. "Educational Policy and Practice in Tropical Africa: A

General Bibliography." *Comparative Education Review* 8 (October 1964): 215-28.

General

Books

932 Ashby, Eric. *African Universities and Western Tradition*. Cambridge, Mass.: Harvard University Press, 1964.

933 Ashby, Eric, and Mary Anderson. *Universities: British, Indian, African*. Cambridge, Mass.: Harvard University Press, 1966.

934 Barkan, Joel D. *An African Dilemma: University Students, Development and Politics in Ghana, Tanzania and Uganda*. New York: Oxford University Press, 1975.

935 Battle, Vincent M., and Charles H. Lyons. *Essays in the History of African Education*. New York: Teacher's College Press, 1970.

936 Berman, Edward. *African Reactions to Missionary Education*. New York: Teacher's College Press, 1975.

937 Bolibaugh, Jerry. *Educational Development in Guinea, Mali, Senegal and the Ivory Coast*. Washington, D.C.: U.S. Office of Education, 1972.

938 Bouche, Denise. *L'enseignement dans les territoires français de l'Afrique Occidentale de 1817-1920*, 2 vols. Paris: Champion, 1975.

939 Brown, G. N., and M. Hiskett, eds. *Conflict and Harmony in Education in Tropical Africa*. London: Allen and Unwin, 1975.

940 Burns, Donald G. *African Education*. London: Oxford University Press, 1965.

941 Cowan, L. Gray, James O'Connell, and David G. Scanlon. *Education and Nation-Building in Africa*. New York: Praeger, 1965.

942 *Educational Development in Africa, Vol. 1: The Planning Process*. Paris: International Institute for Educational Planning, 1969.

943 Fafunwa, A. Babs. *New Perspectives in African Education*. London: Macmillan, 1967.

944 Hanna, William, and Judith Hanna, eds. *University Students and African Politics*. New York: Africana, 1975.

945 Jolly, Richard. *Education in Africa: Research and Action*. Evanston, Ill.: Northwestern University Press, 1969.

946 Jolly, Richard. *Planning Education for African Development*. Nairobi, Kenya: East African Publishing House, 1969.

947 King, Kenneth. *Pan Africanism and Education*. Oxford: Clarendon Press, 1971.

948 Kitchen, Helen. *The Educated African*. New York: Praeger, 1962.

949 Lyons, Charles H. *To Wash an Aethiop White: British Ideas about Black African Educability 1530-1960*. New York: Teacher's College Press, 1975.

950 Mazrui, Ali A. *Political Values and the Educated Class in Africa*. London: Heinemann, 1978.

951 Moumouni, A. *Education in Africa*. New York: Praeger, 1968.

952 Murphy, E. Jefferson. *Creative Philanthropy: Carnegie Corporation and Africa, 1953-1973*. New York: Teacher's College Press, 1976.

953 Roach, Penelope. *Political Socialization in the New Nations of Africa*. New York: Teacher's College Press, 1967.

954 Sarsnett, M., and Inez Sepmeyer. *Educational Systems of Africa*. Berkeley: University of California Press, 1966.

955 Scanlon, David G., ed. *Church, State and Education in Africa*. New York: Teacher's College Press, 1966.

956 Scanlon, David, ed. *Traditions of African Education*. New York: Bureau of Publications, Teacher's College, Columbia University, 1964.

957 Uchendu, Victor, ed. *Education and Politics in Tropical Africa*. Buffalo, N.Y.: Conch, 1980.

958 Yesufu, T. M., ed. *Creating the African University: Emerging Issues in the 1970's*. Ibadan, Nigeria: Oxford University Press, 1973.

Articles

959 Anderson, C. Arnold. "Central-Local Tensions and the Involvement of Education Within Developing Countries." *African Studies Review* 15 (December 1972): 467-88.

960 Anderson, C. Arnold, and P. Foster. "The Outlook for Education in Middle Africa." In *Africa in the Seventies and Eighties: Issues in Development*, edited by F. S. Arkhurst. New York: Praeger, 1970.

961 Berman, Edward. "American Influence on African Education: The Role of the Phelps-Stokes Fund's Education Commissions." *Comparative Education Review* 15 (June 1971): 132-45.

962 Brown, Godfrey N. "British Educational Policy in West and Central Africa." *Journal of Modern African Studies* 2 (November 1964): 365-77.

963 Bugnicourt, Jacques. "Disparités scolaires en Afrique." *Tiers Monde* 48 (1971): 751-86.

964 Callaway, Archibald. "Unemployment Among African School Leavers." *Journal of Modern African Studies* 1 (September 1963): 351-71.

965 Cash, Webster C. "A Critique of Manpower Planning and Educational Change in Africa." *Economic Development and Cultural Change* 14 (October 1965): 33-47.

966 Champion, Jacques. "Linguistic and Cultural Diversities in French Speaking African Countries." *Compare* 8 (April 1978): 113-18.

967 Clignet, Remi. "Damned if You Do, Damned if You Don't: The Dilemmas of Colonized-Colonizer Relations." *Comparative Education Review* 15 (October 1971): 296-312.

968 Clignet, Remi. "Inadequacies of the Notion of Assimilation in African Education." *Journal of Modern African Studies* 8 (October 1970): 425-44.

969 Clignet, Remi. "Social Change and Sexual Differentiation in the Cameroons and the Ivory Coast." *Signs* 3 (Autumn 1977): 244-60.

970 Clignet, Remi, and Philip Foster. "French and British Colonial Education in Africa." *Comparative Education Review* 8 (October 1964): 191-98.

971 Colclough, Christopher. "Formal Education Systems and Poverty-Focused Planning." *Journal of Modern African Studies* 15 (December 1977): 555-95.

972 "Educational Problems in Africa—Special Issue." *Canadian Journal of African Studies* 8 (1974): 463-620.

973 Eliou, Marie. "Educational Inequality in Africa: An Analysis." *Prospects* 6, no. 4 (1976): 558-71.

974 Eliou, Marie. "Scolarisation et promotion feminines en Afrique." *International Review of Education* 19, no. 1 (1973): 30-46.

975 Eliou, Marie. "The Education and Advancement of Women in Africa (Ivory Coast, Upper Volta, Senegal)." *International Review of Education* 19, no. 1 (1973): 30-46.

976 Fafunwa, A. B. "Sub-Saharan Africa." In *International Encyclopedia of Higher Education*, edited by A. Knowles, pp. 198-205. San Francisco: Jossey-Bass, 1977.

977 Farine, Avigdor. "Society and Education: The Content of Education in the French African School." *Comparative Education* 5 (February 1969): 51-67.

978 Gardinier, David E. "Schooling in the States of Equatorial Africa." *Canadian Journal of African Studies* 8 (1974): 517-38.

979 Gifford, Prosser, and Timothy Weiskel. "African Education in a Colonial Context: French and British Styles." In *France and Britain in Africa: Imperial Rivalry and Colonial Rule*, edited by Gifford Prosser and William Roger Louis, pp. 663-711. New Haven: Yale University Press, 1971.

980 Hargreaves, John D. "The Idea of a Colonial University." *African Affairs* 72 (January 1973): 26-36.

981 Kouyate, Maurice. "The Teacher Shortage and Peer Teaching in Africa." *Prospects* 8, no. 1 (1978): 33-47.

982 Martin, Jean-Yves. "Sociologie de l'enseignment en Afrique noire." *Cahiers Internationaux de Sociologie* 53 (July-December 1972): 337-62.

983 Marvick, Dwaine. "African University Students: A Presumptive Elite." In *Education and Political Development*, edited by J. S. Coleman, pp. 463-97. Princeton: Princeton University Press, 1964.

984 Mass, Jacob van Lustenberg. "Educational Change in Pre-Colonial Societies: The Cases of Buganda and Ashanti." *Comparative Education Review* 14 (June 1970): 174-85.

985 Mazuri, Ali. "The African University as a Multi-National Corporation: Problems of Penetration and Dependency." *Harvard Educational Review* 45 (May 1975): 191-210.

986 McQueen, Albert J. "Education and Marginality of African Youth." *Journal of Social Issues* 24 (April 1968): 179-94.

987 Ocaya-Lakidi, Dent. "Towards an African Philosophy of Education." *Prospects* 10, no. 1 (1980): 13-26.

988 Ofuatey-Kodjoe, W. "Education and Social Change in Africa: Some Proposals." *Journal of African Studies* 3 (Summer 1976): 229-46.

989 Peshkin, Alan. "Educational Reform in Colonial and Independent Africa." *African Affairs* 64 (July 1965): 210-16.

990 Shils, Edward. "The Implantation of Universities: Reflections on a Theme of Ashby." *Universities Quarterly* 22 (March 1968): 142-66.

991 Stabler, Ernest. "Pressures and Constraints in Planning African Education: A Review Article." *Comparative Education Review* 12 (October 1968): 350-56.

992 Verhaegen, Benoit. "L'Université dans l'Afrique indépendante." *Cultures et Développement* 1 (1968): 555-84.

993 Van den Berghe, Pierre. "European Languages and Black Mandarins." *Transition* 7 (December-January 1968): 19-23.

994 Ward, Ted. "Cognitive Processes and Learning: Reflections on a Comparative Study of 'Cognitive Style' in Fourteen African Societies." *Comparative Education Review* 17 (February 1973): 1-10.

East Africa

Books

995 African Education Commission. *Education in East Africa: A Study of East, Central and South Africa*. Westport, Conn.: Negro University Press, 1979.

996 Cameron, John. *The Development of Education in East Africa*. New York: Teacher's College Press, 1970.

997 Prewitt, K., ed. *Education and Political Values: Essays on East Africa*. Nairobi: East African Publishing House, 1969.

998 Weeks, Sheldon. *Divergence in Educational Development: The Case of Kenya and Uganda*. New York: Teacher's College Press, 1967.

Articles

999 Beck, Ann. "Colonial Policy and Education in British East Africa, 1900-1950." *Journal of British Studies* 5 (May 1966): 115-38.

1000 Court, David. "East African Higher Education from the Community Standpoint." *Higher Education* 6 (February 1977): 45-66.

1001 Court, David. "The Idea of Social Science in East Africa: An Aspect of the Development of Higher Education." *Minerva* 17 (Summer 1979): 244-82.

1002 Crawford, Malcolm. "Government and the Universities in East Africa. I. On Academic Freedom in East Africa." *Minerva* 5 (Spring 1967): 376-81.

1003 Gould, W. T. S. "Secondary School Admissions Policies in Eastern Africa: Some Regional Issues." *Comparative Education Review* 18 (October 1974): 374-87.

1004 Mumford, W. Byrant. "Malangali Schools." *Africa* 3 (July 1930): 265-90.

1005 O'Connor, Edmund. "Contrasts in Educational Development in Kenya and Tanzania." *African Affairs* 73 (January 1974): 67-84.

1006 Pratt, R. Cranford. "African Universities and Western Tradition—Some East African Reflections." *Journal of Modern African Studies* 3 (October 1965): 421-28.

1007 Ranger, Terrence O. "African Attempts to Control Education in East and Central Africa." *Past and Present* 32 (December 1965): 57-85.

1008 Sifuna, D. N. "Industrial or Literary Training? A History of Curriculum Development in East Africa." *Présence Africaine* 105/106 (1st and 2nd quarters 1978): 151-61.

1009 Tignor, Robert L. "Continuities and Discontinuities in East African Education." *History of Education Quarterly* 13 (Winter 1973): 409-13.

West Africa

Books

1010 Bolibaugh, Jerry B. *Educational Development in Guinea, Mali, Senegal, and Ivory Coast*. Washington, D.C.: U.S. Office of Education, 1972.

1011 Bouche, Denise. *L'enseignement dans les territoires français de l'Afrique Occidentale de 1817 à 1920*, 2 vols. Paris: Champion, 1975.

1012 Jones, Thomas Jesse. *Education in Africa*. New York: Phelps-Stokes Fund, 1922.

1013 Wise, C. G. *A History of Education in British West Africa*. London: Longmans, Green, 1956.

Articles

1014 Berg, Elliot J. "Education and Manpower in Senegal, Guinea, and the Ivory Coast." In *Manpower and Education: Country Studies in Economic Development*, edited by Frederick Harbison and Charles Myers, pp. 232-67. New York: McGraw-Hill, 1965.

1015 Clignet, Remi. "Ethnicity, Social Differentiation and Secondary Schooling in West Africa." *Cahiers d'Etudes Africaines* 7 (1967): 360-78.

1016 Clignet, Remi. "The Legacy of Assimilation in West African Educational Systems: Its Meaning and Ambiguities." *Comparative Education Review* 12 (February 1968): 57-67.

1017 Clignet, R. P., and Philip Foster. "Potential Elites in Ghana and Ivory Coast: A Preliminary Comparison." *American Journal of Sociology* 70 (November 1964): 349-62.

1018 Debeauvas, Michel. "Education in Former French West Africa." In *Education and Political Development*, edited by James S. Coleman, pp. 75-91. Princeton: Princeton University Press, 1965.

Affars and Issas

Articles

1019 "Affars and Issas, French Territory of the." In *International Encyclopedia of Higher Education*, edited by A. Knowles, pp. 178-79. San Francisco: Jossey-Bass, 1977.

1020 Castagno, Alphonso A. "French Somaliland." In *The Educated African*, edited by Helen Kitchen, pp. 108-13. New York: Praeger, 1962.

Angola

Books

1021 Samuels, Michael Anthony. *Education in Angola, 1878-1914: A History of Culture Transfer and Administration*. New York: Teacher's College Press, 1970.

Articles

1022 Kohler, Hans-Peter. "Erste Schritte zur Uberwindung des kolonialen Erbes im Bildungswesen der Volksrepublik Angola." *Vergleichende Pädagogik* 14, no. 1 (1978): 422-26.

1023 Lisboa, E. "Education in Angola and Mozambique." In *Education in Southern Africa*, edited by B. Rose. Johannesburg, South Africa: Macmillan, 1970.

Benin

Books

1024 Houenassou, L. K. *Dualisme de l'éducation dans les pays de la Côte du Bénin (Togo)*. Lome, Togo: Institut National de la Recherche Scientifique, 1973.

Articles

1025 Diskson, A. G. "Mass Education in Togoland." *African Affairs* 49 (1950): 136-50.

1026 Guezodje, Vincent. "Educational Reform in Benin." *Prospects* 7, no. 4 (1977): 455-71.

1027 Pliya, Jean. "Educational Reform and Available Resources: An Example from the People's Republic of Benin." In *Educational Reforms: Experiences and Prospects*, pp. 188-200. Paris: UNESCO, 1979.

1028 "Togo." In *International Encyclopedia of Higher Education*, edited by A. Knowles, pp. 4091-97. San Francisco: Jossey-Bass, 1977.

Botswana

Books

1029 *National Policy on Education. Government Paper, No. 1, 1977.* Gaberone, Botswana: Government Printers, 1977.

1030 Rose, Brian. *Education for Development in Southern Africa.* Johannesburg: South African Institute of International Affairs, 1974.

Articles

1031 Chirenje, J. Mutero. "Church, State and Education in Bechuanaland in the Nineteenth Century." *International Journal of African Historical Studies* 9, no. 3 (1976): 401-18.

1032 Kidd, Ross, and Alan Etherington. "Radio Learning Campaigns: The Botswana Experience." *Convergence* 11, no. 3/4 (1978): 83-92.

1033 Raum, O. F. "The Imbalance of Educational Development in Southern Africa." (Botswana, Leshotho, Swaziland, and South Africa). *South African Journal of African Affairs* 1 (1971): 8-30.

1034 Setidisho, N. O. H. "Botswana." In *International Encyclopedia of Higher Education*, edited by A. Knowles, pp. 652-57. San Francisco: Jossey-Bass, 1977.

1035 Ulin, Richard O. "African Leadership: National Goals and the Values of Botswana University Students." *Comparative Education* 12 (June 1976): 145-56.

Burundi

Books

1036 Lingappa, S. *Education and the Socio-economic Environment: Recent Developments in Burundi.* Paris: UNESCO, 1977.

Articles

1037 Greenland, J. "The Reform of Education in Burundi: Enlightened Theory Faced with Political Reality." *Comparative Education* 10 (March 1974): 57-64.

Cameroon

Books

1038 Lallez, Raymond. *An Experiment in the Ruralization of Education: IPAR and the Cameroonian Reform.* Paris: UNESCO, 1974.

1039 Santerre, Renaud. *Pédagogie musulmane d'Afrique noire: L'école Coranique peuple du Cameroun.* Montreal: Presses de l'Université de Montreal, 1973.

1040 Vernon-Jackson, H. O. H. *Language, Schools, and Government in Cameroon.* New York: Teacher's College Press, 1967.

Articles

1041 Bergmann, H., and U. Bude. "A Survey of Primary Schools and Their Communities for General Education Policy-Making: The Case of Two Provinces in Cameroon." *International Review of Education* 23, no. 1 (1977): 3-34.

1042 Clignet, Remi. "Education, emploi et succès professionnel au Cameroun." *Canadian Journal of African Studies* 9, no. 2 (1975): 193-212.

1043 Clignet, Remi. "Educational and Occupational Differentiation in a New Country: The Case of Cameroon." *Economic Development and Cultural Change* 25 (July 1977): 731-45.

1044 Constable, D. "Bilingualism in the United Republic of Cameroon: Proficiency and Distribution." *Comparative Education* 10 (October 1974): 233-46.

1045 Fonlon, Bernard. "The Language Problem in Cameroon: An Historical Perspective." *Comparative Education* 5 (February 1969): 25-49.

1046 Gwei, S. N. "Cameroon." In *International Encyclopedia of Higher Education*, edited by A. Knowles, pp. 771-80. San Francisco: Jossey-Bass, 1977.

1047 Marchand, Claude. "Tentatives d'adaption de l'enseignement aux réalités camerounaises: l'enseignement agicole, 1921-1970." *Canadian Journal of African Studies* 8, no. 3 (1974): 539-51.

1048 Martin, Jean-Yves. "Inégalités régionales et inégalités sociales: L'enseignement secondaire au Cameroun septentrional." *Revue Française de Sociologie* 16 (July-September 1975): 317-34.

1049 Vander Ploeg, Arie J. "Education in Colonial Africa: The German Experience." *Comparative Education Review* 21 (February 1977): 91-109.

Chad

Articles

1050 "Chad." In *International Encyclopedia of Higher Education*, edited by A. Knowles, pp. 856-61. San Francisco: Jossey-Bass, 1977.

1051 Delacroix, M. Y. "L'éducation en milieu tedda." *Dossiers Pédagogiques* 1 (November-December 1972): 24-31.

1052 Miaro, Mahamat. "Les déterminants de l'aspiration scolaire et professionnelle chez les élèves de l'enseignement de secondaire du Tchad." *Canadian Journal of African Studies* 8, no. 3 (1974): 565-74.

1053 Teisserenc, Pierre. "Milieu urbain et recherche d'une identité culturelle: les lycéens de fort-Archambault et d'Abéché (Tchad)." *Cahiers d'Etudes Africaines* 13 (1973): 511-48.

Congo, Democratic Republic

Articles

1054 Clung, James C. "Public Education Trends in the Democratic Republic of the Congo, 1960-1967." *Comparative Education Review* 12 (October 1968): 323-37.

1055 "Dix ans d'éducation des adultes en République Populaire du Congo." *Convergence* 11, no. 2 (1978): 51-56.

1056 Lucas, Gerald. "Congo-Brazzaville." In *Church, State and Education in Africa*, edited by D. G. Scanlon, pp. 109-34. New York: Teacher's College Press, 1966.

Dahomey

Articles

1057 Adejuhmobi, S. A. "Problems of Education in Dahomey: A Nigerian View." *Journal of Negro Education* 45 (Summer 1976): 275-83.

1058 Asiwaju, A. J. "Formal Education in Western Yorabaland, 1889-1960: A Comparison of the French and British Colonial Systems." *Comparative Education Review* 19 (October 1975): 434-50.

1059 Bunche, Ralph J. "French Educational Policy in Togo and Dahomey." *Journal of Negro Education* 3 (January 1934): 69-97.

1060 Ronen, Dov. "The Colonial Elite in Dahomey." *African Studies Review* 17 (April 1974): 55-74.

1061 Tardits, C. "Réflexions sur le problème de la scolarisation des filles au Dahomey." *Cahiers d'Etudes Africaines* 3, no. 10 (1962): 266-81.

Ethiopia

Books

1062 Kalewood, Alaka Imbakom. *Traditional Ethiopian Church Education.* New York: Teacher's College Press, 1970.

1063 Wagaw, Teshome E. *Education in Ethiopia: Prospect and Retrospect*. Ann Arbor: University of Michigan Press, 1979.

Articles

1064 Abir, Mordechai. "Education and National Unity in Ethiopia." *African Affairs* 69 (January 1970): 44-59.

1065 Bekele, M. "Ethiopian Education: Challenge of the 70s." *Educational Leadership* (March 1968): 511-17.

1066 Gillett, Margaret. "Western Academic Role Concepts in the Ethiopian University." *Comparative Education Review* 7 (October 1963): 149-51.

1067 Korten, David C., and Frances F. Korten. "The Impact of a National Service Experience Upon its Participants: Evidence from Ethiopia." *Comparative Education Review* 13 (October 1969): 312-24.

1068 Lovegrove, Malcolm N. "Educational Growth and Economic Constraints: The Ethiopian Experience." *Comparative Education* 9 (March 1973): 17-27.

1069 Milkais, Paulos. "Traditional Institutions and Traditional Elites: The Role of Education in the Ethiopian Body-Politic." *African Studies Review* 19 (December 1976): 79-94.

1070 Pankhurst, Richard. "Ethiopia." In *Church, State and Education in Africa*, edited by D. G. Scanlon, pp. 23-58. New York: Teacher's College Press, 1966.

1071 Wodajo, Mulugeta. "Postwar Reforms in Ethiopian Education." *Comparative Education Review* 2 (February 1959): 24-30.

Gabon

Articles

1072 Gardinier, D. "Gabon Republic." In *International Encyclopedia of Higher Education*, edited by A. Knowles, pp. 1789-95. San Francisco: Jossey-Bass, 1977.

Ghana

Books

1073 Curle, Adam. *Educational Problems of Developing Societies: With Case Studies of Ghana, Pakistan, and Nigeria*. New York: Praeger, 1973.

1074 George, Betty. *Education in Ghana*. Washington, D.C.: U.S. Office of Education, 1976.

1075 Grindal, Bruce. *Growing Up in Two Worlds: Education and Transition Among the Sisala of Northern Ghana*. New York: Holt, Rinehart and Winston, 1972.

Articles

1076 Anim, Nicholas O. "Ghana." In *Church, State and Education in Africa*, edited by D. G. Scanlon, pp. 165-96. New York: Teacher's College Press, 1966.

1077 Austin, Dennis. "Et in Arcadia Ego: Politics and Learning in Ghana." *Minerva* 13 (Summer 1975): 236-70.

1078 Ayisi, C. H. "Educational Provision and Prospects for Employment in Ghana." *West African Journal of Education* 17 (February 1973): 89-99.

1079 Bibby, J. "The Social Base of Ghanaian Education: Is It Still Broadening?" *British Journal of Sociology* 24 (September 1973): 365-74.

1080 Blakemore, Kenneth P. "Resistance to Formal Education in Ghana: Its Implications for the Status of School Leavers." *Comparative Education Review* 19 (June 1971): 237-51.

1081 Curle, Adam. "Nationalism and Higher Education in Ghana." *Universities Quarterly* 16 (June 1962): 229-42.

1082 Darkwa, K. Ampon. "Education for Cultural Integrity: The Ghanaian Case." *Teachers College Record* 64 (November 1962): 106-11.

1083 Finlay, David J. "Education and Polity in Ghana." *History of Education Quarterly* 11 (Fall 1971): 319-27.

1084 Foster, Philip. "Comment on Hurd and Johnson 'Education and Social

Mobility in Ghana.'" *Sociology of Education* 41 (Winter 1968): 150-71.

1085 Foster, Philip. "Ethnicity and the Schools in Ghana." *Comparative Education Review* 6 (October 1962): 127-36.

1086 Foster, Philip. "Secondary Schooling and Social Mobility in a West African Nation." *Sociology of Education* 37 (Winter 1963): 111-15.

1087 Hurd, G. E., and T. J. Johnson. "Education and Social Mobility in Ghana." *Sociology of Education* 40 (Winter 1967): 55-79.

1088 Jahoda, Gustav. "The Social Background of a West African Student Population." *British Journal of Sociology* 5 (December 1954): 355-65.

1089 Jahoda, Gustav. "The Social Background of a West African Student Population." *British Journal of Sociology* 6, no. 1 (1955): 71-79.

1090 Kissack, J. J. "Language Inadequacy and Intellectual Potential: An Educational Priority in Ghana." *Comparative Education* 7 (November 1971): 68-71.

1091 Lloyd, Barbara. "Education and Family Life in the Development of Class Identification Among the Yoruba." In *The New Elites of Tropical Africa*, edited by P. C. Lloyd, pp. 163-84. London: Oxford University Press, 1966.

1092 Martin, Charles A. "Significant Trends in the Development of Ghanaian Education." *Journal of Negro Education* 45 (Winter 1976): 46-60.

1093 Masemann, Vandra. "The 'Hidden Curriculum' of a West African Girls' Boarding School." *Canadian Journal of African Studies* 8, no. 3 (1974): 479-94.

1094 Peil, Margaret. "Ghanaian University Students: The Broadening Base." *British Journal of Sociology* 16 (March 1965): 19-28.

1095 Thomas, Roger G. "Education in Northern Ghana, 1906-1940: A Study in Colonial Paradox." *International Journal of Historical Studies* 7, no. 3 (1974): 427-67.

1096 Weis, Lois. "Education and the Reproduction of Inequality: The Case of Ghana." *Comparative Education Review* 23 (February 1979): 41-50.

1097 Williams, T. David. "Sir Gordon Guggisberg and Educational Reform in the Gold Coast, 1919-1927." *Comparative Education Review* 8 (December 1964): 290-306.

Guinea

Books

1098 Bolibaugh, Jerry. *Educational Development in Guinea, Mali, Senegal, and Ivory Coast*. Washington, D.C.: U.S. Office of Education, 1970.

1099 Friere, Paulo. *Pedagogy in Process: The Letters to Guinea-Bissau*. New York: Seabury Press, 1978.

Articles

1100 Guilavogui, Galema. "The Basis of the Educational Reform in the Republic of Guinea." *Prospects* 5, no. 4 (1975): 435-54.

1101 Leunda, X. "La réforme de l'enseignement et son incidence sur l'évolution rurale en Guinée." *Civilisations* 22 (1972): 232-62.

1102 Stern, T. Noel. "Political Aspects of Guinean Education." *Comparative Education Review* 8 (June 1964): 98-103.

1103 Pretty, Margaret. "L'éducation en Guinée, 1878-1962." *West African Journal of Education* 12 (June 1968): 134-38.

Ivory Coast

Books

1104 Clignet, Remi, and Philip Foster. *The Fortunate Few: A Study of Secondary Schools and Other Students in the Ivory Coast*. Evanston, Ill.: Northwestern University Press, 1966.

1105 Cerych, Ladislav. *L'aide extérieure et la planification de l'éducation en Côte-d'Ivoire*. Paris: UNESCO, 1967.

1106 UNESCO. *Enquête sur les possibilités d'éducation, de formation et d'emploi offertes aux femmes en Côte d'Ivoire*. Paris: UNESCO, 1974.

Articles

1107 Clignet, Remi. "Ivory Coast." In *World Perspectives on Education*, edited by C. Beck, pp. 407-14. Dubuque, Iowa: Brown, 1970.

1108 Foster, Philip, and Remi Clignet. "La prééminence de l'enseignement classique en Côte d'Ivoire: Une exemple d'assimilation." *Revue Française de Sociologie* 7 (January-March 1966): 32-47.

1109 "Ivory Coast." In *International Encyclopedia of Higher Education*, edited by A. Knowles, pp. 2347-54. San Francisco: Jossey-Bass, 1977.

1110 Konan-Daure, A. N. "Educational Reform and Technological Innovation: The Ivory Coast Experiment." In *Educational Reforms: Experiences and Prospects*, pp. 132-46. Paris: UNESCO, 1979.

1111 Zolberg, Aristide. "Political Generations in Conflict: The Ivory Coast Case." In *University Students and African Politics*, edited by W. Hanna and J. Hanna, pp. 103-34. New York: Africana, 1975.

Kenya

Books

1112 Anderson, J. E. *Organization and Financing of Self-help Education in Kenya*. Paris: International Institute for Educational Planning, 1973.

1113 Brownstein, L., ed. *Education and Development in Rural Kenya*. New York: Praeger, 1972.

1114 Court, David, and D. Ghai, eds. *Education, Society and Development: New Perspectives From Kenya*. Nairobi: Oxford University Press, 1974.

1115 Cowan, L. Gray. *The Cost of Learning: The Politics of Primary Education in Kenya*. New York: Teacher's College Press, 1970.

1116 King, Kenneth. *The African Artisan: Education and the Informal Sector in Kenya*. New York: Teacher's College Press, 1977.

1117 Raju, Beulah M. *Education in Kenya*. London: Heinemann, 1973.

1118 Sheffield, James. *Education in Kenya: An Historical Study*. New York: Teacher's College Press, 1973.

1119 Sheffield, J. R. *Education in the Republic of Kenya*. Washington, D.C.: U.S. Office of Education, 1971.

1120 Sheffield, James R., ed. *Education, Employment and Rural Development*. Nairobi: East African Publishing House, 1967.

1121 Stabler, Ernest. *Education Since Uhuru: Kenya's Schools*. Middletown, Conn.: Wesleyan University Press, 1969.

1122 Weeks, Sheldon. *Divergence in Educational Development: The Case of Kenya and Uganda*. New York: Teacher's College Press, 1967.

Articles

1123 Anderson, J. E. "The Kenya Education Commission Report: An African View of Educational Planning." *Comparative Education Review* 9 (June 1965): 201-7.

1124 Carnoy, Martin, and Hans Thias. "Educational Planning with Flexible Wages: The Case of Kenya." *Economic Development and Cultural Change* 20 (April 1972): 438-73.

1125 Carnoy, Martin, and Hans Thias. "The Rates of Return to Schooling in Kenya." *Eastern Africa Economic Review* 3 (December 1972): 63-103.

1126 Court, David. "Dilemmas of Development: The Village Polytechnic Movement as a Shadow System of Education in Kenya." *Comparative Education Review* 17 (October 1973): 331-49.

1127 Evans, Emmit B., Jr. "Secondary Education, Unemployment and Crime in Kenya." *Journal of Modern African Studies* 13 (March 1975): 55-66.

1128 Godfrey, Martin. "Education, Productivity and Income: A Kenyan Case Study." *Comparative Education Review* 21 (February 1977): 29-36.

1129 Heyman, Richard. "The Initial Years of the Jeanes School in Kenya, 1924-1931." In *Essays in the History of African Education*, edited by Vincent J. Battle and Charles V. Lyons, pp. 105-23. New York: Teacher's College Press, 1970.

1130 Heyman, Richard D. "Pre-Independence African Demands for Educational Reforms—Kenya." In *Studies in Educational Change*, edited by Richard D. Heyman, Robert F. Lawson, and Robert M. Stamp, pp. 107-34. Toronto: Holt, Rinehart and Winston, 1972.

1131 Hopkins, Richard L. "The Self, Political Socialization, and Education: Kenya as a Case Study." *International Education* 3 (Fall 1973): 40-54.

1132 Kay, Stafford. "African Roles, Responses and Initiatives in Colonial Education: The Case of Western Kenya." *Paedagogica Historica* 16, no. 2 (1976): 272-94.

1133 Kay, Stafford. "Curriculum Innovations and Traditional Culture: A Case Study of Kenya." *Comparative Education* 11 (October 1975): 183-92.

1134 Keller, E. J. "Political Socialization of Adolescents in Contemporary Africa: The Role of the School in Kenya." *Comparative Politics* 10 (January 1978): 227-50.

1135 McKown, Roberta. "Kenya University Students and Politics." In *University Students and African Politics*, edited by W. Hanna and J. Hanna, pp. 215-56. New York: Africana, 1975.

1136 Olela, Henry. "Kenya." In *International Encyclopedia of Higher Education*, edited by A. Knowles, pp. 2387-93. San Francisco: Jossey-Bass, 1977.

1137 Olson, Jerry B. "Secondary Schools and Elites in Kenya: A Comparative Study of Students in 1961 and 1968." *Comparative Education Review* 16 (February 1972): 44-53.

1138 Prewitt, Kenneth. "Education and Social Equality in Kenya." In *Education, Society, and Development: New Perspectives from Kenya*, edited by David Court and Dharam Ghai, pp. 199-216. Nairobi: Oxford University Press, 1974.

1139 Schilling, Donald G. "The Dynamics of Education Policy Formation: Kenya, 1928-1934." *History of Education Quarterly* 20 (Spring 1980): 51-76.

1140 Urch, George E. "Education and Colonialism in Kenya." *History of Education Quarterly* 11 (Fall 1971): 249-64.

1141 Sifuna, D. N. "Reform in Primary Education in Kenya." *Présence Africaine* 95 (3rd quarter 1975): 284-99.

Lesotho

Articles

1142 Seithleko, A. N. "Lesotho." In *International Encyclopedia of Higher Education*, edited by A. Knowles, pp. 2522-27. San Francisco: Jossey-Bass, 1977.

Liberia

Books

1143 Gay, John, and Michael Cole. *The New Mathematics in an Old Culture.* New York: Holt, Rinehart and Winston, 1967.

1144 UNESCO. *Community Schools, Programme for Integrated Rural Education and Community Development: Liberia.* Paris: UNESCO, 1977.

Articles

1145 Drewal, Henry John. "Methodist Education in Liberia, 1833-1856." In *Essays in the History of African Education*, edited by Vincent J. Battle and Charles V. Lyons, pp. 33-60. New York: Teacher's College Press, 1970.

1146 Henries, A. D. B. "Liberia." In *World Perspectives on Education*, edited by C. Beck, pp. 415-22. Dubuque, Iowa: Brown, 1970.

1147 Livingston, Thomas W. "The Exportation of American Higher Education to West Africa: Liberia College, 1850-1900." *Journal of Negro Education* 45 (Summer 1976): 246-62.

1148 Mehmet, Ozay. "Educational Inequality and Dependence on Foreign Manpower in Liberia." *Canadian and International Education* 6 (June 1977): 65-79.

Malagasy Republic

Articles

1149 Hugon, P. "L'enseignement enjeu de la competition sociale à Madagascar." *Tiers Monde* 15 (July-December 1974): 491-510.

1150 Razafindrakoto, Andre. "Educational Reform and Decentralization: An Example from Madagascar." In *Educational Reforms: Experiences and Prospects*, pp. 201-11. Paris: UNESCO, 1979.

Malawi

Books

1151 Charlton, A. R. *Malawi Educational Planning*. Paris: UNESCO, 1973.

1152 Read, Margaret. *Children of Their Fathers: Growing Up Among the Ngoni of Malawi*. New York: Holt, Rinehart and Winston, 1968.

Articles

1153 Blackwell, James E. "Malawi." In *World Perspectives on Education*, edited by C. Beck, pp. 423-31. Dubuque, Iowa: Brown, 1970.

1154 Heyneman, Stephen P. "The Formal School as a Traditional Institution in an Underdeveloped Society: The Case of Northern Malawi." *Paedagogica Historica* 12, no. 2 (1972): 460-72.

1155 MacDonald, Roderick J. "The Socio-Political Significance of Educational Initiatives in Malawi, 1899-1939." *Transafrican Journal of History* 2 (1972): 69-93.

1156 Michael, Ian, and Felix Mnthali. "Political Independence and Higher Education in Malawi." In *Higher Education in a Changing World*, edited by B. Holmes and D. Scanlon, pp. 348-56. New York: Harcourt Brace Jovanovich, 1971.

1157 Rimmington, Gerald T. "Education for Independence: A Study of Changing Educational Administration in Malawi." *Comparative Education* 2 (June 1966): 217-24.

Mali

Books

1158 Boundy, K. *Management and Administration of Educational Services and Establishments.* Paris: UNESCO, 1976.

Articles

1159 Belloncle, Guy. "Use of the Bambara Language in Training Young People: An Experiment in Rural Mali." *Prospects* 10, no. 1 (1980): 107-16.

1160 Zolberg, Vera L. "National Goals, Social Mobility, and Personal Aspirations: Students in Mali." *Revue Canadienne d'Etudes Africaines* 10, no. 1 (1976): 125-42.

Mauritania

Articles

1161 Logan, Rayford W. "Education in Former French West and Equatorial Africa and Madagascar." *Journal of Negro Education* 30 (Summer 1961): 277-85.

1162 "Mauritania, Islamic Republic of." In *International Encyclopedia of Higher Education*, edited by A. Knowles, pp. 2786-90. San Francisco: Jossey-Bass, 1977.

Mozambique

Articles

1163 Azevedo, Mario J. "The Legacy of Colonial Education in Mozambique (1876-1976)." *Current Bibliography on African Affairs* 11, no. 1 (1978-79): 3-46.

1164 Delegation from Maputo to the Conference of African Ministries of Education held in Legon, 27 January to 4 February 1976. "Education Policy in The People's Republic of Mozambique." *Journal of Modern African Studies* 14 (June 1976): 331-39.

Nigeria

Books

1165 Abernathy, David B. *The Political Dilemma of Popular Education: An African Case.* Stanford, Calif.: Stanford University Press, 1969.

1166 Ayandele, E. A. *The Missionary Impact on Modern Nigeria, 1842-1914.* New York: Humanities Press, 1966.

1167 Callaway, A., and A. Musone. *Financing of Education in Nigeria.* Paris: International Institute for Educational Planning, 1968.

1168 Cerych, L. *The Integration of External Assistance with Educational Planning in Nigeria.* Paris: International Institute for Educational Planning, 1967.

1169 Fafunwa, A. Babs. *A History of Nigerian Education.* Lagos: Macmillan, 1971.

1170 Fafunwa, A. B. *A History of Nigerian Higher Education.* London: Allen and Unwin, 1974.

1171 Graham, C. K. *A History of Education in Ghana from the Earliest Times to the Declaration of Independence.* London: Frank Cass, 1971.

1172 Graham, Sonia. *Government and Mission Education in Northern Nigeria, 1900-1919.* Ibadan, Nigeria: Ibadan University Press, 1966.

1173 Ike, V. C. *University Development in Africa: The Nigerian Experience.* Ibadan, Nigeria: Oxford University Press, 1976.

1174 Ikejiani, O. *Education in Nigeria.* New York: Praeger, 1965.

1175 Lewis, L. J. *Society, Schools and Progress in Nigeria.* Elmsford, N.Y.: Pergamon, 1976.

1176 Nduka, Otonti. *Western Education and the Nigerian Cultural Background.* Ibadan, Nigeria: Oxford University Press, 1964.

1177 Ogunsola, Albert F. *Legislation and Education in Northern Nigeria.* Ibadan, Nigeria and New York: Oxford University Press, 1974.

1178 Okafur, Nduka. *The Development of Universities in Nigeria, 1868-1967.* London: Longmans, 1971.

1179 Peshkin, A. *Kanuri Schoolchildren: Education and Social Mobilization in Nigeria.* New York: Holt, Rinehart and Winston, 1972.

1180 Smythe, Hugh, and Mable Smythe. *The New Nigerian Elite.* Stanford: Stanford University Press, 1960.

1181 Van den Berghe, Pierre. *Power and Privilege in an African University.* Cambridge, Mass.: Schenkman, 1973.

Articles

1182 Abernathy, David B. "Teachers in Politics: The Southern Nigerian Case." In *The Social Sciences and the Comparative Study of Educational Systems*, edited by J. Fischer, pp. 409-29. Scranton, Pa.: International Textbook, 1970.

1183 Anosike, Benji J. O. "Education and Economic Development in Nigeria: The Need for a New Paradigm." *African Studies Review* 20 (September 1977): 17-26.

1184 Armer, M., and R. Youtz. "Formal Education and Individual Modernity in an African Society." *American Journal of Sociology* 76 (January 1971): 604-26.

1185 Asiwaju, A. I. "Ashby Revisited: A Review of Nigeria's Educational Growth, 1961-1971." *African Studies Review* 15 (April 1972): 1-16.

1186 Awoniyi, Timothy A. "The Place of Yoruba in the Formal School Sytem of Nigeria: A Historical Survey, 1800-1882." *Paedagogica Historica* 16 (1976): 216-26.

1187 Awoniyi, Timothy A. "The Yoruba Language and the Formal School System: A Study of Colonial Language Policy in Nigeria, 1882-1952." *International Journal of African Historical Studies* 8, no. 1 (1975): 63-80.

1188 Beckett, Paul A., and James O'Connell. "Education and the Situation of Women. Background and Attitudes of Christian and Muslim Female Students at a Nigerian University." *Culture et Développement* 8, no. 2 (1976): 242-65.

1189 Chukunta, N. K. Onuoha. "Education and National Integration in Africa: A Case Study of Nigeria." *African Studies Review* 21 (September 1978): 67-76.

1190 Clarke, Peter B. "Islam, Education and the Development Process in Nigeria." *Comparative Education* 14 (June 1978): 133-42.

1191 Koehl, Robert. "The Uses of the University: Past and Present in Nigerian Educational Culture, Part I." *Comparative Education Review* 15 (June 1971): 116-31.

1192 Koehl, Robert. "The Uses of the University: Past and Present in Nigerian Educational Culture, Part II." *Comparative Education Review* 15 (October 1971): 367-77.

1193 Kurtz, Donn M., II. "Education and Elite Integration in Nigeria," *Comparative Education Review* 17 (February 1973): 58-70.

1194 Lloyd, Barbara. "Education and Family Life in the Development of Class Identification Among the Yoruba." In *The New Elites of Tropical Africa*, edited by P. Lloyd, pp. 163-83. London: Oxford University Press, 1966.

1195 Nwagwu, Nicholas A. "The Politics of Universal Primary Education in Nigeria, 1955-1977." *Compare* 8, no. 2 (1978): 149-58.

1196 Omolewa, Michael. "The Question of University Leadership in the Development of Secondary Education in Nigeria." *International Review of Education* 24, no. 1 (1978): 35-52.

1197 Peshkin, Alan. "Education and Modernism in Bornu." *Comparative Education Review* 14 (October 1970): 283-300.

1198 Williams, Grace Alele. "Education and Government in Northern Nigeria." *Présence Africaine* 87 (3rd Quarter 1973): 156-77.

1199 Wilson, David N. "National Educational Planning Influenced by Military Government: Nigeria." *Educational Planning* 2 (March 1976): 64-83.

1200 Wilson, David. N. "Universal Primary Education in Nigeria: An Appraisal of Plan Implementation." *Canadian and International Education* 7 (December 1978): 28-53.

Rwanda

Books

1201 Hanf, Theodor, et al. *Education et Développement au Rwanda*. Munich: Weltforum Verlag, 1974.

1202 Hanf, T., P. V. Dias, W. Mann, and J. Wolff. *Erziehung und Entwicklung in Ruwanda*. Frankfurt am Main: Deutsches Institut für Internationale Pädagogische Forschung, 1973.

Articles

1203 Albert, Hugues. "Le rôle de l'université au Rwanda." *Informateur* 9 (March 1976): 40-65.

1204 Erny, Pierre. "Aspects de l'évolution quantitative de l'enseignement rwandais de 1962 à 1973." *Informateur* 9 (December 1975): 13-49.

1205 Erny, Pierre. "L'enseignement au Rwanda." *Tiers Monde* 15 (July-December 1974): 707-22.

1206 Erny, Pierre. "Pour une professionnalisation de l'enseignement secondaire." *Dialogue* (September-October 1975): 27-50.

Senegal

Articles

1207 Barthel, Denise. "The Rise of a Female Professional Elite: The Case of Senegal." *African Studies Review* 18 (December 1975): 1-18.

1208 Blakemore, Priscella. "Assimilation and Association in French Educational Policy and Practice: Senegal, 1903-1939." In *Essays in the History of African Education*, edited by Vincent J. Battle and Charles V. Lyons, pp. 85-103. New York: Teacher's College Press, 1970.

1209 Bouche, Denise. "Autrefois notre pays s'appelait la Gaule . . . Remarques sur l'adaptation de l'enseignement au Senégal de 1817 à 1960." *Cahiers d'Etudes Africaines* 8 (1968): 110-22.

1210 Bouche, Denise. "L'école française et les musulmans au Senégal de 1850 à 1920." *Revue Française d'Histoire d'Outre-Mer* 61 (April 1974): 218-35.

1211 Coulon, Christian. "L'université de Dakar a la recherche de son identité." *Revue Française d'Etudes Politiques Africaines* 101 (May 1974): 93-99.

Sierra Leone

Books

1212 Anderson, E. C., and Earl DeWitt Baker. *Educational Development in Sierra Leone*. Ann Arbor: University of Michigan Comparative Dissertation Series (No. 15), 1969.

1213 UNESCO. *Educational Development: Sierra Leone*. Paris: UNESCO, 1973.

Articles

1214 Anderson, E. Christian. "Early Muslim Schools and British Policy in Sierra Leone." *West African Journal of Education* 14 (October 1970): 177-80.

1215 Donald, Leland H. "Arabic Literacy Among the Yalunka of Sierra Leone." *Africa* 44 (January 1974): 71-81.

1216 Proudfoot, L., and H. S. Wilson. "Muslim Attitudes to Education in Sierra Leone." *The Muslim World* 50 (April 1960): 86-98.

1217 Windham, Gerald O. "Occupational Aspirations of Secondary School Students in Sierra Leone." *Rural Sociology* 35 (March 1970): 40-53.

Somalia

Articles

1218 Castagno, Alphonso. "Education and Political Evolution in an African Society." *Institute of International Education News Bulletin* 33 (February 1958): 2-10.

1219 Dawson, George A. "Education in Somalia." *Comparative Education Review* 8 (October 1964): 199-214.

1220 Clifford, W. Gilpin. "Somali Democratic Republic." In *International Encyclopedia of Higher Education*, edited by A. Knowles, pp. 3885-90. San Francisco: Jossey-Bass, 1977.

1221 Hamblur, F. N., and Nancy Bennet Turney. "Somalia." In *The Encyclopedia of Education*, edited by Lee C. Deighton, vol. 8, pp. 323-24. New York: Macmillan, 1971.

1222 Lewis, I. H. "Literacy in a Nomadic Society: The Somali Case." In *Literacy in Traditional Societies*, edited by Jack Goody, pp. 265-76. Cambridge: Cambridge University Press, 1968.

South Africa

Books

1223 Auerbach, F. E. *The Power of Prejudice in South African Education*. Capetown: A. A. Balkema, 1965.

1224 Behr, A. L. *New Perspectives on South African Education*. Durban, South Africa: Butterworths, 1978.

1225 Behr, A. L., and R. G. MacMillan. *Education in South Africa*. Pretoria: Van Schaik, 1971.

1226 Davis, R. Hunt. *Bantu Education and the Education of Africans in South Africa*. Athens: Ohio University Center for International Studies, 1972.

1227 Duming, P. A., ed. *Trends and Challenges in the Education of the South African Bantu*. Pretoria: Van Schaik, 1967.

1228 Legassick, Martin. *The National Union of South African Students*. Los Angeles: University of California Press, 1967.

1229 Malherbe, E. G. *Education in South Africa, Vol. 2 (1923-1975)*. Capetown: Juta, 1977.

1230 Morrel, Muriel. *Bantu Education to 1968*. Johannesburg: South African Institute of Race Relations, 1968.

1231 Robertson, Neville L., and Barbara L. Robertson. *Education in South Africa*. Bloomington, Ind.: Phi Delta Kappa Educational Foundation, 1977.

1232 Rose, Brian, ed. *Education in Southern Africa*. London: Collier Macmillan, 1970.

1233 Rose, Brian, and Raymond Tunmer. *Documents in South African Education*. Johannesburg: Donker, 1975.

1234 Troup, Freda. *Forbidden Pastimes: Education under Apartheid*. London: International Defence and Aid Fund, 1976.

1235 UNESCO. *Apartheid, Its Effects in Education, Science, Culture and Information*. Paris: UNESCO, 1972.

1236 Van der Merwe, H. W., and David Welsh, eds. *The Future of the University in Southern Africa*. New York: St. Martin's, 1978.

1237 Watson, Graham. *Passing for White: A Study of Racial Assimilation in a South African School*. London: Tavistock, 1970.

Articles

1238 "Academic Freedom in South Africa: The Open University in South Africa and Academic Freedom, 1957-1974." *Minerva* 12 (Autumn 1975): 428-65.

1239 Ashley, M. J. "The Education of White Elites in South Africa." *Comparative Education* 7 (August 1971): 32-46.

1240 Ashley, M. J., and H. W. Van der Merwe. "Academic Contrasts in South Africa." *Sociology of Education* 42 (Summer 1969): 284-91.

1241 Dickie-Clark, H. F. "The Dilemma of Education in Plural Societies: The South African Case." In *South Africa: Sociological Perspectives*, edited by H. Adam. London: Oxford University Press, 1971.

1242 Hugo, Pierre J. "Academic Dissent and Apartheid in South Africa." *Journal of Black Studies* 7 (March 1977): 208-17.

1243 Hunter, A. P. "South Africa." In *Church, State and Education in Africa*, edited by D. G. Scanlon, pp. 245-306. New York: Teacher's College Press, 1966.

1244 Ireland, Ralph R. "Apartheid and the Education of the Coloureds in the Republic of South Africa." *Plural Societies* 5 (Summer 1974): 9-24.

1245 Ireland, Ralph. "Education for What? A Comparison of the Education of Black South Africans and Black Americans." *Journal of Negro Education* 41 (Summer 1972): 227-40.

1246 Ireland, Ralph R. "Transkei: The Significance of Education for the Development of the Republic of South Africa's First Bantustan." *Plural Societies* (Spring 1972): 39-58.

1247 Low, Victor N. "Education for the Bantu: A South African Dilemma." *Comparative Education Review* 2 (October 1958): 21-27.

1248 MacMillan, R. G. "Education and Legislation in South Africa." *Comparative Education Review* 6 (June 1962): 58-63.

1249 Mphahlele, E. "South Africa." In *International Encyclopedia of Higher Education*, edited by A. Knowles, pp. 3890-902. San Francisco: Jossey-Bass, 1977.

1250 Munroe, David. "The Education of Europeans in South Africa." *Comparative Education Review* 5 (October 1961): 105-11.

1251 Oberholzer, C. K. "Problems and Trends of Education in South Africa." *International Review of Education* 5, no. 2 (1959): 129-41.

1252 Rathbone, Richard. "Students and Politics: South Africa." *Journal of Commonwealth and Comparative Politics* 15 (July 1977): 103-11.

1253 Rebusoajoang (pseud.). "Education and Social Control in South Africa." *African Affairs* 78 (April 1979): 228-39.

1254 Rose, Brian W. "Bantu Education as a Facet of South African Policy." *Comparative Education Review* 9 (June 1965): 208-12.

1255 Sevry, Jean. "Education et apartheid en Afrique du Sud." *Présence Africaine* (1976): 60-80.

1256 Zungu, Yeyedwa. "Education for Africans in South Africa." *Journal of Negro Education* 46 (Summer 1977): 202-18.

Sudan

Books

1257 Beshir, Mohamed Omer. *Educational Development in the Sudan 1898 to 1956*. New York: Oxford University Press, 1969.

1258 Bowles, F., and C. Duke, et al. *Higher Education in Sudan*. Paris: UNESCO, 1971.

1259 Sanyal, B. C., and A. Yacoub El-Samani. *Higher Education and Employment in the Sudan.* Paris: International Institute for Educational Planning, 1975.

Articles

1260 Akrawi, Matta. "Educational Planning in a Developing Country–the Sudan." *International Review of Education* 6, no. 2 (1960): 257-84.

1261 Battle, Vincent J. "The American Mission and Educational Development in Southern Sudan, 1900-1929." In *Essays in the History of African Education*, edited by Vincent J. Battle and Charles V. Lyons, pp. 63-83. New York: Teacher's College Press, 1970.

1262 Beshir, M. O. "Some Problems of University Education in the Sudan." *Comparative Education Review* 5 (June 1961): 50-53.

1263 Beshir, Mohamed Omer. "Sudan." In *Encyclopedia of Education*, edited by Lee C. Deighton, vol. 8, pp. 543-45. New York: Macmillan, 1971.

1264 Blakely, Edward J., and Charles E. Hess. "Designing a National System for Development: The Sudanese Experiment." *Educational Planning* 3 (October 1976): 80-89.

1265 Bouche, Denise. "Les écoles françaises au Soudan à l'époque de la conquête 1884-1900." *Cahiers d'Etudes Africaines* 6 (1966): 228-67.

1266 Hasan, Yusuf Fadl. "Interaction Between Traditional and Western Education in the Sudan: An Attempt Towards a Synthesis." In *Conflict and Harmony in Education in Tropical Africa*, edited by Godfrey N. Brown and Mervyn Hiskelt, pp. 116-33. London: George Allen and Unwin, 1975.

1267 King, K. J. "Nationalism, Education and Imperialism in Southern Sudan." In *Conflict and Harmony in Education in Tropical Africa*, edited by Godfrey N. Brown and Mervyn Hiskelt, pp. 296-318. London: George Allen and Unwin, 1975.

1268 Sammak, A. "Work-Oriented Adult Literacy Project in the Sudan." *Literacy Discussion* 2 (Spring 1971): 75-90.

1269 Sanderson, Lilian. "A Survey of Material Available for the Study of Educational Development in the Modern Sudan, 1900-1963." *Sudan Notes and Records* 44 (1963): 69-81.

1270 Sanderson, Lilian M. "Conflict, Education and New Awareness in the Southern Sudan (1898-1956)." In *Conflict and Harmony in Education in Tropical Africa*, edited by Godfrey N. Brown and Mervyn Hiskelt, pp. 104-15. London: George Allen and Unwin, 1975.

1271 Sanderson, Lilian. "Education and Administrative Control in Colonial Sudan and Northern Nigeria." *African Affairs* 74 (October 1975): 427-41.

1272 Sanderson, Lilian. "Girls' Education in the Northern Sudan, 1898-1956." In *Conflict and Harmony in Education in Tropical Africa*, edited by Godfrey N. Brown and Mervyn Hiskelt. London: George Allen and Unwin, 1975.

1273 Sanderson, Lilian. "The Development of Girls' Education in the Northern Sudan, 1898-1960." *Paedagogica Historica* 8, no. 1 (1968): 120-52.

1274 "Sudan, Democratic Republic." In *International Encyclopedia of Higher Education*, edited by A. Knowles, pp. 4005-11. San Francisco: Jossey-Bass, 1977.

Swaziland

Articles

1275 Guma, S. M. "Swaziland." In *International Encyclopedia of Higher Education*, edited by A. Knowles, pp. 4017-23. San Francisco: Jossey-Bass, 1977.

1276 Nsibandze, M. H. J., and Clifford Green. "In-Service Teacher Training in Swaziland." *Prospects* 8, no. 1 (1978): 110-15.

1277 Sislian, Jack. "African Dimensions in Education: The Case of Swaziland." *Compare* 10, no. 1 (1980): 61-74.

Tanzania

Books

1278 Cameron, John, and W. A. Dodd. *Society, Schools and Progress in Tanzania*. Elmsford, N.Y.: Pergamon Press, 1970.

1279 Chau, Ta Ngoc, and Françoise Caillods. *Educational Policy and Its Financial Implications in Tanzania*. Paris: UNESCO Press, 1975.

1280 Dodd, William A. *Education for Self-Reliance in Tanzania: A Study of Its Vocational Aspects*. New York: Teacher's College Press, 1969.

1281 Dolan, Louis Francis. *Transition from Colonialism to Self Reliance in Tanzanian Education*. Ann Arbor: University of Michigan Comparative Education Dissertation Series, 1970.

1282 Gillette, Arthur L. *Beyond the Non-Formal Fashion: Towards Educational Revolution in Tanzania*. Amherst, Mass.: Center for International Education, University of Massachusetts, 1977.

1283 Hall, Budd L. *Adult Education and the Development of Socialism in Tanzania*. Dar-Es-Salaam: East African Literature Bureau, 1975.

1284 Kurtz, Laura S. *An African Education: The Social Revolution in Tanzania*. New York: Pageant-Poseidon, 1972.

1285 Mbilingi, Marjorie. *The Education of Girls in Tanzania*. Dar-Es-Salaam: University of Dar-Es-Salaam, 1969.

1286 Morrison, David R. *Education and Politics in Africa: The Tanzanian Case*. Montreal: McGill Queens University Press, 1976.

1287 Mwingira, A. C., and Simon Pratt. *The Process of Educational Planning in Tanzania*. Paris: International Institute for Educational Planning, 1967.

1288 Nyerere, J. K. *Education for Self Reliance*. Dar-Es-Salaam: Tanzania Government Printer, 1967.

1289 Resnick, Idrian. *Tanzania: Revolution by Education*. Arusha: Longmans of Tanzania, 1968.

1290 Sanyal, B. C., and M. J. Kinunda. *Higher Education for Self-Reliance: The Tanzanian Experience*. Paris: International Institute for Educational Planning, 1977.

1291 Skorov, George. *Integration of Educational and Economic Planning in Tanzania*. Paris: International Institute for Educational Planning, 1966.

Articles

1292 Brooke-Smith, Robin. "The Politics of High-Level Manpower Supply in Tanzania." *Comparative Education* 14 (June 1978): 143-50.

1293 Cameron, John. "The Integration of Education in Tanganyika." *Comparative Education Review* 11 (February 1967): 38-56.

1294 Court, D. "The Experience of Higher Education in East Africa: The University of Dar Es Salaam as a New Model?" *Comparative Education* 11 (October 1975): 193-218.

1295 Dodd, William. "Centralization in Education in Mainland Tanzania." *Comparative Education Review* 12 (October 1968): 268-80.

1296 Gillette, Arthur. "L'éducation en Tanzanie: Une réforme de plus ou une révolution éducationnelle?" *Tiers Monde* 16 (October-December 1975): 735-56.

1297 Kirkland, Beverly G. "The Language of Self Reliance: Swahili-Medium Secondary Education in Tanzania." *African Languages* 2 (1976): 105-18.

1298 Koff, David, and George Von Der Muhll. "Political Socialization in Kenya and Tanzania—A Comparative Analysis." *Journal of Modern African Studies* 5 (May 1967): 13-53.

1299 Martin, B. G. "Notes on Some Members of the Learned Classes of Zanzibar and East Africa in the Nineteenth Century." *African Historical Studies* 4, no. 3 (1971): 525-45.

1300 Mhaihi, Paul Joseph. "Self-reliance in Educational Reform in the United Republic of Tanzania." In *Educational Reforms: Experiences and Prospects*, pp. 159-69. Paris: UNESCO, 1979.

1301 Mmari, G. R. V. "Attempts to Link School with Work: The Tanzanian Experience." *Prospects* 7, no. 3 (1977): 379-88.

1302 Odia, Solomon. "Rural Education and Training in Tanzania." *International Labour Review* 103 (January 1971): 13-28.

1303 Prewitt, Kenneth, George van der Muhll, and David Cause. "School Experiences and Political Socialization: A Study of Tanzanian Secondary

School Students." *Comparative Political Studies* 3 (July 1970): 203-25.

1304 Smith, Anthony. "British Colonial Education Policy—Tanganyika: A Variation on the Theme." *Paedagogica Historica* 5, No. 2 (1965): 435-54.

1305 "Tanzania." In *International Encyclopedia of Higher Education*, edited by A. Knowles, pp. 4053-62. San Francisco: Jossey-Bass, 1977.

Uganda

Books

1306 Almy, Millie C., Joel R. Davitz, and Mary Alice White. *Studying School Children in Uganda*. New York: Teacher's College Press, 1970.

1307 Chesswas, J. D. *Educational Planning and Development in Uganda*. Paris: International Institute for Educational Planning, 1966.

1308 Evans, David E. *Teachers as Agents of National Development: A Case Study of Uganda*. New York: Praeger, 1971.

1309 Goldthorpe, J. E. *An African Elite: Makerere College Students, 1922-1960*. Nairobi: Oxford University Press, 1965.

1310 Macpherson, Margaret. *They Built for the Future: A Chronicle of Makerere University College*. New York: Cambridge University Press, 1964.

1311 Octitti, J. P. *African Indigenous Education as Practiced by the Acholi of Uganda*. Nairobi: East African Literature Bureau, 1973.

1312 Otaala, Barnabas. *The Development of Operational Thinking in Primary School Children: An Examination of Some Aspects of Piaget's Theory Among the Iteso Children of Uganda*. New York: Teacher's College Press, 1972.

1313 Weeks, Sheldon. *Divergence in Educational Development: The Case of Kenya and Uganda*. New York: Teacher's College Press, 1967.

Articles

1314 Currie, Janice. "The Occupational Attainments Process in Uganda: Effects of Family Background and Academic Achievement on Occupational

Status among Ugandan Secondary School Graduates." *Comparative Education Review* 21 (February 1977): 14-28.

1315 Elkan, Susan. "Primary Schools Leavers in Uganda." *Comparative Education Review* 4 (October 1960): 102-10.

1316 Evans, David R. "Image and Reality: Career Goals of Educated Ugandan Women." *Canadian Journal of African Studies* 6, no. 2 (1972): 213-32.

1317 Heyneman, Stephen. "A Brief Note on The Relationship Between Socio-economic Status and Test Performance Among Ugandan Primary School Children." *Comparative Education Review* 20 (February 1976): 42-47.

1318 Heyneman, Stephen P. "Changes in Efficiency and Equity Accruing from Government Involvement in Ugandan Primary Education." *African Studies Review* 18 (April 1975): 51-60.

1319 Heyneman, Stephen P. "Influences on Academic Achievement: A Comparison of Results from Uganda and More Industrialized Societies." *Sociology of Education* 49 (July 1976): 200-10.

1320 Heyneman, Stephen P. "Relationship between the Primary School Community and Academic Achievement in Uganda." *Journal of Developing Areas* 11 (January 1977): 245-59.

1321 Heyneman, Stephen P. "Why Impoverished Children Do Well in Ugandan Schools." *Comparative Education* 15 (June 1979): 175-87.

1322 Heyneman, Stephen P., and Dean T. Jamison. "Student Learning in Uganda: Textbook Availability and Other Factors." *Comparative Education Review* 24 (June 1980): 206-19.

1323 Hindmarsh, Roland. "Uganda." In *Church, State and Education in Africa*, edited by D. G. Scanlon, pp. 135-64. New York: Teacher's College Press, 1966.

1324 Langlands, Bryant. "Students and Politics in Uganda." *African Affairs* 76 (January 1977): 3-20.

1325 Livingston, Thomas W. "Paradox in Early Mission Education in Buganda." *Journal of African Studies* 2 (Summer 1975): 161-76.

1326 Prewitt, Kenneth. "University Students in Uganda: Political Consequences of Selection Patterns." In *University Students and African Politics*, edited by W. Hanna and J. Hanna, pp. 167-86. New York: Africana, 1975.

1327 Smyth, John. "The Political Economy of Educational Planning in Uganda." *Comparative Education Review* 14 (October 1970): 350-62.

Upper Volta

Books

1328 Caty, R. *Haute Volta: Intégration d'un enseignement rural dans l'enseignement général*. Paris: UNESCO, 1968.

1329 Reif, H. W., and A. Salifou. *Education et développement en Haute Volta: Propositions pour une coopération internationale concentrée sur la région du sahel*. Paris: UNESCO, 1977.

Articles

1330 Fonseca, C. "Functional Literacy for Village Women: An Experiment in Upper Volta." *Prospects* 5, no. 3 (1975): 380-86.

1331 Mulassan, Mbela Hiza. "L'éducation rurale et la participation au développement en milieu rural traditionnel." *Africa* 30 (June 1975): 199-232.

Zaire

Books

1332 George, B. *Educational Developments in the Congo* (Leopoldville). Washington, D.C.: U.S. Office of Education, 1966.

1333 Golan, Tamar. *Educating the Bureaucracy in a New Polity: A Case Study of l'Ecole Nationale de Droit et d'Administration (ENDA) Kinshasa, Congo*. New York: Teacher's College Press, 1968.

1334 Verheust, Therese. *L'enseignement en République du Zaire*. Brussels: Les Cahiers du Cedaf, 1974.

Articles

1335 Dauphin, Henri. "Etre étudiant zairois." *Revue Française d'Etudes Politiques Africaines* 120 (December 1975): 54-70.

1336 Dodson, R. "Congo-Leopoldville." In *Church, State and Education in Africa*, edited by D. G. Scanlon. New York: Teacher's College Press, 1966.

1337 Erny, Pierre. "Aspects de l'évolution de l'enseignement colonial belge." *Revue Zairois de Psychologie et Pédagogie* 3 (July 1974): 93-106.

1338 Erny, P. "Vie universitaire au Zaire." *Education et Développement* 97 (1974): 48-56.

1339 Ponomarev, D. K. "Education in the Belgian Congo." *Soviet Education* 1 (July 1959): 46-51.

1340 Yates, Barbara A. "Structural Problems in Education in the Congo (Leopoldville)." *Comparative Education Review* 7 (October 1963): 152-62.

1341 Yates, Barbara A. "The Triumph and Failure of Mission Vocational Education in Zaire 1879-1908." *Comparative Education Review* 20 (June 1976): 193-208.

1342 Yates, Barbara A. "White Views of Black Minds: Schooling in King Leopold's Congo." *History of Education Quarterly* 20 (Spring 1980): 27-50.

1343 "Zaire." In *International Encyclopedia of Higher Education*, edited by A. Knowles, pp. 4463-68. San Francisco: Jossey-Bass, 1977.

Zambia

Books

1344 Mwanakatwe, J. M. *The Growth of Education in Zambia since Independence*. Dar-Es-Salaam: Oxford University Press, 1968.

1345 Sanyal, B. C., John H. Case, Philips Dow, and Mary E. Jackman. *Higher Education and the Labour Market in Zambia—Expectations and Performance*. Paris: UNESCO and University of Zambia, 1976.

Articles

1346 Burawoy, Michael. "Consciousness and Control: A Study of Student Protest in Zambia." *British Journal of Sociology* 27 (March 1978): 78-98.

1347 Coombe, Trevor. "The Origins of Secondary Education in Zambia, Part 2: Anatomy of a Decision, 1934-1936." *African Social Research* 4 (December 1967): 283-315.

1348 Etheredge, D. A. "The Role of Education in Economic Development: The Example of Zambia." *Journal of Administration Overseas* 6 (October 1967): 229-36.

1349 Musonda, Moses. "Zambia." In *International Encyclopedia of Higher Education*, edited by A. Knowles, pp. 7768-75. San Francisco: Jossey-Bass, 1977.

1350 Serpell, Robert. "Preference for Specific Orientation of Abstract Shapes Among Zambian Children." *Journal of Cross-Cultural Psychology* 2 (September 1971): 225-39.

1351 Small, N. J. "Alternative Educational Systems: The Zambian Proposals." *Prospects* 7, no. 1 (1977): 134-44.

1352 Tembo, L. P. "University of Zambia." In *Creating the African University*, edited by T. Yesufu, pp. 226-43. Ibadan, Nigeria: Oxford University Press, 1973.

1353 Vanzetti, N. R., and J. E. Bessell. "Education and the Development of Farming in Two Areas of Zambia." *Journal of Development Studies* 11 (October 1974): 41-54.

Zimbabwe

Books

1354 Parker, F. *African Development and Education in Southern Rhodesia.* Columbus: Ohio State University Press, 1960.

1355 UNESCO. *Southern Rhodesia: The Effects of a Conquest Society on Education, Culture, and Information.* Paris: UNESCO, 1977.

Articles

1356 Cefkin, J. Leo. "Rhodesian University Students in National Politics." In *University Students in African Politics*, edited by W. Hanna and J. Hanna, pp. 135-66. New York: Africana, 1975.

1357 Challiro, R. J. "The Origins of the Educational System of Southern Rhodesia." *Rhodesian History* 4 (1973): 57-77.

1358 Chideya, N. T., and M. J. M. Sibanda. "A Campus Decolonized? The Urgent Question of Succession at the University of Rhodesia." *Times Higher Education Supplement*, No. 374 (December 21, 1979), pp. 10-11.

1359 Kee, A. Alistair. "Underdevelopment—And How to Maintain It (Rhodesia)." *Teachers College Record* 69 (January 1968): 321-29.

1360 Parker, Franklin. "Education of Africans in Southern Rhodesia." *Comparative Education Review* 3 (October 1959): 27-32.

ASIA

Bibliographies

Books

1361 Neff, Kenneth L. *Selected Bibliography on Education in Southeast Asia.* Washington, D.C.: U.S. Office of Education, 1963.

1362 Stark, Craig. *Annotated Bibliography: Purpose and Process in Formal Education in Asia.* Berkeley: University of California, School of Education, 1973.

General

Books

1363 Adams, Don. *Education and Modernization in Asia.* Reading, Mass.: Addison-Wesley, 1970.

1364 Chomachai, P., ed. *Meeting the Challenges of the Seventies: Managing the University.* Bangkok: Association of Southeast Asian Institutions of Higher Learning, 1973.

1365 Fischer, J. *Universities in South East Asia*. Columbus: Ohio State University Press, 1964.

1366 Furnivall, John S. *Educational Progress in Southeast Asia*. New York: Institute of Pacific Relations, 1943.

1367 Hayden, Harold, et al. *Higher Education and Development in Southeast Asia*, 2 vols. Paris: UNESCO, 1967.

1368 Hoong, Yip Yat, ed. *Role of Universities in National Development Planning in Southeast Asia*. Singapore: Regional Institute of Higher Education and Development, 1971.

1369 Huq, Mohammad Shamsul. *Education, Manpower and Development in South and South-East Asia*. New York: Praeger, 1965.

1370 Medlin, W. K., W. M. Cave, and F. Carpenter. *Education and Development in Central Asia*. Leiden: E. J. Brill, 1971.

1371 Miller, T. W. G., ed. *Education in Southeast Asia*. Sydney: Novak, 1968.

1372 Myrdal, Gunnar. *Asian Drama: An Inquiry into the Poverty of Nations*, Vol. 3, Chs. 29–33. New York: Pantheon, 1958.

1373 Postelthwaite, T. Neville, and R. Murray Thomas, eds. *Schooling in the ASEAN Region*. Elmsford, N.Y.: Pergamon, 1980.

1374 *Progress of Education in the Asian Region: Statistical Supplement*. Bangkok: UNESCO Regional Office for Education in Asia, 1972.

1375 Shah, A. B., ed. *Education, Scientific Policy and Developing Societies*. Bombay: Manaktalas, 1967.

1376 Silock, T. H. *Southeast Asian University*. Durham, N.C.: Duke University Press, 1964.

1377 Thompson, Virginia, and Richard Adloff. *Cultural Institutions and Educational Policy in Southeast Asia*. New York: Institute for Pacific Relations, 1948.

1378 Wittig, Horst. *Bildungswelt Ostasien*. Paderborn, West Germany: Schoningh, 1972.

1379 Wong Hoy Kee, Francis. *Comparative Studies in South-East Asian Education*. Singapore: Heinemann Educational Books, 1973.

Articles

1380 Chang, P. "Educational Trends in Southeast Asia with Special Reference to Problems of Improving the Quality of Education." *International Review of Education* 17, no. 2 (1971): 150-64.

1381 Dore, R. P. "Schools and States in Asia and Africa: Review Article." *Pacific Affairs* 38 (Fall and Winter 1965-66): 345-52.

1382 Duke, Benjamin C. "The Karachi Plan—Master Design for Compulsory Education in Asia." *International Review of Education* 12, no. 1 (1966): 73-80.

1383 Durand, Maurice, and Nicole Louis. "Etude des systèmes d'éducation dans les différentes zones de l'Asie du Sud-Est." In *Education and Development in Southeast Asia*, pp. 61-87. Brussels: Editions de l'Institut de Sociologie, Université Libre de Bruxelles, 1967.

1384 Fischer, Joseph. "The University Student in South and Southeast Asia." *Minerva* 2 (Autumn 1963): 39-53.

1385 Fischer, Joseph. "Universities and the Political Process in Southeast Asia." *Pacific Affairs* 36 (Spring 1963): 3-15.

1386 Hans, Nicholas. "Nationalism and Education in Asia." *Comparative Education Review* 2 (October 1958): 4-12.

1387 Hayhoe, Ruth. "Written Language Reform and the Modernization of the Curriculum: A Comparative Study of China, Japan and Turkey." *Canadian and International Education* 8, no. 2 (1980): 14-33.

1388 Keller, Robert J. "The Role of Higher Education in National Development in Southeast Asia." *Higher Education* 6 (November 1977): 487-98.

1389 Kirpal, Prem. "Modernization of Education in South Asia: The Search for Quality." *International Review of Education* 17, no. 2 (1971): 138-50.

1390 Murray, Douglas P. "Chinese Education in South East Asia." *China Quarterly* 20 (October-December 1964): 67-95.

1391 Myint, H. "The Universities of Southeast Asia and Economic Development." *Pacific Affairs* 35 (Summer 1967): 116-27.

1392 Pieris, Ralph. "The Implementation of Sociology in Asia." *International Social Science Journal* 21, no. 3 (1969): 433-44.

1393 Rahman, A. F. M. K. "Educational Developments in Asia." *International Review of Education* 8, no. 3-4 (1963): 257-75.

1394 Seah, C. M. "Student Activism and the Political Process of ASEAN Countries." *Pacific Community* 7 (July 1976): 551-66.

1395 Silcock, T. H. "The Development of Universities in Southeast Asia to 1960." *Minerva* 2 (Winter 1964): 169-96.

1396 Silverstein, Josef. "Students in Southeast Asian Politics." *Pacific Affairs* 49 (Summer 1976): 189-212.

1397 Van Der Kroef, Justus M. "Asian Education and Unemployment: The Continuing Crisis." *Comparative Education Review* 7 (October 1963): 173-80.

1398 Van Der Kroef, Justus M. "Asia's Brain Drain." *Higher Education* 39 (May 1968): 241-53.

1399 Van Der Kroef, Justus M. "The Educated Unemployed in Southeast Asia: A Common Problem in India, Indonesia and the Philippines." *Journal of Higher Education* 31 (April 1960): 177-84.

Afghanistan

Books

1400 Sassain, Abul H. K. *Education in Afghanistan.* Washington, D.C.: U.S. Office of Education, 1961.

Articles

1401 "Afghanistan." In *International Encyclopedia of Higher Education*, edited by A. Knowles, pp. 189-94. San Francisco: Jossey-Bass, 1977.

1402 Eberhard, Wolfram. "Afghanistan's Young Elite." *Asian Survey* 1 (February 1962): 3-22.

1403 Linton, Clarence. "Afghanistan." In *World Perspectives on Education*, edited by C. Beck, pp. 227-36. Dubuque, Iowa: Brown, 1970.

1404 Sirat, Abdul Satar. "Sharia and Islamic Education in Modern Afghanistan." *Middle East Journal* 23 (Spring 1969): 217-21.

Bangladesh

Articles

1405 "Bangladesh." In *International Encyclopedia of Higher Education*, edited by A. Knowles, pp. 595-600. San Francisco: Jossey-Bass, 1977.

1406 Latif, A. H. "Educational Administration in Bangladesh." *Bulletin of the UNESCO Regional Office for Education in Asia* No. 15 (June 1974), pp. 20-34.

Burma

Books

1407 Neff, Kenneth Lee. *Burma: Education Data*. Washington, D.C.: U.S. Office of Education, 1965.

1408 Nyi, Nyi. *Higher Education in Burma*. Rangoon: Sarpay Beikman Press, 1972.

Articles

1409 Guyot, James F. "The Clerk Mentality in Burmese Education." In *Man, State and Society in Contemporary Southeast Asia*, edited by Robert O. Tilmon, pp. 212-27. New York: Praeger, 1969.

1410 Fischer, Joseph. "Education and Political Modernization in Burma and Indonesia." *Comparative Education Review* 9 (October 1965): 282-87.

1411 Kyi, D. H. M. "Burma." In *International Encyclopedia of Higher Education*, edited by A. Knowles, pp. 697-703. San Francisco: Jossey-Bass, 1977.

1412 Nash, Manning. "Education in a New Nation: The Village School in Upper Burma." *International Journal of Comparative Sociology* 2 (September 1961): 135-43.

1413 Nash, Manning, "Education in Burma: An Anthropological Perspective." In *The Social Sciences and the Comparative Study of Educational Systems*, edited by J. Fischer, pp. 148-68. Scranton, Pa.: International Textbook, 1970.

1414 Nash, M. "Rural Education for Development: Burma and Malaysia: A Contract for Cultural Meaning and Structural Relations." In *Education and Rural Development: The World Yearbook of Education*, edited by J. Sheffield, pp. 338-39. London: Evans Brothers, 1973.

1415 Nyi, Nyi. "The Development of University Education in Burma." *Journal of the Burma Research Society* 47 (June 1964): 11-76.

1416 Orata, Pedro T. "Towards a New School System in Burma." *International Review of Education* 5 (1959): 38-45.

1417 Sarkisyanz, H. "Cultural and Political Factors Affecting Changes in Education in Burma." In *Education et développement dans le Sud-Est de l'Asie*, pp. 199-207. Brussels: Université Libre de Bruxelles, 1967.

Cambodia

Books

1418 Bilodeau, Charles. *Compulsory Education in Cambodia, Laos, and Vietnam.* Paris: UNESCO, 1955.

1419 Duvieusart, B., and B. Ughelto. *Project de restructuration du système d'éducation: République Khemère.* Paris: UNESCO, 1976.

1420 Osborne, Milton. *The French Colonial Presence in Cambodia and Cochin China: Rule and Response, 1859-1905.* Ithaca, N.Y.: Cornell University Press, 1969.

1421 Tan, Kim Huon. *Role of Universities in Development Planning, the Khmer Republic Case.* Singapore: Regional Institute of Higher Education and Development, 1974.

Articles

1422 Delvert, Jean. "Le Cambodge: problèmes universitaires et évolution politique." *Compte Rendu Trimestriels des Séances de l'Académie des Sciences d'Outre-Mer* 32 (1972): 251-61.

1423 Dim, M. "Educational Administration in the Khmer Republic." *Bulletin of the UNESCO Regional Office for Education in Asia* 15 (June 1974): 85-100.

1424 Eilenberg, Jeanette H. "New Directions in Cambodian Education." *Comparative Education Review* 4 (February 1961): 188-92.

1425 Kiefer, Mildred S. "Cambodia." In *World Perspectives on Education*, edited by C. Beck, pp. 135-41. Dubuque, Iowa: Brown, 1970.

1426 Sou, Khim. "Status and Organization of Educational Planning in the Khmer Republic." *Bulletin of the UNESCO Regional Office of Education in Asia*, No. 16 (June 1975), pp. 44-58.

China

Books

1427 Ayres, William. *Chang Chih tung and Educational Reform in China.* Cambridge, Mass.: Harvard University Press, 1971.

1428 Barendsen, Robert D. *Education in the People's Republic of China: A Selective Annotated Bibliography of Materials Published in the English Language: 1971-1976.* Washington, D.C.: U.S. Office of Education, 1980.

1429 Barendsen, Robert D. *Half-Work, Half-Study Schools in Communist China.* Washington, D.C.: U.S. Office of Education, 1964.

1430 Beggerstaff, Knight. *The Earliest Government Schools in China.* Ithaca, N.Y.: Cornell University Press, 1961.

1431 Chen, Theodore H. *The Maoist Educational Revolution.* New York: Praeger, 1974.

1432 Chien, Chun-jui. *Educational Theory in the People's Republic of China.* Honolulu: University of Hawaii Press, 1971.

1433 Chow Tse-Tsung. *The May Fourth Movement: Intellectual Revolution in Modern China.* Stanford, Calif.: Stanford University Press, 1960.

1434 Doolin, Dennis J. *Communist China: The Politics of Student Opposition.* Stanford, Calif.: Hoover Institution on War, Revolution and Peace, Stanford University, 1964.

1435 Franke, Wolfgang. *Reform and Abolition of the Traditional Chinese Examination System*. Cambridge, Mass.: Harvard University Press, 1968.

1436 Fraser, Stewart E. *Chinese Communist Education: Records of the First Decade*. Nashville, Tenn.: Vanderbilt University Press, 1965.

1437 Fraser, Stewart E. *Education and Communism in China*. London: Pall Mall Press, 1971.

1438 Fraser, Stewart E., and Kuang-liang Hsu. *Chinese Education and Society: A Bibliographic Guide*. White Plains, N.Y.: International Arts and Sciences Press, 1972.

1439 Gamberg, Ruth. *Red and Expert: Education in the People's Republic of China*. New York: Schoken, 1977.

1440 Gregory, Peter B., and Noele Krenkel. *China: Education Since the Cultural Revolution; A Selected Partially Annotated Bibliography of English Translations*. San Francisco: Evaluation and Research Analysts, 1972.

1441 Hawkins, John N. *Mao Tse-Tung and Education: His Thoughts and Teachings*. Hamden, Conn.: Linnet Books, 1974.

1442 Hinton, William. *Hundred Day War: The Cultural Revolution at Tsinghua University*. New York: Monthly Review Press, 1972.

1443 Hu, C. T., ed. *Aspects of Chinese Education*. New York: Teacher's College Press, 1969.

1444 Hu, Shi Ming, and Eli Seifman. *Toward a New World Outlook: A Documentary History of Education in the People's Republic of China, 1949-1976*. New York: A. M. S. Press, 1976.

1445 Israel, John. *Student Nationalism in China, 1927-1937*. Stanford, Calif.: Stanford University Press, 1966.

1446 Keenan, Barry. *The Dewey Experiment in China: Educational Reform and Political Power in the Early Republic*. Cambridge: Cambridge University Press, 1977.

1447 Kessen, William, ed. *Childhood in China*. New Haven: Yale University Press, 1975.

1448 Kwong, Julia. *Chinese Education in Transition: Prelude to the Cultural Revolution*. Montreal: McGill Queens University Press, 1979.

1449 Montaperto, Ronald, and Jan Henderson, eds. *China's Schools in Flux*. White Plains, N.Y.: M. E. Sharpe, 1979.

1450 Orleans, Leo. *Professional Manpower and Education in Communist China*. Washington, D.C.: National Science Foundation, 1961.

1451 Peake, Cyrus. *Nationalism and Education in Modern China*. New York: Howard Fertig, 1970.

1452 Price, R. F. *Education in Communist China*. New York: Praeger, 1975.

1453 Price, R. F. *Education in Modern China*. London: Routledge and Kegan Paul, 1979.

1454 Rawski, Evelyn Sakakida. *Education and Popular Literacy in Ch'ing China*. Ann Arbor: University of Michigan Press, 1979.

1455 Ridley, Charles Price, Paul Goodwin, and Dennis J. Doolin. *The Making of a Model Citizen in Communist China*. Stanford, Calif.: Hoover Institute Press, 1971.

1456 Seybolt, Peter J., ed. *Revolutionary Education in China: Documents and Commentary*. New York: International Arts and Sciences Press, 1972.

1457 Seybolt, Peter J., and Gregory Knei-ko Chiang, eds. *Language Reform in China: Documents and Commentary*. New York: M. E. Sharpe, 1979.

1458 Swetz, F. *Mathematics Education in China: Its Growth and Development*. Cambridge, Mass.: M.I.T. Press, 1974.

1459 Tsang, Chiu-Sam. *Society, Schools, and Progress in China*. Oxford: Pergamon Press, 1968.

1460 Wang, Y. C. *Chinese Intellectuals and the West, 1872-1949*. Chapel Hill: University of North Carolina Press, 1966.

Articles

1461 Abe, Munemitsu. "Spare-Time Education in Communist China." *China Quarterly*, No. 8 (October-December 1961): 149-60.

1462 Alitto, Susan Biele. "The Language Issue in Communist Chinese Education." *Comparative Education Review* 13 (February 1969): 43-59.

1463 Bastid, Marianne. "Economic Necessity and Political Ideals in Educational Reform During the Cultural Revolution." *China Quarterly*, No. 42 (April-June 1970): 16-45.

1464 Baum, Richard. "Revolution and Reaction in the Chinese Countryside: The Socialist Education Movement in Cultural Revolutionary Perspective." *China Quarterly*, No. 38 (April-June 1969): 92-119.

1465 Chambers, D. I. "The 1975-76 Debate Over Higher Education in the People's Republic of China." *Comparative Education* 13 (March 1977): 3-14.

1466 Chen, Theodore H. E. "Elementary Education in Communist China." *China Quarterly*, No. 10 (April-June 1962): 98-122.

1467 Fraser, Stewart E. "Administration et contrôle de l'éducation en Chine." *International Review of Education* 22, no. 4 (1976): 491-503.

1468 Fraser, Stewart E. "Bibliography—China: School and Society." *Comparative Education Review* 18 (October 1974): 463-81.

1469 Fraser, Stewart E. "China's International, Cultural, and Educational Relations: With Selected Bibliography." *Comparative Education Review* 13 (February 1969): 60-87.

1470 Fraser, Stewart E. "Notes on Policy Formulation Process in China and Differential Levels of Educational Responsibility." *Viewpoints* 51 (May 1975): 87-107.

1471 Fraser, Stewart, and John Hawkins. "Chinese Education: Revolution and Development." *Phi Delta Kappan* 53 (April 1972): 487-500.

1472 Gardner, John, and Idema Witt. "China's Educational Revolution." In *Authority, Participation and Cultural Change in China*, edited by Stuart R. Schram, pp. 257-89. Cambridge: Cambridge University Press, 1973.

1473 Glassman, Joel. "The Political Experience of Primary School Teachers in the People's Republic of China." *Comparative Education* 15 (June 1979): 159-75.

1474 Hsu, Immanuel C. Y. "The Reorganization of Higher Education in Communist China, 1949-1961." *China Quarterly*, No. 19 (July-September 1964): 128-60.

1475 Hu, C. T. "Chinese Education: Theory and Practice." *China Quarterly*, No. 10 (April-June 1962): 84-97.

1476 Hunt, R. C. "Change in Higher Education in the People's Republic of China." *Higher Education* 4 (February 1975): 45-60.

1477 Kobayashi, Fumio. "The Great Cultural Revolution and the Educational Reform: The Image of Socialist Man." *Developing Economies* 9 (December 1971): 577-98.

1478 Keenan, Barry C. "Educational Reform and Politics in Early Republican China." *Journal of Asian Studies* 33 (February 1974): 225-37.

1479 Lee, Hong Yung. "The Radical Students in Kwantung during the Cultural Revolution." *China Quarterly*, No. 64 (October-December 1975): 645-83.

1480 Lewis, John W. "Party Codes in Communist China." In *Education and Political Development*, edited by James S. Coleman, pp. 408-36. Princeton: Princeton University Press, 1965.

1481 Lubot, Eugene. "Peking University Fifty-Five Years Ago: Perspectives on Higher Education in China Today." *Comparative Education Review* 17 (February 1973): 44-57.

1482 Lucas, C. J. "Towards A History of Chinese Education: Selected Resources." *Educational Studies* 5 (Fall 1974): 115-27.

1483 Machetzki, Rudiger. "China's Education Since the Cultural Revolution." *Political Quarterly* 45 (January-March 1974): 59-74.

1484 Martin, R. "Socialization of Children in China and on Taiwan: An Analysis of Elementary School Textbooks." *China Quarterly*, No. 62 (April-June 1975): 242-62.

1485 "May 7 Cadre Schools." *Chinese Education* 10 (Spring 1977): 3-84.

1486 McDowell, S. G. "Educational Reform in China as a Readjusting Country." *Asian Studies* 11 (March 1971): 256-70.

1487 Munro, Donald J. "Egalitarian Ideal and Educational Fact in Communist China." In *China: Management of a Revolutionary Society*, edited by John Lindbeck, pp. 256-301. Seattle: University of Washington Press, 1971.

1488 Munro, D. J. "Man, State and School." In *China's Developmental Experience*, edited by Michael Oksenberg, pp. 121-43. New York: Praeger, 1973.

1489 Pepper, Suzanne. "Education and Political Development in Communist China." *Studies in Comparative Communism* 3 (July and October 1971): 132-57.

1490 Pepper, Suzanne. "Education and Politics: The Chinese Model Revisited." *Asian Survey* 18 (October 1978): 843-90.

1491 Price, R. F. "Educating Successors to Which Revolution in China." *Canadian and International Education* 8, no. 2 (1980): 34-46.

1492 Price, R. F. "Labour and Education in Russia and China." *Comparative Education* 10 (March 1974): 13-24.

1493 Saywell, W. G. "Education in China Since Mao." *Canadian Journal of Higher Education* 10, no. 1 (1980): 1-28.

1494 Seybolt, Peter. "Higher Education in China." *Higher Education* 3 (August 1974): 265-84.

1495 Seybolt, Peter. "The Yenan Revolution in Mass Education." *China Quarterly* (October-December 1971): 643-69.

1496 Shirk, Susan L. "Educational Reform and Political Backlash: Recent Changes in Chinese Educational Policy." *Comparative Education Review* 23 (June 1979): 183-217.

1497 Shirk, Susan L. "The 1963 Temporary Work Regulations for Full-Time Middle and Primary Schools: Commentary and Translation." *China Quarterly*, No. 55 (July-September 1973): 511-46.

1498 Shirk, Susan L. "Work Experience in Chinese Education." *Comparative Education* 14 (March 1978): 5-18.

1499 Tien, Joseleyne Slade. "A Lesson From China: Percy Bysshe Shelley and the Cultural Revolution at Wuhan University." *Harvard Educational Review* 45 (May 1975): 211-23.

1500 Tsang, C. S. "The Red Guards and the Great Proletarian Cultural Revolution." *Comparative Education* 3 (June 1967): 195-207.

1501 Unger, Jonathan. "Bending the School Ladder: The Failure of Chinese Educational Reform in the 1960's." *Comparative Education Review* 24 (June 1980): 221-38.

1502 Unger, Jonathan. "Post Cultural Revolution Primary School Education: Selected Texts." *Chinese Education* 10 (Summer 1977): 3-106.

1503 Unger, Jonathan. "The Chinese Controversy over Higher Education." *Pacific Affairs* 53 (Spring 1980): 29-47.

1504 Whyte, Martin K. "Educational Reform: China in the 1970's and Russia in the 1920's." *Comparative Education Review* 18 (February 1974): 112-28.

1505 Yang, Chen Ning. "Education and Scientific Research in China." *Asia*, No. 26 (Summer 1972): 74-84.

1506 Zweig, David S. "The Peita Debate on Education and the Fall of Teng Hsiao-p'ing." *China Quarterly*, No. 73 (January-March 1978): 140-58.

Hong Kong

Articles

1507 Cheng, S. C., and R. Edwards. "Individual Versus Cooperative Research in Comparative Education: An Extension of the I. E. A. Enquiry to Hong Kong." *Comparative Education* 7 (December 1971): 107-20.

1508 Crames, John Francis. "The Chinese Colleges in Hong Kong." *Comparative Education Review* 3 (June 1959): 26-29.

1509 "Hong Kong." In *International Encyclopedia of Higher Education*, edited by A. Knowles, pp. 2052-59. San Francisco: Jossey-Bass, 1977.

1510 To, Cho-Yee. "The Development of Higher Education in Hong Kong." *Comparative Education Review* 9 (February 1965): 74-80.

India

Books

1511 Altbach, Philip G. *Student Politics in Bombay*. Bombay: Asia, 1968.

1512 Altbach, Philip, ed. *Turmoil and Transition: Higher Education and Student Politics in India*. New York: Basic Books, 1969.

1513 Ashby, Eric. *Universities, British, Indian, African*. Cambridge, Mass.: Harvard University Press, 1966.

1514 Basu, Aparna. *The Growth of Education and Political Development in India, 1878-1920*. Delhi: Oxford University Press, 1974.

1515 Blaug, M., P. R. G. Layard, and M. Woodhall. *The Causes of Graduate Unemployment in India*. London: Penguin Press, 1969.

1516 Chitnis, Suma, and Philip G. Altbach, eds. *The Indian Academic Profession*. New Delhi: Macmillan, 1979.

1517 Das Gupta, J. *Language Conflict and National Development: Group Politics and National Language Policy in India*. New York: Oxford University Press, 1970.

1518 DiBona, Joseph. *Change and Conflict in the Indian University*. Bombay: Lalvani, 1973.

1519 *Education in India: Index and Bibliography*. Ann Arbor: University of Michigan Press, 1966.

1520 Gore, M. S., I. D. Desai, and Suma Chitnis, eds. *Papers in the Sociology of Education in India*. New Delhi: National Council of Educational Research and Training, 1967.

1521 India. Ministry of Education. *Report of the Education Commission, 1964-66: Education and National Development*. New Delhi: Ministry of Education, 1966.

1522 Kamat, A. R. *Two Studies in Education*. Bombay: Asia, 1968.

1523 Kaul, J. N. *Higher Education in India, 1951-1971: Two Decades of Planned Drift*. Simla: Indian Institute of Advanced Study, 1974.

1524 Kopf, David. *British Orientalism and the Bengal Renaissance*. Berkeley: University of California Press, 1969.

1525 Laska, John A. *Planning and Educational Development in India*. New York: Teacher's College Press, 1968.

1526 Lindsay, J. K. *Primary Education in Bombay: Introduction to a Social Study*. Oxford: Pergamon Press, 1978.

1527 McCully, Bruce. *English Education and the Rise of Indian Nationalism*. New York: Columbia University Press, 1940.

1528 Misra, L. *Education of Women in India, 1921-1966*. Bombay: Macmillan, 1966.

1529 Naik, J. P. *Equality, Quality and Quantity: The Elusive Triangle in Indian Education*. Bombay: Allied, 1975.

1530 Nurullah, Syed, and J. P. Naik. *A Students' History of Education in India*. Bombay: Macmillan, 1964.

1531 Rudolph, Susanne H., and Lloyd I. Rudolph. *Education and Politics in India: Studies in Organization, Society and Policy*. Cambridge, Mass.: Harvard University Press, 1972.

1532 Sargent, Sir John. *Society, Schools and Progress in India*. Elmsford, N.Y.: Pergamon Press, 1967.

1533 Singh, Amrik, and Philip G. Altbach, eds. *The Higher Learning in India*. Delhi: Vikas, 1974.

1534 Srivastava, H. S. *Examination Reforms in India*. Paris: UNESCO, 1979.

Articles

1535 Altbach, Philip G. "Bibliography on Higher Education in India." *New Frontiers in Education* 4 (October-December 1974): 85-106; and 5 (January-March 1975): 75-101.

1536 Altbach, Philip G. "Higher Education in India." In *Higher Education in Nine Countries*, edited by B. Burn, pp. 317-45. New York: McGraw-Hill, 1971.

1537 Basu, Aparna. "Policy and Conflict in India: The Reality and Perception of Education." In *Education and Colonialism*, edited by P. G. Altbach and G. P. Kelly, pp. 53-68. New York: Longmans, 1978.

1538 Chaurasia, G., and G. K. Kaul. "Recent Trends and Developments in Primary and Secondary Education in India." *International Review of Education* 13, no. 3 (1967): 345-54.

1539 Dave, Ravindra H., and Walker Hill. "Educational and Social Dynamics of an Educational System: A Case Study of India." *Comparative Education Review* 18 (February 1974): 24-38.

1540 Elder, Joseph W. "The Decolonization of Educational Culture: The Case of India." *Comparative Education Review* 15 (October 1971): 288-95.

1541 Gilbert, Irene. "The Indian Academic Profession: The Origins of a Tradition of Subordination." *Minerva* 10 (July 1972): 384-411.

1542 Gusfield, Joseph. "Education and Social Segmentation in Northern India." In *The Social Sciences and the Comparative Study of Educational Systems*, edited by J. Fischer, pp. 240-76. Scranton, Pa.: International Textbook, 1970.

1543 Ilchman, Warren F. "'People in Plenty': Educated Unemployment in India." *Asian Survey* 9 (October 1969): 781-95.

1544 Ilchman, Warren F., and Trilok N. Dhar. "Optimal Ignorance and Excessive Education: Educational Inflation in India." *Asian Survey* 11 (June 1971): 523-43.

1545 Jones, Dawn E., and Rodney W. Jones. "The Scholars Rebellion: Educational Interests and Agitational Politics in Gujarat." *Journal of Asian Studies* 36 (May 1977): 457-76.

1546 Kale, Pratima. "The Guru and the Professional: The Dilemma of the Secondary School Teacher in Poona, India." *Comparative Education Review* 14 (October 1970): 371-76.

1547 Kirpal, P. "Modernization of Education in South Asia: The Search for Quality." *International Review of Education* 17 (1971): 138-49.

1548 Lindsey, J. K. "School, State, Caste, and Class in Bombay." *Canadian and International Education* 7 (December 1978): 64-80.

1549 Lindsey, J. K. "Social Class and Primary School Age in Bombay: The Role of Education in Transition to Capitalism." *Canadian and International Education* 6 (June 1977): 75-97.

1550 McDonald, Ellen. "English Education and Social Reform in Late Nineteenth Century Bombay: A Case Study in the Transmission of a Cultural Ideal." *Journal of Asian Studies* 25 (May 1966): 453-70.

1551 Rosenthal, Donald B. "Educational Politics and Public Policy Making in Maharashtra, India." *Comparative Education Review* 18 (February 1974): 79-95.

1552 Shukla, Snehlata. "Achievements of Indian Children in Mother Tongue (Hindi) and Science." *Comparative Education Review* 18 (June 1974): 237-47.

1553 Singh, R. P. "India." In *World Perspectives on Education*, edited by C. Beck, pp. 152-64. Dubuque, Iowa: Brown, 1970.

1554 Zachariah, Mathew. "The Durability of Academic Secondary Education in India." *Comparative Education Review* 14 (June 1970): 152-61.

1555 Zachariah, M. "Positive Discrimination for India's Scheduled Castes: A Review of Problems, 1950-1970." *Comparative Education Review* 16 (February 1972): 16-29.

Indonesia

Books

1556 Beeby, C. E. *Assessment of Indonesian Education: A Guide in Planning.* Wellington, New Zealand: Oxford University Press, 1979.

1557 Hutasoit, M. *Compulsory Education in Indonesia.* Paris: UNESCO, 1954.

1558 Junge, Gerhard. *The Universities of Indonesia: History and Structure.* Bremen, West Germany: Bremen Economic Research Society, 1973.

1559 Kersteins, Thom. *The New Elite in Asia and Africa: A Comparative Study of Indonesia and Ghana.* New York: Praeger, 1966.

1560 Thomas, R. Murray. *A Chronicle of Indonesian Higher Education.* Singapore: Chopmen Enterprises, 1973.

1561 Thomas, R. Murray, S. Z. Arbi, and Soedijarto. *Indonesian Education: An Annotated Bibliography*. Santa Barbara: University of California, 1973.

1562 Van de Veur, Paul W. *Education and Social Change in Colonial Indonesia*. Athens, Ohio: Southeast Asia Program, Center for International Studies, Ohio University, 1969.

1563 Van Neil, Robert. *The Emergence of the Modern Indonesian Elite*. The Hague: W. Van Hoeve, 1965.

Articles

1564 Budiman, Aref. "Student Movements in Indonesia." *Asian Survey* (June 1978): 609-25.

1565 Fischer, Joseph. "Education and Political Modernization in Burma and Indonesia." *Comparative Education Review* 9 (October 1965): 282-87.

1566 Fischer, Joseph. "Indonesia." In *Education and Political Development*, edited by J. S. Coleman, pp. 92-122. Princeton: Princeton University Press, 1965.

1567 Jones, Gavin W. "Religion and Education in Indonesia." *Indonesia* 22 (October 1976): 19-56.

1568 Lee, Kam Hing. "The Taman Siswa in Postwar Indonesia." *Indonesia* 25 (April 1978): 41-59.

1569 McVey, Ruth. "Taman Siswa and the Indonesian National Awakening." *Indonesia* 4 (October 1967): 128-49.

1570 Pearse, R. "The Role of Selection Based on Academic Criteria in the Recruitment Process at an Indonesian Government University." *Higher Education* 7 (May 1978): 157-76.

1571 Radcliffe, David. "Ki Hadjar Dewantara and the Taman Siswa Schools: Notes on an Extra-Colonial Theory of Education." *Comparative Education Review* 15 (June 1971): 219-27.

1572 Sarumpact, J. P. "New Era in Indonesian Education." *Comparative Education Review* 7 (June 1963): 66-73.

1573 Smith, T. M., et al. "Indonesian University Students and Their Career Aspirations." *Asian Survey* 14 (September 1974): 807-26.

1574 Soedijarto, et al. "Indonesia." In *Schooling in the ASEAN Region*, edited by T. N. Postelthwaite and R. M. Thomas, pp. 49-97. Elmsford. N.Y.: Pergamon Press, 1980.

1575 Surakhmad, Winarno. "Indonesia." In *Teacher Education in ASEAN*, edited by Francis H. K. Wang, pp. 35-55. Kuala Lumpur, Malaysia: Heinemann Educational Books, 1976.

1576 Taylor, Jean. "'Educate the Javanese!' A 1903 Memorial by Radin Ajeng Kartini." *Indonesia* 17 (April 1974): 83-98.

1577 Thomas, R. Murray. "Appraising the Community School—The Indonesian Case." *International Review of Education* 12 (1966): 416-31.

1578 Thomas, R. Murray. "Effects of Indonesian Population Growth on Educational Development, 1940-1968." *Asian Survey* 9 (July 1969): 498-514.

1579 Thomas, R. Murray. "Indonesia: Four Educational Development Problems in the 1970's." *Asian Profile* 5 (December 1977): 579-90.

1580 Thomas, R. Murray. "Toward Quality in the Face of Quantity: The Role of Consortia in Indonesian Higher Education." *International Review of Education* 19, no. 4 (1973): 489-95.

1581 Thomas, R. Murray. "Who Shall be Educated?: The Indonesian Case." In *The Social Sciences and the Comparative Study of Educational Systems*, edited by J. Fischer, pp. 277-346. Scranton, Pa.: International Textbook, 1970.

1582 Tsuchiya, Kenji. "The Taman Siswa Movement—Its Early Eight Years and Javanese Background." *Journal of Southeast Asian Studies* 6 (September 1975): 164-77.

1583 Van der Kroef, Justus M. "Educational Development and Social Change in Indonesia." *Harvard Educational Review* 24 (Fall 1954): 239-55.

1584 Van der Kroef, Justus. "Social Disfunctions of Indonesian Education." *Comparative Education Review* 2 (October 1958): 15-21.

1585 Williams, Lea E. "Nationalistic Indoctrination in the Chinese Minority Schools of Indonesia." *Comparative Education Review* 1 (February 1958): 15-21.

1586 Wilson, Greta. "Dutch Educational Policy in Indonesia, 1850-1900." *Asian Profile* 3 (February 1975): 59-72.

1587 Wong, Hoy-Kee. "The Development of National Language in Indonesia and Malaysia." *Comparative Education* 7 (November 1971): 71-81.

Japan

Books

1588 Beauchamp, Edward R., ed. *Learning to be Japanese: Selected Readings on Japanese Society and Education*. Hamden, Conn.: Linnet Books, 1978.

1589 Brameld, Theodore. *Japan: Culture, Education, and Change in Two Communities*. New York: Holt, Rinehart and Winston, 1968.

1590 Cummings, William K. *Education and Equality in Japan*. Princeton: Princeton University Press, 1980.

1591 Cummings, W., I. Amano, and K. Kitamura. *Changes in the Japanese University—A Comparative Perspective*. New York: Praeger, 1979.

1592 Dore, Ronald. *Education in Tokugawa Japan*. Berkeley: University of California Press, 1965.

1593 Duke, Benjamin. *Japan's Militant Teachers: A History of the Left-Wing Teachers Movement*. Honolulu: University of Hawaii Press, 1973.

1594 Hall, Robert King. *Education for a New Japan*. New Haven, Conn.: Yale University Press, 1959.

1595 Kobayashi, Tatsuya. *Society, Schools, and Progress in Japan*. Oxford: Pergamon, 1976.

1596 Kokusai Bunka Shinkokai. *Higher Education and the Student Problem in Japan: K. B. S. Bibliography*. Tokyo: Kokusai Bunka Shinkokai, 1972.

1597 Krauss, Ellis S. *Japanese Radicals Revisited: Student Protest in Postwar Japan*. Berkeley: University of California Press, 1974.

1598 Nagai, Michio. *Higher Education in Japan. Its Take-Off and Crash*. Tokyo: Tokyo University Press, 1971.

1599 Organization for Economic Cooperation and Development. *Reviews of National Policies for Education: Japan*. Paris: OECD, 1971.

1600 Passin, Herbert. *Japanese Education: A Bibliography of Materials in the English Language*. New York: Teacher's College Press, 1970.

1601 Passin, Herbert. *Society and Education in Japan*. New York: Bureau of Publications, Teacher's College, Columbia University, 1965.

1602 Pempel, T. J. *Patterns of Japanese Policymaking: Experiences from Higher Education*. Boulder, Col.: Westview Press, 1978.

1603 Shimahara, Nobuo. *Adaptation and Education in Japan*. New York: Praeger, 1979.

1604 Singleton, John C. *Nichu—A Japanese School*. New York: Holt, Rinehart and Winston, 1967.

1605 Teichler, Ulrich, and Friedrich Voss. *Bibliography on Japanese Education: Postwar Publications in Western Languages*. Munich: Verlag Dokumentation, 1974.

1606 Thurston, Donald R. *Teachers and Politics in Japan*. Princeton: Princeton University Press, 1973.

Articles

1607 Allen, G. C. "Education, Science and the Economic Development of Japan." *Oxford Review of Education* 4, no. 1 (1978): 27-36.

1608 Beauchamp, Edward. "Shiken Jigoku: The Problem of Entrance Examinations in Japan." *Asian Profile* 6 (December 1978): 543-60.

1609 Burn, Barbara. "Higher Education in Japan." In B. Burn, *Higher Education in Nine Countries*, pp. 227-76. New York: McGraw-Hill, 1971.

1610 Cummings, William K. "The Changing Role of the Japanese Professor." *Higher Education* 6 (May 1977): 209-34.

1611 Cummings, William K. "Understanding Behavior in Japan's Academic Marketplace." *Journal of Asian Studies* 34 (February 1975): 313-40.

1612 Dore, R. P. "Education: Japan." In *Political Modernization in Turkey and Japan*, edited by R. E. Ward and D. Rustow, pp. 176-203. Princeton: Princeton University Press, 1964.

1613 Dore, Ronald P. "The Legacy of Tokugawa Education." In *Changing Japanese Attitudes Toward Modernization*, edited by M. B. Jansen, pp. 99-131. Princeton: Princeton University Press, 1965.

1614 Duke, Ben. "American Educational Reforms in Japan 12 Years Later." *Harvard Educational Review* 34 (1964): 525-37.

1615 Duke, Ben. "Irony of Postwar Japanese Education." *Comparative Education Review* 6 (February 1963): 212-18.

1616 Duke, Benjamin C. "Statistical Trends in Post-War Japanese Education." *Comparative Education Review* 19 (June 1975): 252-66.

1617 Kida, Hiroshi. "Higher Education in Japan." *Higher Education* 4 (August 1975): 261-72.

1618 Kitamura, Kazuyuki, and William K. Cummings. "The 'Big Bang' Theory and Japanese University Reform." *Comparative Education Review* 16 (June 1972): 303-24.

1619 Kobayashi, Tetsuya. "Tokugawa Education as a Foundation of Modern Education in Japan." *Comparative Education Review* 9 (October 1965): 288-302.

1620 Kojima, Sigeo. "IEA Science Study in Japan with Special Reference to the Practical Test." *Comparative Education Review* 18 (June 1974): 262-67.

1621 Kruss, E., and J. Fendrich. "Political Identification and Behavior of Former Student Activists." *Japan Interpreter* 11 (Winter 1977): 313-36.

1622 Nagai, Michio. "Westernization and Japanization: The Early Meiji Transformation of Education." In *Tradition and Modernization in Japanese
Culture*, edited by D. Shively, pp. 35-76. Princeton: Princeton University Press, 1971.

1623 Passin, Herbert. "Japan." In *Education and Political Development*, edited
by J. S. Coleman, pp. 272-312. Princeton: Princeton University Press,
1964.

1624 Passin, Herbert. "Japanese Education: Guide to a Bibliography of Materials in the English Language." *Comparative Education Review* 9 (February 1965): 81-101.

1625 Pempel, T. J. "The Politics of Enrollment Expansion in Japanese Universities." *Journal of Asian Studies* 33 (November 1973): 67-86.

1626 Wray, Harry. "Nationalism and Internationalism in Japanese Elementary
Textbooks, 1918-1931." *Asian Forum* 5 (October-December 1973):
46-62.

Korea, People's Democratic Republic of (North)

Books

1627 Fraser, S., H. C. Kim, and S. H. Kim. *North Korean Education and Society: A Select and Partially Annotated Bibliography Pertaining to the
Democratic Peoples Republic of Korea*. London: University of London Institute of Education, 1972.

Articles

1628 Kim, Hyung-Chan. "Ideology and Indoctrination in the Development of
North Korean Education." *Asian Survey* 4 (November 1969): 831-41.

1629 Kim, Hyung-Chan. "Teaching Social Studies in North Korean Schools
Under Communism." *Social Education* 34 (May 1970): 528-42.

1630 Kim, S. H. "Korea, Democratic Republic." In *International Encyclopedia
of Higher Education*, edited by A. Knowles, pp. 2394-401. San Francisco: Jossey-Bass, 1977.

1631 Ou, Nam Djin. "Some Aspects of the Educational System in the Democratic People's Republic of Korea." *Prospects* 8, no. 1 (1978): 116-20.

Korea, Republic of (South)

Books

1632 Korean Commission for UNESCO. *Report on Major Trends in Educational Development in 1971-75.* Seoul: Korean Commission for UNESCO, 1971-75.

1633 Korean Commission for UNESCO. *Educational Development in Korea 1975-78.* Seoul: Korean Commission for UNESCO, 1975-78.

1634 Lee, Yong Dug. *Educational Innovation in the Republic of Korea.* Paris: UNESCO Press, 1974.

1635 McGinn, Noel, et al. *Education and Development in Korea.* Cambridge, Mass.: Harvard University Press, 1980.

1636 Morgan, Robert M., and Clifton B. Chadwick, eds. *Systems Analysis for Educational Change: The Republic of Korea.* Gainesville: University of Florida Press, 1971.

Articles

1637 Abe, Hiroshi. "Higher Learning in Korea Under Japanese Rule: Keijo Imperial University and the 'People's University' Campaign." *Developing Economies* 9 (June 1971): 174-96.

1638 Adams, Don. "Problems of Reconstruction in Korean Education." *Comparative Education Review* 3 (February 1960): 27-33.

1639 Bae, Chong-Keuh. "Impact of the Brain Drain on Korea." *Journal of Social Sciences and Humanities* 41 (June 1975): 79-92.

1640 Kim, Eugene C. I., and Chester Hunt. "Education and Political Development: A Comparison of Korea and the Philippines." *Journal of Developing Areas* 2 (April 1968): 407-20.

1641 "Korea, Republic." In *International Encyclopedia of Higher Education,* edited by A. Knowles, pp. 2401-7. San Francisco: Jossey-Bass, 1977.

1642 Oh, Byung Hun. "University Students and Politics in Korea." *Koreana Quarterly* 9 (Winter 1967): 1-41.

1643 Oh, Seung Shik. "Economic Development and Human Resources: With Reference to University Education." *Koreana Quarterly* 8 (Spring 1966): 37-48.

Laos

Books

1644 Lingappa, S. *L'éducation et l'environnement socio-économique: développements récents au Laos*. Paris: UNESCO, 1977.

Articles

1645 Brindley, Thomas A. "American Educational Efforts in Laos." *Educational Forum* 34 (March 1970): 365-70.

1646 Butler, L. "Lao Secondary Education Enrollment Review." *Malaysian Journal of Education* 9 (June 1972): 1-20.

1647 Butler, Lucius. "Secondary Education in Laos." *International Education* 2 (Fall 1972): 61-65.

1648 Cohen, David N. "A History of Education in Laos." *International Education* 7 (Spring 1978): 24-42.

1649 Halpern, Joel M., and Marilyn Clark Tinsman. "Education and Nation Building in Laos." *Comparative Education Review* 10 (October 1966): 499-507.

1650 "Laos." In *International Encyclopedia of Higher Education*, edited by A. Knowles, pp. 2438-42. San Francisco: Jossey-Bass, 1977.

1651 Outsama, K. "Educational Administration in Laos." *Bulletin of the UNESCO Regional Office for Education in Asia*, No. 15 (June 1974), pp. 115-28.

Malaysia

Books

1652 Bock, John C. *Education in a Plural Society*. Stanford, Calif.: Stanford University Press, 1978.

1653 Hon-Chan, C. *Education and Nation Building in Plural Societies: The West Malaysian Experience.* Canberra: Australian National University Press, 1977.

1654 Loh, Philip. *Seeds of Separatism—Education Policy in Malaysia, 1874-1940.* Kuala Lumpur: Oxford University Press, 1975.

1655 McMeekin, Robert W., Jr. *Educational Planning and Expenditure Decisions in Developing Countries: With a Malaysian Case Study.* New York: Praeger, 1975.

1656 Roff, W. R. *The Origins of Malay Nationalism.* New Haven: Yale University Press, 1967.

1657 Stevenson, Rex. *Cultivators and Administrators—British Educational Policy Towards the Malays, 1875-1906.* Kuala Lumpur: Oxford University Press, 1975.

1658 Tham, Seong Chee. *Malays and Modernization: A Sociological Interpretation.* Singapore: Singapore University Press, 1977.

1659 Wong, Francis H. K., and Paul Chang. *The Changing Pattern of Teacher Education in Malaysia, 1874-1940.* Kuala Lumpur: Oxford University Press, 1975.

1660 Wong, Francis Hoy Kee. *Education in Malaysia.* Kuala Lumpur: Heinemann Educational Books, 1971.

1661 Wong, F. H. K., ed. *Readings in Malaysian Education.* Kuala Lumpur: Penerbit University Malaya, 1977.

1662 Wong, Francis Hoy Kee, and Gwee Yee Hean. *Perspectives: The Development of Education in Malaysia and Singapore.* Kuala Lumpur: Heinemann Educational Books, 1972.

Articles

1663 Colletta, N. J., and A. S. Wong. "The Education of Chinese Workers' Children on Malaysia's Plantation Frontier: Myths and Realities." *Asian Survey* 14, no. 9 (1974): 827-44.

1664 Cooke, D. F. "The Mission Schools of Malaya, 1815-1942." *Paedagogica Historica* 6 (1966): 364-99.

1665 Fook-Seng, Philip Loh. "A Review of the Educational Developments in the Federated Malay States to 1939." *Journal of Southeast Asian Studies* 5 (September 1974): 225-38.

1666 Gwee, Y. H., and Y. C. Yen. "Primary and Mass Education in Malaysia." In *World Yearbook of Education*, pp. 407-19. London: Evans Brothers, 1965.

1667 Hirschman, Charles. "Educational Patterns in Colonial Malaya." *Comparative Education Review* 16 (October 1972): 486-502.

1668 Hoerr, O. D. "Education, Income, and Equity in Malaysia." *Economic Development and Cultural Change* 21 (January 1973): 247-73.

1669 Lim, David. "The Role of the University in Development Planning in Malaysia." *Minerva* 12 (January 1974): 18-31.

1670 Loh, Philip. "A Review of the Educational Developments in the Federated Malay States to 1939." *Journal of Southeast Asian Studies* 5, no. 2 (1974): 225-38.

1671 Loh, Philip. "British Politics and the Education of Malays, 1909-1939." *Paedagogica Historica* 14 (1974): 355-84.

1672 Nash, Manning. "Ethnicity, Centrality and Education in Pasir Mas, Kelantan." *Comparative Education Review* 16 (February 1972): 4-15.

1673 Seymour, J. Madison. "The Rural School as an Acculturating Institution: The Iban of Malaysia." *Human Organization* 33 (Fall 1974): 277-90.

1674 Strange, Heather. "Education and Employment Patterns of Rural Malay Women, 1965-1975." *Journal of Asian and African Studies* 13 (January-April 1978): 50-64.

1675 Takei, Yoshimitsu, John C. Bock, and Rex Wailand. "Aspirations and Expectations of West Malaysian Youth: Two Models of Social Class Values." *Comparative Education Review* 17 (June 1973): 216-30.

1676 Takei, Yoshimitsu, and Michael Kleiman. "Participation and Feelings of Political Efficacy: An Examination of the Transference Model." *Comparative Education Review* 20 (October 1976): 381-99.

1677 Tilman, Robert O. "Education and Political Development in Malaysia." In *Man, State, and Society in Contemporary Southeast Asia*, edited by Robert O. Tilman, pp. 228-42. New York: Praeger, 1969.

1678 Wang, Bee-Lau. "Governmental Intervention in Ethnic Stratification: Effects on the Distribution of Students Among Fields of Study." *Comparative Education Review* 21 (February 1977): 110-23.

1679 Wang, Chen Hsiu Chin. "Education in Malaysia: A Bibliography." *Malaysian Journal of Education* 1 (October 1964): 125-40.

1680 Watson, J. K. P. "The Problem of Chinese Education in Malaysia and Singapore." *Journal of Asian and African Studies* 8 (January-April 1973): 77-87.

1681 Wicks, Peter C. "Education, British Colonialism and a Plural Society in West Malaysia, 1786-1874." *History of Education Quarterly* 20 (Summer 1980): 163-88.

Mongolia

Articles

1682 Boldoyev, R. L. "Public Education in the Mongolian People's Republic." *Soviet Education* 1 (January 1959): 61-66.

1683 Krueger, John R. "Education in the Mongolian People's Republic." *Comparative Education Review* 4 (February 1961): 183-87.

1684 Pritchatt, Derrick. "Education in the Mongol People's Republic." *Asian Affairs* 61 (February 1974): 32-40.

1685 Pritchatt, Derrick. "Teacher Training in the Mongol People's Republic." *Asian Affairs* 61 (October 1974): 267-71.

1686 Rupen, Robert A. "Mongolian People's Republic." In *International Encyclopedia of Higher Education*, edited by A. Knowles, pp. 2890-94. San Francisco: Jossey-Bass, 1977.

Nepal

Books

1687 Aryal, Krishna Raj. *Education for the Development of Nepal.* Kathmandu: Shanti Prakashan, 1970.

1688 Reed, H. S., and M. J. Reed. *Nepal in Transition: Education Innovation.* Pittsburgh: University of Pittsburgh Press, 1968.

1689 Shrestka, Bihar K., and S. B. Gurung. *Equality of Access of Women to Education in Pokhara, Nepal.* Paris: UNESCO, 1973.

1690 Wood, Hugh B. *The Development of Education in Nepal.* Washington, D.C.: U.S. Office of Education, 1965.

Articles

1691 Hayes, Louis. "Educational Reform and Student Political Behaviour in Nepal." *Asian Survey* 16 (August 1976): 752-69.

1692 Murray, Margaret. "Nepal's Great Educational Leap Forward—to What?" *Compare* 10, no. 1 (1980): 31-46.

1693 Sharma, C. L. "Education in Nepal—Its Problems and Prospects." *Journal of Abstracts in International Education* 3 (Fall-Winter 1972-73): 22-27.

1694 Wood, Hugh B. "Mobile Normal Schools in Nepal." *Comparative Education* 1 (March 1965): 119-24.

Pakistan

Books

1695 Curle, Adam. *Educational Problems of Developing Societies, with Case Studies of Ghana, Pakistan, and Nigeria.* New York: Praeger, 1973.

1696 Curle, Adam. *Planning for Education in Pakistan: A Personal Case Study.* Cambridge, Mass.: Harvard University Press, 1966.

1697 Rauf, Abdur. *West Pakistan: Rural Education and Development.* Honolulu: East West Center Press, 1970.

Articles

1698 Klitgaard, Robert E., Fatima Akbar, Sofia Hakeken, Rabia Raffi, Tazeem-ur Rehman. "Merit and Admission Policy: Case Studies from Pakistan." *Comparative Education Review* 23 (June 1979): 271-82.

1699 Peshkin, Alan. "Education, the Muslim Elite, and the Creation of Pakistan." *Comparative Education Review* 6 (October 1962): 152-59.

1700 Peshkin, Alan. "The Shaping of Secondary Education in Pakistan." *History of Education Quarterly* 3 (March 1963): 4-18.

1701 Rahman, Fazlur. "The Qur'anic Solution of Pakistan's Educational Problems." *Islamic Studies* 6 (December 1967): 315-26.

1702 Thomas, Hendrik. "Literacy Without Formal Education: A Case Study in Pakistan." *Economic Development and Cultural Change* 22 (April 1974): 489-95.

Philippines

Books

1703 Carson, Arthur L. *The Story of Philippine Education.* Quezon City, Philippines: New Day Publishers, 1978.

1704 Case, Harry, and Robert Bonnell. *The University of the Philippines: External Assistance and Development.* East Lansing, Mich.: Institute of International Studies, Michigan State University, 1970.

1705 Foley, Douglas E. *Philippine Rural Education: An Anthropological Perspective.* DeKalb, Ill.: Center for Southeast Asian Studies, Northern Illinois University, 1976.

1706 Jocano, F. Landis. *Growing Up in a Philippine Barrio.* New York: Holt, Rinehart and Winston, 1969.

1707 Manalang, Priscila. *A Philippine Rural School: Its Cultural Dimension.* Quezon City: University of Philippines Press, 1977.

1708 Pascasio, E. M. *The Philipino Bilingual: Studies on Philippine Bilingualism and Bilingual Education.* Quezon City: Ateneo de Manila University Press, 1977.

Articles

1709 Cortes, Josefina R. "Philippines." In *Schooling in the ASEAN Region*, edited by T. N. Postelthwaite and R. M. Thomas, pp. 146-83. Elmsford, N.Y.: Pergamon Press, 1980.

1710 Encarnacion, José. "Family Income, Education, Labour Force Participation and Fertility." In *A Demographic Path to Modernity: Patterns of Early-Transition in the Philippines*, edited by Wilhelm Flieger and Peter C. Smith. Quezon City: University of the Philippines Press, 1975.

1711 Foley, Douglas. "Colonialism and Schooling in the Philippines from 1898 to 1970." In *Education and Colonialism*, edited by P. G. Altbach and G. P. Kelly, pp. 69-95. New York: Longmans, 1978.

1712 Green, Justin J. "Children and Politics in the Philippines: Socialization for Stability in a Highly Stratified Society." *Asian Survey* 17 (July 1977): 667-78.

1713 Green, Justin J. "Social Backgrounds, Attitudes and Political Behavior—A Study of a Philippine Elite." *South East Asia* 2 (Summer 1973): 301-38.

1714 Hernandez, Dolores F. "Renewing Elementary Science in the Philippines." *Prospects* 8, no. 1 (1978): 99-104.

1715 Hunt, Chester L., and Thomas R. McHale. "Education and Philippine Economic Development." *Comparative Education Review* 9 (February 1965): 63-73.

1716 Jacano, F. Landa. "Youth in a Changing Society: A Case Study from the Philippines." *Youth and Society* 1 (September 1969): 73-84.

1717 Lande, Carl. "The Philippines." In *Education and Political Development*, edited by J. Coleman, pp. 313-50. Princeton: Princeton University Press, 1965.

1718 Lear, Elmer N. "Education in Guerrilla Territory Under a Regime of Enemy Occupation." *History of Education Quarterly* 7 (Fall 1967): 312-29.

1719 May, Glenn. "Social Engineering in the Philippines: The Aims and Execution of American Educational Policy, 1900-1913." *Philippine Studies* 24 (2nd Quarter 1976): 135-83.

1720 Orata, Pedro T. "Philippine Education Today." *International Review of Education* 2, no. 2 (1956): 159-73.

1721 Pernie, Ernesto M. "The Question of the Brain Drain from the Philippines." *International Migration Review* 10 (Spring 1976): 63-72.

1722 Samonte, Quirico S. "Land Tenure and Public School Enrollment in the Philippines." *Comparative Education Review* 5 (October 1961): 136-41.

1723 Schumacher, John N. "Philippine Higher Education and the Origins of Nationalism." *Philippine Studies* 23 (1st and 2nd Quarters, 1975): 53-65.

1724 Schwartz, Karl. "Filipino Education and Spanish Colonialism: Toward an Autonomous Perspective." *Comparative Education Review* 15 (June 1971): 202-18.

1725 Tilman, Robert O. "The Impact of American Education on the Philippines." *Asia* 21 (Spring 1971): 66-80.

Singapore

Books

1726 Beach, N., and N. De Witt. *Administration and Financing of Education: Singapore*. Paris: UNESCO, 1973.

1727 Gopinathan, Saravanan. *Towards a National System of Education in Singapore, 1945-1973*. Singapore: Oxford University Press, 1974.

1728 Lau, W. H. *Qualitative Evaluation for Primary Teacher Education in Singapore*. Paris: International Institute for Educational Planning, 1972.

1729 Wong, Ruth H. K. *Education Innovation in Singapore*. Paris: UNESCO Press, 1974.

Articles

1730 Cheng, S. H. "Singapore Women: Legal Status, Educational Attainment, and Employment Patterns." *Asian Survey* 17 (April 1977): 358-74.

1731 Gopinathan, Saravanan. "Moral Education in a Plural Society: A Singapore Case Study." *International Review of Education* 26, no. 2 (1980): 171–86.

1732 Gopinathan, Saravanan. "Singapore's Language Policies: Strategies for a Plural Society." In *Southeast Asian Affairs, 1979*. Singapore: Heinemann Educational Books, 1979.

1733 Puccetti, Roland. "Authoritarian Government and Academic Subservience: the University of Singapore." *Minerva* 10 (April 1972): 223–41.

1734 Pye, Lucian, and A. Singer. "Higher Education and Politics in Singapore." *Minerva* 3 (Spring 1965): 321–35.

1735 "Singapore." In *International Encyclopedia of Higher Education*, edited by A. Knowles, pp. 3833–39. San Francisco: Jossey-Bass, 1977.

1736 Thomas, R. M., et al. "Singapore." In *Schooling in the ASEAN Region*, edited by T. N. Postelthwaite and R. M. Thomas, pp. 181–223. Elmsford, N.Y.: Pergamon Press, 1980.

Sri Lanka

Books

1737 Diyasena, W. *Pre-vocational Education in Sri Lanka*. Paris: UNESCO, 1976.

1738 Hallak, Jacques. *Financing and Educational Policy in Sri Lanka*. Paris: International Institute for Educational Planning, 1972.

1739 Jayasuriya, J. E. *Education in Ceylon Before and After Independence: 1939-1968*. Colombo, Sri Lanka: Associated Educational Publishers, 1969.

1740 Jayaweera, S., ed. *A Study of Educational Opportunities and Employment Opportunities Open to Women in Sri Lanka: A Report on an Investigation Conducted for UNESCO*. Paris: UNESCO, 1974.

Articles

1741 Ames, M. M. "Impact of Western Education on Religion and Society in Ceylon." *Pacific Affairs* 40 (Spring/Summer 1967): 19–42.

1742 Corea, J. C. A. "One Hundred Years of Education in Ceylon." *Modern Asian Studies* 3 (April 1969): 151-75.

1743 de Saram, D. D. "Education: An Era of Reforms." *Asian Survey* 13 (December 1973): 1169-78.

1744 de Silva, Kingsley. "The Universities and the Government in Sri Lanka." *Minerva* 16 (Summer 1978): 251-72.

1745 Green, T. L. "Social Education for Teachers in Ceylon." *International Review of Education* 2, no. 2 (1956): 200-14.

1746 Gunawardena, Chandra. "Ethnic Representation, Regional Imbalance and University Admissions in Sri Lanka." *Comparative Education* 15 (October 1979): 301-13.

1747 Hewage, Lankaputra, and David Radcliffe. "Sri-Lanka: The Relevance of Culture in Adult Education and Development." *Convergence* 10, no. 2 (1977): 63-74.

1748 Jayasuriya, J. E. "Current Educational Trends and Controversies in Ceylon." *International Review of Education* 8, no. 3-4 (1963): 292-301.

1749 Jayasuriya, J. E. "Educational Dilemmas of a Developing Country—Ceylon." *Journal of Social Issues* 24 (April 1968): 199-205.

1750 Jayaweera, Swarna. "British Educational Policy in Ceylon in the Nineteenth Century." *Paedagogica Historica* 9, no. 1 (1969): 68-90.

1751 Jayaweera, Swarna. "Language and Colonial Educational Policy in Ceylon in the Nineteenth Century." *Modern Ceylon Studies* 2 (July 1971): 123-50.

1752 Jayaweera, Swarna. "Recent Trends in Educational Expansion in Ceylon." *International Review of Education* 15, no. 3 (1969): 277-94.

1753 Jayaweera, Swarna. "Religious Organizations and the State in Ceylonese Education." *Comparative Education Review* 12 (June 1968): 159-70.

1754 Kapferer, Judith. "Four Schools in Sri Lanka: Equality of Opportunity for Rural Children?" *Comparative Education* 11 (March 1975): 31-43.

1755 Kearney, Robert N. "Educational Expansion and Volatility in Sri Lanka: The 1971 Insurrection." *Asian Survey* 15 (September 1975): 721-46.

1756 "Report of the Ceylon Universities Commission." *Minerva* 2 (Summer 1964): 492-518.

1757 Ruberu, T. Ranjit. "Educational Tradition Indigenous to Ceylon." *Paedagogica Historica* 14, no. 1 (1974): 106-117.

1758 Ryan, Bryce. "The Dilemmas of Education in Ceylon." *Comparative Education Review* 4 (October 1960): 84-93.

1759 Sirisena, U. D. I. "Educational Legislation and Educational Development: Compulsory Education in Ceylon." *History of Education Quarterly* 7 (Fall 1967): 329-48.

1760 Siriwardena, Subadra. "The Education of Girls and Women in Ceylon." *International Review of Education* 19, no. 1 (1973): 115-20.

Taiwan

Books

1761 Ysurumi, E. P. *Japanese Colonial Education in Taiwan, 1895-1945.* Cambridge, Mass.: Harvard University Press, 1977.

1762 Wilson, Richard. *Learning to be Chinese.* Cambridge, Mass.: M.I.T. Press, 1970.

Articles

1763 Appleton, Sheldon. "Silent Students and the Future of Taiwan." *Pacific Affairs* 43 (Summer 1970): 227-39.

1764 Appleton, Sheldon. "Taiwanese and Mainlanders on Taiwan: A Survey of Student Attitudes." *China Quarterly*, No. 44 (October-December 1970): 38-65.

1765 Appleton, Sheldon. "The Social and Political Impact of Education in Taiwan." *Asian Survey* 16 (August 1976): 703-20.

1766 Speare, Alden, Jr., Mary C. Speare, and Hui-Shang Lin. "Urbanization, Non-Familial Work, Education and Fertility in Taiwan." *Population Studies* 27 (July 1973): 323-34.

1767 Tsurumi, E. P. "Attempting to Create a Colonial Mentality: Japanese Elementary Education in Taiwan, 1895-1945." *Canadian and International Education* 5 (June 1976): 29-46.

1768 Wu, P. L. "Educational Modernization in Taiwan." *Catholic Educational Review* 66 (March 1969): 760-73.

Thailand

Books

1769 Bennett, Nicholas. *Problems of Financing the Thai Educational System in the 60s and 70s*. Paris: International Institute for Educational Planning, 1975.

1770 Gue, L. R. *Educational Reorganization in Thailand*. Washington, D.C.: American Educational Research Association, 1972.

1771 Montgomery, Warner M. *The Purpose and Problems of AID Educational Assistance to Thailand*. Ann Arbor: University of Michigan Comparative Education Dissertation Series, 1970.

1772 Porter, Willis P. *Institution Building: The College of Education Bangkok, Thailand: Its Role in National Development*. Bloomington: Indiana University Press, 1965.

1773 Sanguanruang, Saeng, and Amnuay Tapingkae, eds. *Development Planning in Thailand: The Role of the University*. Singapore: Regional Institute of Higher Education and Development, 1973.

1774 Tapingkae, Amnuay, and Louis J. Setti, eds. *Education in Thailand: Some Thai Perspectives*. Washington, D.C.: U.S. Office of Education, 1973.

1775 Wyatt, David K. *The Politics of Reform in Thailand: Education in the Reign of King Chulalongkorn*. New Haven: Yale University Press, 1969.

Articles

1776 Buripakdi, Chalio, and P. Mahakhan. "Thailand." In *Schooling in the ASEAN Region*, edited by T. N. Postelthwaite and R. M. Thomas, pp. 224-73. Elmsford, N.Y.: Pergamon Press, 1980.

1777 Danskin, Edith. "Quality and Quantity in Higher Education in Thailand and Philippines." *Comparative Education* 15 (October 1979): 313-25.

1778 Fry, Gerald W. "Education and Success: A Case Study of the Thai Civil Service." *Comparative Education Review* 24 (February 1980): 21-34.

1779 Goldstein, Sidney, et al. "The Influence of Labour Force Participation and Education on Fertility in Thailand." *Population Studies* 26, no. 3 (1972): 419-36.

1780 Gurevich, Robert. "Teachers, Rural Development and The Civil Service in Thailand." *Asian Survey* 15 (October 1975): 870-81.

1781 Guskin, Alan E. "Tradition and Change in a Thai University." In *Cultural Frontiers of the Peace Corps*, edited by R. B. Textor, pp. 88-106. Cambridge, Mass.: M.I.T. Press, 1966.

1782 Mezey, Susan. "Political Socialization and Participation Among University Students in Thailand." *Asian Survey* 15 (June 1975): 499-510.

1783 Muangchai Tajaroensuk. "Educational Planning in Thailand: Status and Organization." *Bulletin of the UNESCO Regional Office for Education*, No. 16 (June 1975), pp. 128-40.

1784 Nimmanheminda, Nai Sukich. "Higher Education in Thailand." In *The Task of the Universities in a Changing World*, edited by Stephen D. Kertesz, pp. 445-54. South Bend, Ind.: University of Notre Dame Press, 1971.

1785 Pin, Malakul. "Education During the Time When His Highness Prince Dhaninivat was Minister of Public Instruction." *Journal of the Siam Society* 63 (January 1975): 9-27.

1786 Prizzia, R., and N. Sinsawasdi. "Evolution of the Thai Student Movement." *Asia Quarterly* (1975): 3-54.

1787 Smythe, Hugh H., and Nihondh Sasidhorn. "Educational Planning in Thailand." *Comparative Education Review* 8 (June 1964): 37-40.

1788 Soen, Dan, and M. Tamir. "Education in the Northern Region of Thailand—An Attempt at Analysis." *Asia Quarterly* (1973): 313-28.

1789 Sukontarangsi, Swat. "The Development of Governmental Control of Public Education in Thailand." *Paedagogica Historica* 6 (1966): 416-39.

1790 Watson, J. K. P. "A Conflict of Nationalism: The Chinese and Education in Thailand, 1900-1960." *Paedagogica Historica* 16, no. 2 (1976): 429-54.

1791 Watson, J. K. P. "Primary Education in Thailand: Plans, Problems and Possibilities." *Comparative Education* 10 (March 1974): 35-48.

1792 Watson, J. K. P. "The Monastic Tradition of Education in Thailand." *Paedagogica Historica* 13, no. 2 (1973): 515-29.

Vietnam

Books

1793 Marr, David G. *Vietnamese Anti-Colonialism, 1885-1925.* Berkeley: University of California Press, 1971.

1794 Nguyn Khanh Toan. *20 Years Development of Education in the Democratic Republic of Vietnam.* Hanoi: Ministry of Education, 1965.

1795 Osborne, Milton E. *The French Presence in Cochinchina and Cambodia: Rule and Response (1859-1905).* Ithaca, N.Y.: Cornell University Press, 1969.

Articles

1796 Chompatong, S. "Some Aspects of Education in the Republic of Vietnam." *Contemporary Education* 45 (Spring 1974): 190-94.

1797 Dodd, Joseph W. "Aspects of Recent Educational Change in South Vietnam." *Journal of Developing Areas* 6 (July 1972): 555-70.

1798 Fraser, Stewart E. "The Three Rs of Vietnamese Education: Revolution, Reunification and Redevelopment." *Phi Delta Kappan* (June 1977): 730-34.

1799 Jones, P. H. M. "Vietnam at School." In *Vietnam: Anatomy of a Conflict,* edited by Wesley Fishel, pp. 648-60. Itasca, Ill.: Peacock, 1968.

1800 Kelly, Gail P. "Colonial Schools as Alternatives to Modern Education: The Case of Vietnam." In *Education and Colonialism*, edited by P. G. Altbach and G. P. Kelly, pp. 96-121. New York: Longmans, 1978.

1801 Kelly, Gail P. "Education and Participation in Nationalist Groups: An Exploratory Study of the Indochinese Communist Party and the UNQDD, 1921-1931." *Comparative Education Review* 15 (June 1971): 227-37.

1802 Khôi, Lê Thành. "Literacy Training and Revolution: the Vietnamese Experience." *Convergence* 8, no. 4 (1975): 29-38.

1803 Morton, B. E. "Education in Vietnam." *Contemporary Education* 45 (Spring 1974): 201-8.

1804 Naughton, Patrick W. "Some Comparisons of Higher Education in Vietnam, 1954-76." *Canadian and International Education* 8, no. 2 (1980): 100-16.

1805 Nguyen-Trong-Huang. "Traditional Education in Vietnam." *Vietnamese Studies* 30 (1971): 127-46.

1806 Quang-Nam, Thai. "Education et travail productif au Vietnam." *Canadian and International Education* 8, no. 2 (1980): 92-99.

1807 "Vietnam." In *International Encyclopedia of Higher Education*, edited by A. Knowles, pp. 4348-58. San Francisco: Jossey-Bass, 1977.

1808 Vu Duc Bang. "The Dong Kinh Free School." In *Aspects of Vietnamese History*, edited by Walter Vella, pp. 30-95. Honolulu: University of Hawaii Press, 1973.

1809 Woodside, Alexander. "Ideology and Integration in Post-Colonial Vietnamese Nationalism." *Pacific Affairs* 44 (Winter 1971-72): 487-510.

EUROPE

Bibliographies

Books

1810 Documentation Centre for Education in Europe. *Educational Research: European Survey 1968*, 4 vols. Strasbourg: Documentation Centre for Education in Europe, 1969.

1811 Fomerand, Jacques, J. van de Graaff, and Henry Wasser. *Higher Education in Western Europe and North America: A Selected and Annotated Bibliography*. New York: Council on European Studies, Columbia University, 1979.

1812 Fraser, Stewart E., and Barbara J. Fraser. *Scandinavian Education: A Bibliography of English-Language Materials*. New York: International Arts and Sciences Press, 1973.

1813 Paulston, Rolland G. *Folk Schools in Social Change: A Partisan Guide to the International Literature*. Pittsburgh: University Center for International Studies, University of Pittsburgh, 1974.

General

Books

1814 Adamski, W. *Continuing Education in Western and Eastern European Societies: Ideology and Reality*. Paris: European Cultural Foundation, 1978.

1815 Anweiler, Oskar, et al. *Bildungssysteme in Europa*. Weinheim, West Germany: Beltz, 1980.

1816 Archer, Margaret S., ed. *Students, Universities and Society: A Comparative Sociological Review*. London: Heinemann, 1972.

1817 Armstrong, John. *The European Administrative Elite*. Princeton: Princeton University Press, 1973.

1818 Ashby, Eric. *Technology and the Academics: An Essay on Universities and the Scientific Revolution*. London: Macmillan, 1958.

1819 Bakke, Wight E., and Mary S. Bakke. *Campus Challenge*. Hamden, Conn.: Archon, 1971.

1820 Beck, Robert H. *Change and Harmonization in European Education*. Minneapolis: University of Minnesota Press, 1971.

1821 Ben-David, Joseph. *Centers of Learning: Britain, France, Germany, United States*. New York: McGraw-Hill, 1977.

1822 Bengtsson, Jarl. *Does Education Have a Future?: The Political Economy of Social and Educational Inequalities in European Society*. The Hague: Nijhoff, 1975.

1823 Berger, Walter. *Schulentwicklungen in vergleichender Sicht. USA, England, Frankreich, BRD, Schweiz und Österreich*. Vienna: Verlag Jugend und Volk, 1978.

1824 Bockstael, Eric, and Otto Feinstein. *Higher Education in the European Community*. Lexington, Mass.: Heath-Lexington Books, 1970.

1825 Boudon, Raymond. *Education, Opportunity and Social Inequality: Changing Prospects in Western Society*. New York: Wiley, 1974.

1826 Cook, T. G., ed. *The History of Education in Europe*. London: Methuen, 1974.

1827 Debeauvais, Michel. *Quelques problèmes de devéloppement de l'enseignement supérieur en Europe*. Bruxelles: Ministère de l'Education, 1969.

1828 Dixon, Cyril Willis. *Society, Schools and Progress in Scandinavia*. Oxford: Pergamon Press, 1965.

1829 Flexner, Abraham. *Universities: American, English, German*. New York: Oxford University Press, 1968.

1830 Gary, Romain. *Education européenne*. Paris: Gallimard, 1965.

1831 Glenny, Lyman A., et al. *Funding Higher Education: A Six Nation Analysis*. New York: Praeger, 1979.

1832 Jensen, Stefan, Jan Tinbergen, Barry Hake, et al. *Possible Futures of European Education*. The Hague: Nijhoff, 1972.

1833 King, Edmund J. *Education and Development in Western Europe*. Reading, Mass.: Addison-Wesley, 1969.

1834 King, Edmund J., Christine H. Moor, and Jennifer A. Mundy. *Post-Compulsory Education*, 2 vols. Beverly Hills, Calif.: Sage Publications, 1974.

1835 Laqueur, Walter, and George L. Mosse, eds. *Education and Social Structure in the 20th Century*. New York: Harper and Row, 1967.

1836 LeGall, A., et al. *Present Problems in the Democratization of Secondary and Higher Education.* Paris: UNESCO, 1973.

1837 Lynch, J., and H. D. Plunkett. *Teacher Education and Cultural Change: England, France and West Germany.* London: Allen and Unwin, 1973.

1838 Majault, J. *Primary and Secondary Education: Modern Trends and Common Problems.* Strasbourg: Council of Europe, 1967.

1839 Mallinson, V. *The Western European Idea in Education.* Oxford: Pergamon Press, 1980.

1840 Matthijssen, M. A., and C. E. Vervoort, eds. *Education in Europe: Sociological Research.* The Hague: Mouton, 1967.

1841 Newcombe, Norman. *Europe at School.* London: Methuen, 1977.

1842 Nicollier, A., ed. *The European Universities 1975-1985.* Oxford: Pergamon Press, 1975.

1843 Organization for Economic Cooperation and Development. *Development of Higher Education 1950-1967.* Paris: OECD, 1971.

1844 Poignant, Raymond. *Education and Development in Western Europe, the United States, and the U.S.S.R.: A Comparative Study.* New York: Teacher's College Press, 1969.

1845 Poignant, Raymond. *Education in the Industrialised Countries.* The Hague: Nijhoff, 1973.

1846 Psacharopoulos, G. *Earnings and Education in OECD Countries.* Paris: OECD, 1975.

1847 Riche, Pierre. *Education and Culture in the Barbarian West: From the Sixth Through the Eighth Century.* Columbia: University of South Carolina Press, 1976.

1848 Ringer, Fritz. *Education and Society in Modern Europe.* Bloomington: Indiana University Press, 1978.

1849 Sauvy, Alfred. *Access to Education: New Possibilities,* vol. 3. The Hague: Nijhoff, 1973.

1850 Shipman, M. D. *Education and Modernisation*. London: Faber and Faber, 1971.

1851 Spolton, Lewis, *The Upper Secondary School: A Comparative Survey*. Oxford: Pergamon Press, 1967.

1852 Ulich, Mary E. *Patterns of Adult Education: A Comparative Study*. New York: Pageant Press, 1965.

Articles

1853 Anderson, D. "Geographic and Economic Factors and the Development of Educational Systems in Western Europe." *Comparative Education Review* 9 (June 1965): 147-54.

1854 Ben-David, Joseph, and Abraham Zloczower. "Universities and Academic Systems in Modern Societies." *European Journal of Sociology* 3 (1962): 45-84.

1855 Blandy, Richard. "'Brain Drains' in an Integrating Europe." *Comparative Education Review* 12 (June 1968): 180-93.

1856 Cerych, Ladislav. "Towards Zero Growth in Higher Education: The Problem." *Paedagogica Europaea* 12, no. 2 (1977): 11-20.

1857 Coombs, Fred S., and Gunther Luschen. "System Performance and Policy Making in West European Education: Effectiveness, Efficiency, Responsiveness and Fidelity." *International Review of Education* 22, no. 2 (1976): 133-55.

1858 "Diversifying Post-Secondary Education in Europe." *Paedagogica Europaea* 3 (1972): 1-149.

1859 Ford, Boris. "Changing Relations Between Universities and Colleges of Education in West Germany, Sweden and Denmark." *Universities Quarterly* 28 (Autumn 1974): 404-37.

1860 Frieden, Pierre. "La compréhension européenne par l'éducation." *International Review of Education* 1, no. 4 (1955): 479-96.

1861 Halls, W. D. "Towards a European Education System?" *Comparative Education* 10 (October 1974): 211-20.

1862 Halsall, Elizabeth. "Intelligence, School and Social Context: Some European Comparisons." *Comparative Education* 2 (June 1960): 181-96.

1863 Husén, Torsten. "Social Determinants of the Comprehensive School." *International Review of Education* 9 (1963-64): 158-73.

1864 King, Edmund J. "Comparative Research for the 16-19 Age Group in Western Europe." *International Review of Education* 21, no. 2 (1975): 149-65.

1865 Kuebart, F., and B. Zymek. "Comparative Aspects of Multilateral Cooperation and Supranational Integration in Educational Politics: The EEC and Comecon." *Slavic and European Education Review* 2 (1977): 21-32.

1866 Levin, Henry M. "Educational Opportunity and Social Inequality in Western Europe." *Social Problems* 24 (December 1976): 148-72.

1867 Little, Alan, and Denis Kallen. "Western European and Secondary School Systems and Higher Education: A Warning for Comparative Education." *Comparative Education* 4 (March 1968): 135-54.

1868 Neave, Guy. "Between Growth and Change: The Influence of External Constraints upon the Development of Higher Education in Europe." *Paedagogica Europaea* 12, no. 2 (1977): 83-90.

1869 O'Connor, Robert E. "Political Activism and Moral Reasoning: Political and A-Political Students in Great Britain and France." *British Journal of Political Science* 4 (January 1974): 53-78.

1870 Premfors, Rune. "Higher Education as a Political Issue Area: A Comparative View of France, Sweden and the United Kingdom." *Higher Education* 9 (May 1980): 325-44.

1871 Shafer, Susanne M. "The Socialization of Girls in the Secondary Schools of England and the Two Germanies." *International Review of Education* 22, no. 1 (1976): 5-25.

1872 Sheehan, John. "Inter-Country Comparisons of Educational Costs: England, Ireland, Portugal, and Quebec." *Comparative Education Review* 15 (February 1971): 59-74.

1873 Weissman, Ann B. "Widening the Base for Higher Education: A Study of Scandinavian Institutions." *Western European Education* 6 (Summer 1974): 5-85.

1874 Whiting, Charles. "A Decade of Educational Reform in Western Europe." *Educational Forum* 34 (March 1970): 297-306.

Eastern Europe

Books

1875 Agoston, G., V. Deri, and I. Hahn. *Case Study on the Development of Higher Education in Some East European Countries.* Paris: UNESCO, 1974.

1876 Anweiler, Oskar, ed. *Bindungsreform in Osteuropa.* Stuttgart: Kohlhammer, 1968.

1877 Anweiler, Oskar, ed. *Erziehungs-und-Sozialisations–problem in der Sowjetunion, der DDR und Polen.* Hannover, West Germany: Schrodel, 1978.

1878 Apanasewicz, Nellie. *Education in Eastern Europe: An Annotated Bibliography of English-language Materials, 1965-1975.* Washington, D.C.: U.S. Office of Education, 1980.

1879 Apanasewicz, Nellie, and Seymour M. Rosen. *Eastern Europe Education: A Bibliography of English-Language Materials.* Washington, D.C.: Office of Education, 1966.

1880 Birzea, C., ed. *Educational Research in Seven European Socialist Countries.* Hamburg: UNESCO Institute for Education, 1962.

1881 Grant, N. *Society, Schools and Progress in Eastern Europe.* Oxford: Pergamon Press, 1969.

1882 King, Edmund J., ed. *Communist Education.* Indianapolis: Bobbs Merrill, 1963.

1883 Novak, Zidenek. *Educational Research in Seven European Socialist Countries. A Survey.* Hamburg: UNESCO Institute for Education, 1972.

1884 Schmidt, Gerling. *Die polytechnische Bildung in der Sowjetunion und in der DDR*. Wiesbaden, West Germany: Verlag Otto Harrassowitz, 1973.

1885 Shimoniak, W. *Communist Education: Its History, Philosophy and Politics*. Chicago: Rand McNally, 1970.

Articles

1886 Anweiler, Oskar. "Towards a Comparative Study of the Educational Systems in the Socialist Countries of Europe." *Comparative Education* 11 (March 1975): 3-11.

1887 Connor, Walter D. "Education and National Development in the European Socialist States: A Model for the Third World?" *Comparative Studies in Society and History* 17 (July 1975): 326-48.

1888 Cornell, Richard. "Students and Politics in the Communist Countries of Eastern Europe." *Daedalus* 97 (Winter 1968): 166-83.

1889 Georgeoff, John. "Nationalism in the History Textbooks of Yugoslavia and Bulgaria." *Comparative Education Review* 10 (October 1966): 422-50.

1890 Grant, Nigel. "Teacher Training in the U.S.S.R. and Eastern Europe." *Comparative Education* 8 (April 1972): 7-29.

1891 Monoszohn, E. I., and J. Szarka. "Educational Research in the Socialist Countries." *International Review of Education* 16, no. 3 (1970): 357-68.

1892 Nica, Julian, and Cezar Birzea. "Educational Innovation in European Socialist Countries: A Comparative Overview." *International Review of Education* 19, no. 4 (1973): 447-59.

1893 Suchodolski, Bogdan. "The East European University." In *Higher Education in a Changing World*, edited by Brian Holmes and David Scanlon, pp. 120-34. London: Evans, 1971.

Albania

Books

1894 Thomas, John I. *Education for Communism: School and State in the People's Republic of Albania*. Stanford, Calif.: Hoover Institution Press, 1969.

Articles

1895 Dilo, Jani I. "Albania." In *Perspectives on World Education*, edited by C. Beck, pp. 12-19. Dubuque, Iowa: Brown, 1970.

1896 Roucek, Joseph S. "The Sovietization of Albanian Education." *Slavic and East European Journal* 16 (Spring 1958): 55-61.

1897 Thomas, John I. "Albania." In *International Encyclopedia of Higher Education*, edited by A. Knowles, pp. 307-11. San Francisco: Jossey-Bass, 1977.

1898 Thomas, John I. "Communist Education in Albania." *Paedagogica Historica* 13, no. 1 (1973): 107-19.

Austria

Books

1899 Organization for Economic Cooperation and Development. *Educational Policy and Planning, Austria*. Paris: OECD, 1968.

1900 Organization for Economic Cooperation and Development. *National Background Reports: Austria*. Paris: OECD, 1968.

1901 Organization for Economic Cooperation and Development. *Reviews of National Policies for Education: Austria*. Paris: OECD, 1970.

1902 Organization for Economic Cooperation and Development. *Reviews of National Policy for Education: Austria: Higher Education and Research*. Paris: OECD, 1976.

1903 Organization for Economic Cooperation and Development. *Reviews of National Policies for Education: Austria: School Policy*. Paris: OECD, 1979.

1904 Papanek, Ernst. *The Austrian School Reform, Its Bases, Principles and Development–The Twenty Years Between the Two World Wars*. New York: F. Fell, 1962.

1905 Schnell, Hermann. *Schools in Vienna*. Wien: Jugend und Volk, 1971.

Articles

1906 "Austria." In *International Encyclopedia of Higher Education*, edited by A. Knowles, pp. 561-72. San Francisco: Jossey-Bass, 1977.

1907 Leitner, Erich. "Current Trends in Austrian Higher Education: The Call for a New Reform." *European Journal of Education* 14, no. 1 (1979): 59-67.

Belgium

Books

1908 Coulon, Marion. *La planification de l'enseignement en Belgique.* Bruxelles: Institut de Sociologie, Université Libre de Bruxelles, 1966.

1909 Dejean, Christian, and Charles-Louis Binnemans. *L'université belge, du pari au défi.* Bruxelles: Editions de l'Institut de Sociologie, Université Libre de Bruxelles, 1971.

1910 Mallinson, Vernon. *Power and Politics in Belgian Education 1815 to 1961.* London, Heinemann, 1963.

1911 Pirson-DeClerco, Jacqueline, and Ronald Pirson. *Le rénovation scolaire: réalités d'une théorie,* 3 vols. Bruxelles: Ministère de l'Education Nationale et de la Culture Française, 1979.

Articles

1912 Coulon, Marion. "La situation actuelle de l'enseignement belge." *International Review of Education* 5, no. 1 (1959): 28-39.

1913 Coulon, Marion. "Tendances et développements récents dans l'education primaire et secondaire en Belgique." *International Review of Education* 13, no. 3 (1967): 285-305.

1914 DeClerck, Karel. "Belgium." In *International Encyclopedia of Higher Education*, edited by A. Knowles, pp. 608-15. San Francisco: Jossey-Bass, 1977.

1915 DeCorte, E. "Recent Innovations in Secondary Education in Belgium." *Journal of Curriculum Studies* 9 (November 1977): 133-43.

1916 de Landsheere, Gilbert, Aletta Grisay, and Georges Henry. "High Achievers in Belgium: A Partial Analysis of IEA Science, Literature and Reading Comprehension Data." *Comparative Education Review* 18 (June 1974): 188-95.

1917 Deprez, Marcel. "L'éducation permanente en Belgique d'expression française." *International Review of Education* 12, no. 2 (1966): 159-75.

1918 Mallinson, Vernon. "Education in Belgium." *Comparative Education Review* 11 (October 1967): 275-87.

1919 Mallinson, Vernon, and Silvain De Coster. "Church and State Education in Belgium." *Comparative Education Review* 4 (June 1960): 43-49.

1920 Pinner, Frank A. "Student Trade-Unionism in France, Belgium and Holland: Anticipatory Socialization and Role-Seeking." *Sociology of Education* 37 (Spring 1964): 177-99.

1921 Swing, Elizabeth Sherman. "Separate But Equal: An Inquiry into the Impact of the Language Controversy on Education in Belgium." *Western European Education* 5 (Winter 1973-74): 6-33.

1922 Van de Vijvere, J. "L'enseignement post-secondaire en Belgique: entre l'évolution et la mutation." *Paedagogica Europaea* 12, no. 1 (1977): 41-62.

1923 Van Vaek, Gilbert, and Henk Vandaele. "Non-University Higher Technical Education in Belgium." *European Journal of Education* 14 (March 1979): 25-36.

Bulgaria

Books

1924 Apanasewicz, N., and S. Rosen. *Education in Bulgaria*. Washington, D.C.: U.S. Office of Education, 1965.

1925 Atanassov, Z. *Education and Science in the People's Republic of Bulgaria*. Sofia: Sofia Press, 1974.

1926 Georgeoff, Peter John. *Educational System of Bulgaria*. Washington, D.C.: U.S. Office of Education, 1977.

1927 Georgeoff, Peter John. *The Social Education of Bulgarian Youth*. Minneapolis: University of Minnesota Press, 1968.

1928 Russell, William. *Schools in Bulgaria*. New York: Teacher's College, Columbia University, 1924.

Articles

1929 Brown, James F. "Educational Policy and the Problems of Youth." In *Bulgaria Under Communist Rule*, pp. 215-39. New York: Praeger, 1970.

1930 Georgeoff, John. "Elementary Education in Bulgaria." *School and Society* 44 (February 11, 1966): 71-74.

1931 Georgeoff, John. "Higher Education in Bulgaria." *Educational Forum* 31 (May 1967): 455-69.

1932 Georgeoff, John. "Sofia." In *Education in Cities: The World Year Book of Education*, edited by J. Lauwerys and D. Scanlon, pp. 315-25. New York: Harcourt, Brace and World, 1970.

1933 Grant, Nigel. "Bulgaria." In N. Grant, *Society, School and Progress in Eastern Europe*, pp. 331-44. Oxford: Pergamon Press, 1969.

1934 Grant, Nigel. "Educational Reform in Bulgaria." *Comparative Education* 6 (November 1970): 179-91.

1935 Kasvin, G. "The Bulgarian School in the 1965/66 Academic Year." *Soviet Education* 9 (December 1966): 34-40.

1936 Mawrow, Georgi. "Zur didaktischen Struktur des neu gestalten Bildungsinhalts der Untersufe in Bulgarien." *Vergleichende Pädagogik* 14 (June 1978): 286-94.

1937 UNESCO. "Bulgaria." In *World Survey of Education—II: Primary Education*, pp. 178-88. Paris: UNESCO, 1958.

1938 UNESCO. "Bulgaria." In *World Survey of Education—III: Secondary Education*, pp. 227-92. New York: Columbia University Press, 1961.

1939 UNESCO. "Bulgaria." In *World Survey of Education—IV: Higher Education*, pp. 240-50. Paris: UNESCO, 1966.

1940 UNESCO. "Bulgaria." In *World Survey of Education–V: Educational Policy, Legislation and Administration*, pp. 225-37. Paris: UNESCO, 1971.

Czechoslovakia

Books

1941 Apanasewicz, Nellie, and Seymour Rosen. *Education in Czechoslovakia*. Washington, D.C.: U.S. Office of Education, 1963.

1942 Apanasewicz, Nellie, and Seymour Rosen. *Selected Bibliography of Materials on Education in Czechoslovakia*. Washington, D.C.: U.S. Office of Education, 1960.

1943 Kaskova, Alena, ed. *Education in Czechoslovakia*. Prague: Statni pedagogicke nakl., 1958.

1944 Slamecka, Vladimir. *Science in Czechoslovakia*. New York: Columbia University Press, 1963.

1945 Toma, Peter A. *The Educational System of Czechoslovakia*. Washington, D.C.: U.S. Office of Education, 1976.

1946 Vodinsky, Stanislav. *Schools in Czechoslovakia*. Prague: State Pedagogical Publishing House, 1965.

Articles

1947 Akhmerova, F. G. "Certain Questions of Organization of the Educational Process in Primary Schools of the Czechoslovak Socialist Republic." *Soviet Education* 8 (June 1966): 52-58.

1948 Cisar, Vaclav. "Grundlagen des Bildungs - und Erzie-hungssystems in der CSSR." *Vergleichende Pädagogik* 14 (June 1978): 258-69.

1949 Dixon, R. T. "Differentiated Education in Czechoslovakia." *Comparative Education* 4 (November 1967): 3-9.

1950 Drapela, Victor R. "Educational Guidance in the United States and Czechoslovakia." *East European Quarterly* 8 (Fall 1974): 295-305.

1951 Johnson, Owen V. "The Post-1945 Study of the History of Slovak Education." *Slavic and European Education Review* 1 (1978): 39-47.

1952 Kasvin, G. A., and A. A. Shivanov. "The Reform of the Schools in the Czechoslovak Republic." *Soviet Education* 1 (February 1959): 64-70.

1953 Kulich, Jindra. "The Communist Party and Adult Education in Czechoslovakia, 1945-1965." *Comparative Education Review* 11 (June 1967): 231-43.

1954 Nekola, J., and J. Zelinka. "Research and Development in Czechoslovakia." *Minerva* 6 (Spring 1968): 3-34.

Denmark

Books

1955 Dauske, Selskab. *Schools and Education in Denmark*. Copenhagen: Det Danske-Selskat, 1972.

1956 Dixon, Willis. *Education in Denmark*. Copenhagen: Centraltrykkeriet, 1958.

1957 Nelleman, Aksel. *Schools and Education in Denmark*. Copenhagen: Det Danske-Selskat, 1964.

1958 Thomsen, Ole B. *Some Aspects of Education in Denmark*. London: Oxford University Press, 1967.

Articles

1959 Canfield, Alvah T. "Folk High Schools in Denmark and Sweden: A Comparative Analysis." *Comparative Education Review* 9 (February 1965): 18-24.

1960 Kulich, Jindra. "The Danish Folk High School: Can it be Transplanted? The Success and Failure of the Danish Folk High School at Home and Abroad." *International Review of Education* 10, no. 4 (1964): 417-29.

1961 Pederson, Mogens. "The Danish University Between the Millstones." *Minerva* 15 (Autumn-Winter 1977): 335-76.

England and Wales

Books

1962 Bamford, T. W. *The Rise of the Public Schools*. London: Nelson, 1967.

1963 Baron, George. *A Bibliographical Guide to the English Educational System*. London: The Athlone Press, University of London, 1965.

1964 Baron, George. *Society, Schools and Progress in England*. Oxford: Pergamon Press, 1965.

1965 Baron, George, and D. A. Howell. *The Government and Management of Schools*. University of London: The Athlone Press, 1974.

1966 Bell, R. E., and N. Grant. *Patterns of Education in the British Isles*. London: Allen and Unwin, 1977.

1967 Bell, Robert, et al., eds. *Education in Great Britain and Ireland: A Source Book*. London: Open University Press, 1973.

1968 Benn, Caroline, and Brian Simon. *Half-Way There: Report on the British Comprehensive School Reform*. London: McGraw-Hill, 1970.

1969 Berg, Leila. *The Death of a Comprehensive School*. London: Penguin, 1968.

1970 Blyth, W. A. L. *English Primary Education: A Sociological Description*, 2 vols. London: Routledge and Kegan Paul, 1967.

1971 Central Advisory Council for Education. *Half Our Future*. London: H. M. S. O., 1963. (The Newson Report)

1972 *Children and Their Primary Schools*. London: H. M. S. O., 1967. (The Plowden Report)

1973 Commission on Higher Education (Robbins Commission). *Higher Education*. London: H. M. S. O., 1963.

1974 Douglas, J. W. B., J. M. Ross, and H. R. Simpson. *All Our Future: A Longitudinal Study of Secondary Education*. London: Peter Davies, 1968.

1975 *Fifteen to Eighteen*. London: H.M.S.O., 1959-60. (The Crowther Report)

1976 Floud, J. E., A. H. Halsey, and F. M. Maxton. *Social Class and Educational Opportunity*. London: Heinemann, 1956.

1977 Halsey, A. H., A. F. Heath, and J. M. Ridge. *Origins and Destinations: Family, Class and Education in Modern Britain*. Oxford: Clarendon Press, 1980.

1978 Halsey, A. H., and M. A. Trow. *The British Academics*. Cambridge, Mass.: Harvard University Press, 1971.

1979 Howson, Geoffrey, ed. *Children at School: Primary Education in Britain Today*. New York: Teacher's College Press, 1970.

1980 Jackson, Brian, and Dennis Marsen. *Education and the Working Class*. Harmondsworth, England: Penguin, 1966.

1981 Kogan, Maurice. *The Politics of Educational Change*. London: Fontana, 1978.

1982 Lawson, John, and Harold Silver. *A Social History of Education in England*. London: Methuen, 1973.

1983 Layard, Richard, et al. *The Impact of Robbins*. London: Penguin, 1969.

1984 Litt, Edgar, and Michael Parkinson. *U.S. and U.K. Educational Policy: A Decade of Reform*. New York: Praeger, 1979.

1985 Lomax, Donald E., ed. *The Education of Teachers in Britain*. London: Wiley, 1973.

1986 Lowndes, G. A. N. *The English Educational System*. London: Hutchinson, 1963.

1987 Murphy, James. *Church, State and Schools in Britain, 1800-1970*. London: Routledge and Kegan Paul, 1971.

1988 Murrow, Casey, and Liza Murrow. *Children Come First: The Inspired World of English Primary Schools*. New York: American Heritage Press, 1971.

1989 Organization for Economic Cooperation and Development. *National Policies for Education: England and Wales*. Paris: OECD, 1975.

1990 Pedley, F. H. *The Educational System in England and Wales*. Oxford: Pergamon Press, 1964.

1991 Pedley, Robin. *The Comprehensive School*. Harmondsworth, England: Penguin, 1968.

1992 Rubenstein, David, and Brian Simon. *The Evolution of the Comprehensive School: 1926-1972*. London: Routledge and Kegan Paul, 1973.

1993 Sanderson, Michael. *The Universities and British Industry, 1850-1970*. London: Routledge and Kegan Paul, 1972.

1994 Simon, Joan. *The Social Origins of English Education*. London: Routledge and Kegan Paul, 1970.

1995 Vaughan, Michalina, and Margaret Archer. *Social Conflict and Educational Change in England and France*. Cambridge: Cambridge University Press, 1971.

1996 Young, Michael. *The Rise of the Meritocracy, 1970-2033*. Harmondsworth, England: Penguin, 1958.

Articles

1997 Bagley, Christopher. "A Comparative Perspective on the Education of Black Children in Britain." *Comparative Education* 15 (March 1979): 63-83.

1998 Burn, Barbara. "Higher Education in Great Britain." In B. Burn, *Higher Education in Nine Countries*, pp. 45-90. New York: McGraw-Hill, 1971.

1999 Glass, David. "Education and Social Change in England." In *Education, Economy and Society*, edited by A. H. Halsey, J. Floud, and C. A. Anderson, pp. 391-413. New York: Free Press, 1962.

2000 Halls, W. D. "Cultural Ideals and Elitist Education in England." *Comparative Education Review* 15 (October 1971): 317-29.

2001 Halsey, A. H. "Towards Meritocracy?: The Case of Britain." In *Power and Ideology in Education*, edited by J. Karabel and A. H. Halsey, pp. 173-85. New York: Oxford University Press, 1977.

2002 McMahon, Walter W. "Policy Issues in the Economics of Higher Education and Related Research Opportunities in Britain and the United States." *Higher Education* 3 (April 1974): 165-84.

2003 Peterson, A. D. C. "Educational Reform in England and Wales 1955-1966." *Comparative Education Review* 11 (October 1967): 288-300.

2004 Peterson, Paul E. "Politics of Educational Reform in England and the United States." *Comparative Education Review* 17 (June 1973): 160-79.

2005 Pidgeon, D. A. "National Analysis: England." *International Review of Education* 15, no. 2 (1969): 142-53.

2006 Scott, Peter. "British Universities 1968-1978." *Paedagogica Europaea* 13, no. 2 (1978): 291-44.

Finland

Books

2007 Ministry of Education. *Educational Development in Finland, 1976-1978.* Helsinki: Ministry of Education, Finland, 1979.

2008 Ojansuu, Raila, ed. *Comprehensive School in Finland: Goals and an Outline for a Curriculum.* Helsinki: Finland Ministry of Education, 1971.

Articles

2009 Karvonen, Juhani. "School Democracy and Social Attitudes of Students and Teachers in Finnish Schools." *Comparative Education Review* 18 (June 1974): 207-16.

2010 Kyostio, O. K. "Contemporary Finnish School Legislation." *Comparative Education Review* 5 (October 1961): 130-35.

2011 Kyostio, O. K. "Finland." In *Perspectives on World Education*, edited by C. Beck, pp. 29-35. Dubuque, Iowa: Brown, 1970.

2012 Malinen, P., and V. Lyytikainen. "National Analysis: Finland." *International Review of Education* 15, no. 2 (1969): 154-62.

2013 Paulston, R. G. "Separate Education as an Ethnic Survival Strategy: The Finlandssvenska Case." *Anthropology and Education Quarterly* 8 (August 1977): 181-88.

2014 Rajavuori, Tapio. "Finland." In *International Encyclopedia of Higher Education*, edited by A. Knowles, pp. 1729-39. San Francisco: Jossey-Bass, 1977.

France

Books

2015 Antoine, Gérald, and Jean-Claude Passeron. *La réforme de l'université*. Paris: Calmann-Lévy, 1966.

2016 Anderson, R. D. *Education in France, 1848-1870*. Oxford: Clarendon Press, 1975.

2017 Barnard, H. C. *Education and the French Revolution*. Cambridge: Cambridge University Press, 1969.

2018 Baudelot, Christian, and Roger Establet. *L'école capitaliste en France*. Paris: Maspero, 1971.

2019 Bourdieu, Pierre, and Jean-Claude Passeron. *The Inheritors: French Students and Their Relation to Culture*. Chicago: University of Chicago Press, 1979.

2020 Capelle, Jean. *Tomorrow's Education: The French Experience*. Oxford: Pergamon Press, 1967.

2021 Cherkaoui, M. *Les paradoxes de la réussite scolaire*. Paris: Presses Universitaires de France, 1979.

2022 Chevallier, Pierre, B. Grosperrin, and J. Maillet. *L'enseignement français de la révolution à nos jours*, 2 vols. The Hague: Mouton, 1969.

2023 Clark, James M. *Teachers and Politics in France: A Pressure Group Study of the Fédération de l'Education Nationale*. Syracuse, N.Y.: Syracuse University Press, 1967.

2024 Clark, Terry Nichols. *Prophets and Patrons: The French University and the Emergence of the Social Sciences*. Cambridge, Mass.: Harvard University Press, 1973.

2025 Cohen, Habiba. *Elusive Reform: The French Universities, 1968-1978*. Boulder, Col.: Westview Press, 1979.

2026 Drouard, Alain. *Analyse comparative des processus de changement et des mouvements de réforme de l'enseignement supérieur française.* Paris: Editions du Centre National de la Recherche Scientifique, 1978.

2027 Faure, Edgar. *L'éducation nationale et la participation.* Paris: Plon, 1968.

2028 Fields, A. Belden. *Student Politics in France: A Study of the Union Nationale des Etudiants de France.* New York: Basic Books, 1970.

2029 Fraser, W. R. *Education and Society in Modern France.* London: Routledge and Kegan Paul, 1963.

2030 Fraser, W. R. *Reforms and Restraints in Modern French Education.* London: Routledge and Kegan Paul, 1971.

2031 Gilpin, Robert. *France in the Age of the Scientific State.* Princeton: Princeton University Press, 1968.

2032 Girard, Alain. *La réussite sociale en France. Ses caractères ses lois ses effets.* Paris: Presses Universitaires de France, 1961.

2033 Halls, W. D. *Education, Culture and Politics in Modern France.* Elmsford, N.Y.: Pergamon Press, 1976.

2034 Halls, W. D. *Society, Schools and Progress in France.* Elmsford, N.Y.: Pergamon Press, 1966.

2035 Moody, Joseph N. *French Education Since Napoleon.* Syracuse, N.Y.: Syracuse University Press, 1978.

2036 Munkin, Patience. *Enseignement et politique en France et en Angleterre depuis 1789.* Paris: Institut Pédagogique National, 1962.

2037 Organization for Economic Cooperation and Development. *National Background Reports: France.* Paris: OECD, 1973.

2038 Organization for Economic Cooperation and Development. *Reviews of National Policies for Education: France.* Paris: OECD, 1971.

2039 Prost, Antoine. *Histoire de l'enseignement en France 1800-1967.* Paris: Colin, 1970.

2040 Robert, J. J. *Un plan pour l'enseignement du primaire au supérieur.* Paris: Plon, 1968.

2041 Segré, Monique. *Ecole, formation, contradiction: De la réforme Berthoin-Fouchet à la réforme Haby*. Paris: Editions Sociales, 1976.

2042 Talbott, John E. *The Politics of Educational Reform in France 1918-1940*. Princeton: Princeton University Press, 1969.

2043 Thabault, Roger. *Education and Change in a Village Community, Mazières-en Gatine, 1848-1914*. London: Routledge and Kegan Paul, 1971.

2044 Titmus, C. *Adult Education in France*. Elmsford, N.Y.: Pergamon Press, 1976.

2045 Vaughan, M., and M. S. Archer. *Social Conflict and Educational Change in England and France 1789-1848*. Cambridge: Cambridge University Press, 1971.

2046 Wylie, Lawrence. *Village in the Vaucluse: An Account of Life in a French Village*. New York: Harper and Row, 1964.

Articles

2047 Ader, Jean. "Développements récents des rapports de la sociologie et de la pédagogie en France." *International Review of Education* 6, no. 2 (1960): 163-75.

2048 Anderson, Robert. "Secondary Education in mid Nineteenth-Century France: Some Social Aspects." *Past and Present* 53 (November 1971): 121-46.

2049 Aron, Raymond. "Quelques problèmes des universités françaises," *European Journal of Sociology* 3 (1962): 102-22.

2050 Bénéton, Philippe, and Jean Touchard. "Les interpretations de la crise de Mai-Juin, 1968." *Revue Française de Science Politique* 20 (June 1970): 503-44.

2051 Bonora, Denis. "Educational Aims and Curriculum in France: An IEA Survey." *Comparative Education Review* 18 (June 1974): 217-27.

2052 Boudon, Raymond. "The French University Since 1968." *Comparative Politics* 10 (October 1977): 89-118.

2053 Boudon, Raymond. "The 1970s in France: A Period of Student Retreat." *Higher Education* 8 (November 1979): 669-81.

2054 Boudon, Raymond, Philippe Cibois, and Janina Lagneau. "Short Cycle Higher Education and the Pitfalls of Collective Action." *Minerva* 14 (Spring 1976): 33-60.

2055 Brickman, William W. "Selected Bibliography on the History of Education in France." *Paedagogica Historica* 10 (1970): 286-92.

2056 Burn, Barbara. "Higher Education in France." In B. Burn, *Higher Education in Nine Countries*, pp. 11-44. New York: McGraw-Hill, 1971.

2057 Chamboulant, Simone. "Conception et pratique de l'orientation scolaires en France." *International Review of Education* 2, no. 4 (1956): 410-18.

2058 de l'Ain, Bertrand Girod. "The Paths of French Higher Education." *Minerva* 17 (Summer 1979): 283-304.

2059 Dobinson, Charles H. "French Educational Reform." *Comparative Education Review* 3 (June 1959): 5-14.

2060 Drouard, A. "La déperdition universitaire en France." *Paedagogica Europaea* 12, no. 3 (1977): 31-52.

2061 Dundas-Grant, Valerie. "Attainment at 16+: the French Perspective." *Comparative Education* 11 (March 1975): 13-22.

2062 Fomerand, Jacques. "The French University: What Happened After the Revolution?" *Higher Education* 6 (February 1977): 93-116.

2063 Fraser, William R. "Progress in French School Reform." *Comparative Education Review* 7 (February 1964): 273-78.

2064 Fraser, William R. "Reform in France." *Comparative Education Review* 11 (October 1967): 300-11.

2065 Gal, Roger. "Guiding Principles of French Educational Reform." *International Review of Education* 3, no. 4 (1957): 469-85.

2066 Girard, A. "Selection for Secondary Education in France." In *Education, Economy and Society*, edited by A. H. Halsey et al., pp. 183-92. New York: Free Press, 1962.

2067 Halls, W. D. "Educational Planning in an Industrial Society: The French Experience." *Comparative Education* 1 (October 1964): 19-28.

2068 Halls, W. D. "Les effets de l'urbanisation sur l'éducation française." *International Review of Education* 13 (1967): 461-69.

2069 Harrigan, Patrick J. "Secondary Education and the Professions in France During the Second Empire." *Comparative Studies in Society and History* 17 (July 1975): 349-71.

2070 Hein, Roland. "The Planning of Vocational-Technical Education and Secondary School Reform in France." *Western European Education* 9 (Fall 1977): 8-104.

2071 Howard, Suzanne. "Sociopolitical Attitudes of French Secondary School Youth." *Comparative Education Review* 18 (February 1974): 39-54.

2072 Lévy-Garbova, Louis. "Les demandes de l'étudiant et les contradictions de l'université de masse." *Revue Française de Sociologie* 17 (January-March 1976): 89-118.

2073 Niesser, Bruno. "Innovations in Primary and Secondary School Education in France." *Western European Education* 10 (Summer 1978): 8-27.

2074 Paulston, Rolland G. "French Influence in American Institutions of Higher Learning, 1784-1825." *History of Education Quarterly* 8 (Summer 1968): 229-45.

2075 Peyre, Christiane. "Regional Variations in Educational Opportunity in France." *International Journal of Comparative Sociology* 2 (September 1961): 167-76.

2076 Tournier, Michèle. "Women and Access to University in France and Germany (1861-1967)." *Comparative Education* 9 (October 1973): 107-17.

2077 "Université." *Esprit* (November-December 1978): 1-275. (special issue)

2078 van de Graaff, John H. "The Politics of Innovation in French Higher Education." *Higher Education* 5 (May 1976): 189-210.

2079 Veyret, B. "French Republic." In *International Encyclopedia of Higher Education*, edited by A. Knowles, pp. 1772-82. San Francisco: Jossey-Bass, 1977.

2080 Vial, Jean. "L'évolution des methodes pédagogiques en France." *International Review of Education* 13, no. 3 (1967): 306-31.

2081 Vincent, G. "Histoire et structure du système scolaire française: l'enseignement primaire." *Revue Française de Sociologie* 13 (January-March 1972): 59-79.

2082 Zeldin, Theodore. "Higher Education in France, 1848-1940." *Journal of Contemporary History* 2 (July 1967): 53-80.

2083 Zolberg, Aristide R., and Vera L. Zolberg. "The Regimentation of Bourgeois Culture: Public Secondary Schools in Modern France." *Comparative Education Review* 15 (October 1971): 330-45.

Germany, Democratic Republic

Books

2084 Akademie der Pädagogischen Wissenschaften. *Das Bildungswesen der Deutschen Demokratischen Republic.* Berlin: Volk und Wissen, 1979.

2085 Baylis, Thomas A. *The Technical Intelligentsia and the East German Elite: Legitimacy and Social Change in Mature Communism.* Berkeley: University of California Press, 1974.

2086 Bodenman, Paul S. *Education in the Soviet Zone of Germany.* Washington, D.C.: U.S. Office of Education, 1959.

2087 Bodenman, Paul S. *The Education System of the German Democratic Republic.* Washington, D.C.: U.S. Office of Education, 1975.

2088 Günther, Karl Heinz, and Gottfried Uhlig. *History of the Schools in the German Democratic Republic, 1945-1968.* Berlin: Volk und Wissen Verlag, 1973.

2089 Hearnden, Arthur. *Education in the Two Germanies.* Boulder, Col.: Westview, 1979.

2090 Hettwer, Hubert. *Das Bildungswesen in der DDR: Strukturelle und inhaltliche Entwicklung seit 1945.* Cologne: Kiepenheuer and Witsch, 1976.

2091 Klein, Helmut. *Bildung in der DDR.* Reinbek bei Hamburg: Rowohlt, 1974.

2092 Klein, Helmut. *Education in a Socialist Country: Report on Educational Policy in the GDR.* East Berlin: Panorama, 1974.

2093 Klein, Helmut, and Ernst Behling. *German Democratic Republic: Education*. Dresden: Verlag Zeit im Bild, 1971.

2094 Moore-Rinvolucri, Mina J. *Education in East Germany*. Newton Abbot, England: David and Charles, 1973.

2095 Richert, Ernst. *"Sozialistische Universität": Die Hochschulpolitik der SED*. Berlin, West Germany: Colloquium Verlag, 1967.

2096 Vogt, Hartmut. *Bildung und Erziehung in der DDR: Sozialistisch-industriegesellschaftliche Curriculum-Reform in Kindergarten, Schule und Berufsbildung*. Stuttgart: Klett, 1969.

Articles

2097 Giles, Geoffrey J. "The Structure of Higher Education in the German Democratic Republic." *Higher Education* 7 (May 1978): 131-56.

2098 Hofmann, Erich. "The Changing School in East Germany." *Comparative Education Review* 6 (June 1962): 48-58.

2099 Lottich, Kenneth V. "Extra-curricular Indoctrination in East Germany." *Comparative Education Review* 6 (February 1963): 209-11.

2100 Nast, Manfred. "Das Recht auf Bildung als Menschenrecht." *Vergleichende Pädagogik* 14 (February 1978): 113-28.

2101 Schaefer, H. D. "German Democratic Republic." In *International Encyclopedia of Higher Education*, edited by A. Knowles, pp. 1831-37. San Francisco: Jossey-Bass, 1977.

2102 Schmidt, Roland. "Die Schulentwicklung der DDR als Bestandteil der internationalen Entwicklung des Sozialismus (II. Arbeitstagung zur Schulgeschichte der DDR)." *Vergleichende Pädagogik* 14 (June 1978): 310-11.

2103 Schmitt, Karl. "Education and Politics in the German Democratic Republic." *Comparative Education Review* 19 (February 1975): 31-50.

Germany, Federal Republic

Books

2104 Arbeitsgruppe am Max Planck Institut für Bildungsforschung. *Das Bildungs-*

wesen in der Bundesrepublik Deutschland. Reinbek bei Hamburg: Rowohlt, 1979.

2105 Boning, E., and Roelffs, K. *Three German Universities: Aachen, Bochum, and Konstanz.* Paris: Organization for Economic Cooperation and Development, 1970.

2106 Friedeburg, Ludwig von, et al. *Freie Universität und politisches Potential der Studenten.* Neuweid, West Germany: Luchterhand, 1968.

2107 Goldschmidt, Dietrich, ed. *Demokratisierung und Mitwirkung in Schule und Hochschule.* Braunschweig, West Germany: Westermann Verlag, 1973.

2108 Hartshorne, E. Y. *The German Universities and National Socialism.* Cambridge, Mass.: Harvard University Press, 1937.

2109 Hearnden, A. *Education, Culture and Politics in West Germany.* Elmsford, N.Y.: Pergamon Press, 1976.

2110 Hearnden, Arthur. *Education in the Two Germanies.* Boulder, Col.: Westview Press, 1979.

2111 Hearnden, A., ed. *The British in Germany: Educational Reconstruction After 1945.* London: Hamish Hamilton, 1978.

2112 Hess, G. *Universities in Germany, 1930-1970.* Bad Godesberg: Internationes, 1968.

2113 Huebener, T. *The Schools of West Germany. A Study of German Elementary and Secondary Schools.* New York: New York University Press, 1962.

2114 International Council for Educational Development. *Access to Higher Education: Two Perspectives. A Comparative Study of the Federal Republic of Germany and the United States of America.* New York: International Council for Educational Development, 1978.

2115 Kluge, Alexander. *Die Universitäts-Selbstverwaltung: Ihre Geschichte und Gegenwärtige Rechtsform.* Frankfurt/Main: Klostermann, 1958.

2116 Lilge, Frederic. *The Abuse of Learning: The Failure of the German University.* New York: Octagon Books, 1975.

2117 Marxistische Gruppe Erlangen, eds. *Kapitalistische Hochschulreform.* Erlangen, West Germany: Politladen, 1972.

2118 McClulland, Charles E. *State, Society and University in Germany, 1700–1914.* Cambridge: Cambridge University Press, 1980.

2119 Nitsch, Wolfgang, et al. *Hochschule in der Demokratie.* Berlin: Luchterhand, 1965.

2120 Organization for Economic Cooperation and Development. *Reviews of National Policies for Education: Germany.* Paris: OECD, 1973.

2121 Peisert, H., and G. Framhein. *Systems of Higher Education: Federal Republic of Germany.* New York: International Council for Educational Development, 1978.

2122 Ringer, Fritz K. *The Decline of the German Mandarins. The German Academic Community 1890–1933.* Cambridge, Mass.: Harvard University Press, 1969.

2123 Warren, Richard L. *Education in Rebhausen: A German Village.* New York: Holt, Rinehart and Winston, 1967.

Articles

2124 Beattie, N. "Public Participation in Curriculum Change. A West German Example." *Compare* 7, no. 1 (1977): 17–29.

2125 Bunn, Ronald F. "Treatment of Hitler's Rise to Power in West German School Textbooks." *Comparative Education Review* 6 (June 1962): 34–43.

2126 Burn, Barbara B. "Access to Higher Education in the Federal Republic of Germany and the United States." *International Review of Education* 22, no. 4 (1976): 193–203.

2127 Burn, Barbara. "Higher Education in the Federal Republic of Germany." In B. Burn, *Higher Education in Nine Countries*, pp. 165-96. New York: McGraw-Hill, 1971.

2128 Dahrendorf, R. "The Crisis in German Education." *Journal of Contemporary History* 2 (July 1967): 139–47.

2129 Dahrendorf, Ralf. "Starre und Offenheit der Deutschen Universität: Die

Chancen der Reform." *European Journal of Sociology* 3 (1962): 263-93.

2130 Edding, F. "Educational Planning in Western Germany." In *Educational Planning*, edited by G. Z. F. Bereday and J. A. Lauwerys, pp. 100-16. London: Evans, 1967.

2131 Fischer, A. "American University Planning and Its Relevance to West German Educational Policy." *International Review of Education* 20, no. 2 (1974): 138-54.

2132 Goldschmidt, Dietrich. "Autonomy and Accountability of Higher Education in the Federal Republic of Germany." In *The University's Response to Societal Demands, An International Perspective*, edited by P. Altbach, pp. 151-72. New York: International Council for Educational Development, 1975.

2133 Goldschmidt, Dietrich. "Participatory Democracy in Schools and Higher Education. Emerging Problems in the Federal Republic of Germany and Sweden." *Higher Education* 5, no. 2 (1976): 113-33.

2134 Goldschmidt, Dietrich, and I. Sommerkorn. "Deprivation and Disadvantage: Federal Republic of Germany." In *Deprivation and Disadvantage: Nature and Manifestations*, edited by A. H. Passow, pp. 119-69. Hamburg: UNESCO Institute for Education, 1970.

2135 Gougher, Ronald L. "Comparison of English and American Views of the German University, 1840-1865: A Bibliography." *History of Education Quarterly* 9 (Winter 1969): 477-91.

2136 Heidenheimer, Arnold. "The Politics of Educational Reform: Explaining Different Outcomes of School Comprehensionization Attempts in Sweden and West Germany." *Comparative Education Review* 18 (October 1974): 388-410.

2137 Karpen, Ulrich. "University Admission Criteria: Some German-American Comparative Observations." *International Review of Education* 22, no. 2 (1976): 203-21.

2138 Kloss, G. "University Reform in West Germany: The Burden of Tradition." *Minerva* 6 (Spring 1968): 323-53.

2139 Lawson, Robert F. "The Political Foundations of German Education." *Comparative Education* 6 (November 1970): 193-204.

2140 Mason, Henry L. "Reflections on the Politicized University: I. The Academic Crisis in the Federal Republic of Germany." *AAUP Bulletin* 60 (Autumn 1974): 299-312.

2141 Merritt, Richard L., Ellen P. Flerlage, and Anna J. Merritt. "Democratizing West German Education." *Comparative Education* 7 (December 1971): 121-36.

2142 Merritt, Richard L., Ellen P. Flerlage, and Anna J. Merritt. "Political Man in Postwar West German Education." *Comparative Education Review* 15 (October 1971): 346-61.

2143 Ringer, F. K. "Higher Education in Germany in the 19th Century." *Journal of Contemporary History* 2 (July 1967): 123-38.

2144 Robinsohn, Saul B., and J. Caspar Kuhlmann. "Two Decades of Non-Reform in West German Education." *Comparative Education Review* 11 (October 1967): 311-30.

2145 Rüegg, Walter. "The Intellectual Situation in German Higher Education." *Minerva* 13 (Spring 1975): 102-20.

2146 Schuppe, Erwin. "The State, Problems and Trends in the Development of the West German Education System." *Comparative Education* 5 (June 1969): 125-38.

2147 Smart, Kenneth. "Vocational Education in the Federal Republic of Germany: Current Trends and Problems." *Comparative Education* 11, no. 2 (1975): 153-64.

2148 Teichler, Ulrich. "Problems of West German Universities on the Way to Mass Higher Education." *Western European Education* 8, no. 1-2 (1976): 81-120.

2149 van de Graaff, John H. "Federal Republic of Germany." in J. H. van de Graaff et al., *Academic Power: Patterns of Authority in Seven National Systems of Higher Education*, pp. 15-36. New York: Praeger, 1978.

2150 Williamson, W. "Patterns of Educational Inequality in West Germany." *Comparative Education* 13 (March 1977): 29-44.

Greece

Books

2151 Massialas, Byron G. *The Educational System of Greece*. Washington, D.C.: U.S. Office of Education, 1980.

Articles

2152 Charis, Constantine P. "The Problem of Bilingualism in Modern Greek Education." *Comparative Education Review* 20 (June 1976): 216-19.

2153 Dimaras, Alexis. "The Movement for Reform: A Historical Perspective." *Comparative Education Review* 22 (February 1978): 11-20.

2154 Elion, Marie. "Those Whom Reform Forgot." *Comparative Education Review* 22 (February 1978): 60-70.

2155 Haniotis, George. "The Situation of the Universities in Greece." *Minerva* 6 (Winter 1968): 163-84.

2156 Kazamias, Andreas M. "Plans and Policies for Educational Reform in Greece." *Comparative Education Review* 11 (October 1967): 331-47.

2157 Kazamias, Andreas M. "The Politics of Education Reform in Greece: Law 309/1976." *Comparative Education Review* 22 (February 1978): 21-45.

2158 Kazamias, A. M. "Transfer and Modernity in Greek and Turkish Education." In *Schools in Transition*, edited by A. Kazamias and E. Epstein, pp. 7-31. Boston: Allyn and Bacon, 1968.

2159 Margaritis, Stephen C. "Higher Education in Greece." *International Review of Education* 10, no. 3 (1965): 297-311.

2160 Melanites, Nicholas G. "Educational Problems in Modern Greece." *International Review of Education* 3, no. 4 (1957): 458-68.

2161 Persianis, P. K. "Values Underlying the 1976-1977 Educational Reform in Greece." *Comparative Education Review* 22 (February 1978): 51-59.

2162 Polydorides, Georgia K. "Equality of Opportunity in the Greek Higher

Education System: The Impact of Reform Policies." *Comparative Education Review* 22 (February 1978): 80-93.

2163 Psacharopoulos, George. "Economic Implications of Raising the School Leaving Age." *Comparative Education Review* 22 (February 1978): 71-79.

2164 Psacharopoulos, G., and A. Kazamias. "Student Activism in Greece: A Historical and Empirical Analysis." *Higher Education* 9 (March 1980): 127-38.

Hungary

Books

2165 Braham, Randolph L. *Education in the Hungarian Peoples' Republic.* Washington, D.C.: U.S. Office of Education, 1970.

2166 Konis, Gyula. *Education in Hungary.* New York: Teacher's College, Columbia University, 1932.

Articles

2167 Bathony, Zolban, and Judit Kádár-Fülop. "Some Conclusions for Curriculum Development Based on Hungarian IEA Data." *Comparative Education Review* 18 (June 1974): 228-36.

2168 Bencedy, J. "Tendances et développments récents dans l'éducation primaire et secondaire en Hongrie." *International Review of Education* 13, no. 3 (1967): 332-50.

2169 Deubler, Hans. "Das Ungarische Schulwesen und die Tendenzen seiner Entwicklung." *Vergleichende Pädagogik* 13, no. 1 (1977): 14-28.

2170 Kádár-Fülop, Judit. "Women's Education in Hungary." *International Review of Education* 19, no. 1 (1973): 109-15.

2171 Korcsog, Andras, and Andras Rohonyi. "Experiments of Two-level Training in Hungarian Higher Education." *Higher Education* 6 (February 1977): 1-44.

2172 Magocsi, Paul R. "The Role of Education in the Formation of a National Consciousness." *Eastern European Quarterly* 7 (Summer 1973): 157-65.

2173 Murray, E. "Higher Education in Communist Hungary: 1948-1956." *American-Slavic Review* 19 (October 1960): 395-413.

2174 Ret, Rosza. "The Hungarian Plan for the School of Tomorrow." *Prospects* 8, No. 2 (1978): 228-38.

2175 Richmond, W. Kenneth. "Educational Planning in Hungary." *Comparative Education* 2 (March 1966): 93-107.

2176 Vladar, Ervin. "Die Neugestaltung der allgemeinbildenen Fächer an den Fachmittelschulen Ungarns." *Vergleichende Pädagogik* 14, no. 4 (1978): 375-85.

Iceland

Books

2177 Björnsson, S., et al. *Exploration in Social Inequality: Stratification Dynamics in Social and Individual Development in Iceland.* Berlin: Ernst Klett Verlag, 1977.

2178 Josepsson, Bragi. *Icelandic Culture and Education: An Annotated Bibliography.* Bowling Green: Western Kentucky University, 1968.

Ireland

Books

2179 Akenson, D. H. *Education and Enmity: The Control of Schooling in Northern Ireland.* Newton Abbot, England: David and Charles, 1973.

2180 Akenson, Donald H. *The Irish Education Experiment: the National System of Education in the Nineteenth Century.* London: Routledge and Kegan Paul, 1970.

2181 Athinson, N. *Irish Education.* Dublin: Allen Figgis, 1969.

2182 Dowling, P. J. *A History of Irish Education.* Cork: Mercier Press, 1971.

2183 McElligott, T. J. *Education in Ireland.* Dublin: Institute of Public Administration, 1966.

2184 Murphy, M. W., ed. *Education in Ireland: Now and the Future*. Cork: Mercier Press, 1970.

2185 Organization for Economic Cooperation and Development. *Reviews of National Policies for Education: Ireland*. Paris: OECD, 1970.

Articles

2186 Atkinson, Norma. "The School Structure in the Republic of Ireland." *Comparative Education Review* 8 (December 1964): 276-80.

2187 Peck, B. "Irish Education and European Integration." *Comparative Education* 2 (June 1966): 197-209.

Italy

Books

2188 Burn, Barbara. *The Emerging System of Higher Education in Italy: Report of a Seminar*. New York: International Council for Educational Development, 1973.

2189 Clark, Burton R. *Academic Power in Italy: A Study of Bureaucracy and Oligarchy in a National University System*. Chicago: University of Chicago Press, 1977.

2190 Organization for Economic Cooperation and Development. *Reviews of National Policies for Education: Italy*. Paris: OECD, 1968.

Articles

2191 Anello, Michael. "Italy." In *International Encyclopedia of Higher Education*, edited by A. Knowles, pp. 2341-47. San Francisco: Jossey-Bass, 1977.

2192 Borghi, Lamberto, and Anthony Scarangello. "Italy's Ten-Year Education Plan." *Comparative Education Review* 4 (June 1960): 26-31.

2193 Codignola, Tristano. "The University Reform." *Western European Education* 3 (Winter 1971-72): 316-29.

2194 Correa, Hector. "Flows of Students and Manpower Planning: Application to Italy." *Comparative Education Review* 13 (June 1969): 167-79.

2195 D'Arcais, G. F. "L'école, l'enseignement et la pédagogie en Italie de 1945 à 1955." *International Review of Education* 1, no. 2 (1955): 182-92.

2196 de Francesco, C., and P. Trivalleto. "Drop-outs from Italian Universities: 1960-1975." *Paedagogica Europaea* 12 (1977): 81-106.

2197 Mancini, Federico. "The Italian Student Movement." *AAUP Bulletin* 54 (Winter 1968): 427-32.

2198 Martinotti, Guido, and Alberto Giasanti. "The Robed Baron: The Academic Profession in the Italian University." *Higher Education* 6 (May 1977): 189-208.

2199 Newport, Angela. "A Comparative Study of Provision Made in Recurrent Education for Workers with Special Reference to the '150 Hours' in Italy." *Comparative Education* 15 (October 1979): 269-77.

2200 Rugiu, Antonio Santioni. "The Evolution of the Italian Educational System, 1956-1966." *Comparative Education Review* 11 (October 1967): 348-59.

2201 Ryan, Desmond. "The University of Calabria in Its Regional Context." *Paedagogica Europaea* 12, no. 1 (1977): 63-92.

2202 Sartori, Giovanni. "The Italian University System." In *Universities in the Western World*, edited by Paul Seabury, pp. 246-56. New York: Free Press, 1975.

2203 Scarangello, Anthony. "Church and State in Italian Education." *Comparative Education Review* 5 (February 1962): 199-208.

2204 Statera, Gianna. "Student Politics in Italy: From Utopia to Terrorism." *Higher Education* 8 (November 1979): 657-68.

2205 Steedman, Hilary. "The Italian Intermediate School: Knowledge and Control." *Comparative Education* 10 (June 1974): 137-46.

2206 von Blumenthal, Victor. "Educational Planning and Secondary School Reform in Italy." *Western European Education* 9 (Spring 1977): 10-81.

2207 Wuliger, Robert. "Italian Universities and the Social Crisis." *AAUP Bulletin* 61 (Autumn 1975): 232-38.

Netherlands

Books

2208 Brickman, William W. *The Educational System of the Netherlands.* Washinton, D.C.: U.S. Office of Education, 1975.

2209 Organization for Economic Cooperation and Development. *Reviews of National Policies for Education: Netherlands.* Paris: OECD, 1969.

Articles

2210 Daalder, Hans. "The Dutch Universities between the 'New Democracy' and the 'New Management.'" *Minerva* 12 (April 1974): 221-57.

2211 de Goede, Martijn P. M., and Rene Hoksbergen. "Part-Time Education at Tertiary Level in the Netherlands." *Higher Education* 7 (November 1978): 443-56.

2212 Hansen, E. "Marxism, Socialism and the Dutch Primary School." *History of Education Quarterly* 13 (Winter 1973): 367-91.

2213 Maas, Jacob van Lutsenburg. "The 'Mammoth Law' Reforms in Dutch Education." *Comparative Education Review* 7 (February 1964): 279-85.

2214 Mason, Henry L. "Reflections on the Polarized University: Triparity and Tripolarity in the Netherlands." *AAUP Bulletin* 60 (December 1974): 383-400.

2215 "Netherlands." In *International Encyclopedia of Higher Education*, edited by A. Knowles, pp. 2996-3003. San Francisco: Jossey-Bass, 1977.

2216 Noordam, N. F., et al. "Netherlands." In *Perspectives on World Education*, edited by C. Beck, pp. 64-75. Dubuque, Iowa: Brown, 1970.

2217 Sloos, Isaac J. "Structure, Organization and Activities of the Leidscheonderwijsinstelliwgen." *International Review of Education* 13, no. 1 (1967): 40-55.

2218 Stellwag, Helena W. F. "On Reform of the Educational System in the Netherlands." *Comparative Education Review* 11 (October 1967): 360-65.

2219 Stellwag, Helena W. F. "Problems and Trends in Dutch Education." *International Review of Education* 3, no. 1 (1957): 54-68.

2220 Velena, Elzo. "Primary and Post-Primary Education in the Netherlands." *Comparative Education Review* 7 (October 1963): 119-24.

2221 Wiegersma, S. "National Analysis: Netherlands." *International Review of Education* 15, no. 2 (1969): 183-94.

2222 Wilson, Norman H. "Dutch Schools and Religious Segmentation." *Comparative Education Review* 3 (October 1959): 19-23.

Norway

Books

2223 Hove, Olav. *An Outline of Norwegian Education.* Oslo: Ministry of Foreign Affairs, 1958.

2224 Hove, O. *The System of Education in Norway.* Oslo: Royal Norwegian Ministry of Church and Education, 1968.

2225 Huus, Helen. *The Education of Children and Youth in Norway.* Pittsburgh: University of Pittsburgh Press, 1960.

2226 Organization for Economic Cooperation and Development. *Policies for Science and Education: Country Reviews, Norway.* Paris: OECD.

2227 Organization for Economic Cooperation and Development. *Reviews of National Policies for Education: Norway.* Paris: OECD, 1976.

Articles

2228 Arnesen, Carl. "Problèmes de l'enseignement en Norvège." *International Review of Education* 6, no. 1 (1960): 1-9.

2229 Eide, Kjell. "Educational Planning in Norway." *Educational Planning* 2 (March 1976): 13-20.

2230 Hansen, Lorraine S. "Ends and Means in Norwegian Educational Reform." *Comparative Education Review* 8 (December 1964): 269-75.

2231 Haywood, Roy. "Recent Reforms in the Organization and the Curricula of Norwegian Secondary Schools." *Comparative Education* 15 (June 1969): 123-43.

2232 Lauglo, Jon. "Upper-Secondary Teachers in Norway: Organizational Participation and its Correlates." *Comparative Education* 12 (June 1976): 93-114.

2233 Sausjord, Gunnar. "Norwegian Educational Reform and the Enhetsskole Idea." *Comparative Education Review* 11 (October 1967): 366-73.

2234 Sirevag, Tönnes. "Ten Years of Norwegian School Experimentation." *International Review of Education* 12 (1966): 1-15.

2235 Stenhouse, Lawrence. "Comprehensive Education in Norway: A Developing System." *Comparative Education* 2 (November 1965): 37-42.

Poland

Books

2236 Apanasewicz, Nellie, and William Medlin. *Selected Bibliography of Materials on Education in Poland.* Washington, D.C.: U.S. Office of Education, 1960.

2237 *Educational System of Poland.* Washington, D.C.: U.S. Office of Education, 1976.

2238 Fiszman, Joseph R. *Revolution and Tradition in People's Poland: Education and Socialization.* Princeton: Princeton University Press, 1973.

2239 Hartmann, Karl. *Hochschulwesen und Wissenschaft in Polen: Entwicklung, Organisation und Stand 1918-1960.* Frankfurt: Mertzner, 1962.

2240 Januszkiewicz, F. *Education in Poland.* Warsaw: Interpress, 1973.

2241 Parnowski, Z. *Education in Poland.* Warsaw: Polonia Publishing House, 1958.

2242 Rosen, Seymour, and Nellie Apanasewicz. *Higher Education in Poland.* Washington, D.C.: U.S. Office of Education, 1964.

2243 Sanyal, B. C., and A. Jozefowicz, eds. *Graduate Employment and Plan-*

ning of Higher Education in Poland. Paris: International Institute for Educational Planning, 1978.

2244 Searing, Marjory E. *Estimates of Educational Attainment in Poland 1950-1969.* Washington, D.C.: U.S. Bureau of the Census, 1970.

2245 Simon, Brian. *Education in the New Poland.* London: Lawrence and Wishart, 1954.

2246 Singer, Gusta. *Teacher Education vs. a Communist State: Poland 1956-1961.* New York: Brookman and Associates, 1965.

Articles

2247 Kaczor, Stanislav. "The Modernization of Education in an Advanced Socialist Society: The Example of Poland." In *Educational Reforms: Experiences and Prospects*, pp. 125-31. Paris: UNESCO, 1979.

2248 Kuberski, Jerzy, and Jerzy Wolcczyk. "The Bases of the Reform of the Educational System in Poland." *Prospects* 5, no. 3 (1975): 301-11.

2249 Okon, Wincenty. "Trends and Problems in Educational Research in Poland." *International Review of Education* 8, no. 3-4 (1963): 302-10.

2250 Oster, Susanne, and Wompel Ilse-Renate. "The Educational Policy and Future Plans of the Polish Communist Party." *Slavic and European Education Review*, no. 1 (1978): 18-28.

2251 Pecherski, M. "Changes in the Polish System of Teacher-Education Since 1972." *International Review of Education* 21, no. 4 (1975): 407-21.

2252 Soroka, W. W. "Poland." In *Perspectives on World Education*, edited by C. Beck, pp. 76-89. Dubuque, Iowa: Brown, 1970.

2253 Suchodolski, B. "Les problèmes de l'éducation et de l'enseignement en Pologne contemporaine." *International Review of Education* 4, no. 1 (1958): 17-35.

2254 Sufin, Zbigniew. "Planning and Implementation of Educational Reform in Poland." *Educational Planning* 2 (March 1976): 45-52.

2255 Szczepanski, Jan. "Social Sciences and the Reform of the Education System," *Canadian Slavonic Papers* 15 (Spring and Summer 1973): 134-43.

Portugal

Articles

2256 Gomez, S. "Portugal." In *Perspectives on World Education*, edited by C. Beck, pp. 90-98. Dubuque, Iowa: Brown, 1970.

2257 Melo, Alberto. "Portugal's Experiences of Reform through Popular Initiative." *Convergence* 11, no. 1 (1978): 28-40.

2258 Teodoro, Antonio. "Die portugiesische Revolution und das Bildungswesen." *Vergleichende Pädagogik* 14 (June 1978): 233-57.

Rumania

Books

2259 Braham, Randolph L. *Education in Rumania: A Decade of Change.* Washington, D.C.: U.S. Office of Education, 1972.

2260 Braham, Randolph L. *The Educational System of Romania: Education Around the World.* Washington, D.C.: U.S. Office of Education, 1978.

2261 Haase, O., and Seymour Rosen. *Education in Rumania.* Washington, D.C.: U.S. Office of Education, 1960.

Articles

2262 Grant, Nigel. "The Changing School in Rumania." *Comparative Education* 2 (June 1966): 167-80.

2263 Gulutsan, Metro. "National Identity, Politics and Education in Romania." *Canadian and International Education* 1 (June 1972): 59-78.

2264 Iazykov, S. "In the Rumanian School." *Soviet Education* 8 (June 1966): 46-51.

2265 Muster, Dumitru, and George Vaideanu. "Romania. Contemporary Romanian Education." *Journal of Education* 152 (February 1970): 64-71.

Scotland

Books

2266 Findlay, Ian R. *Education in Scotland*. Newton Abbot: David and Charles, 1973.

2267 Hunter, S. Leslie. *The Scottish Educational System*. Elmsford, N.Y.: Pergamon Press, 1972.

2268 Mackintosh, M. *Education in Scotland, Yesterday and Today*. Glasgow: Robert Gobson and Sons, 1962.

2269 Nisbet, John, ed. *Scottish Education Looks Ahead*. Edinburgh: Chambers, 1969.

2270 Osborne, G. S. *Scottish and English Schools*. Pittsburgh: University of Pittsburgh Press, 1966.

2271 Powell, J. L. *Selection for University in Scotland*. London: University of London Press, 1973.

Articles

2272 Bullough, Vern L. "Intellectual Achievement in Eighteenth Century Scotland: A Computer Study of the Importance of Education." *Comparative Education Review* 14 (February 1970): 90-102.

2273 McIntosh, Douglas. "Scottish Education, Past, Present and Future." *International Review of Education* 6, no. 2 (1960): 176-87.

2274 McPherson, Andrew. "The Dainton Report—A Scottish Dissent." *Universities Quarterly* 22 (June 1968): 254-73.

2275 Neave, Guy. "The Development of Scottish Education 1958-1972." *Comparative Education* 12 (June 1976): 129-44.

2276 Neave, Guy, and Henry Cowper. "Higher Education in Scotland." *European Journal of Education* 14 (March 1979): 7-24.

Soviet Union

Books

2277 Ablin, Fred, ed. *Contemporary Soviet Education: A Collection of Readings from Soviet Journals.* White Plains, N.Y.: International Arts and Science Press, 1969.

2278 Alston, Patrick L. *Education and the State in Tsarist Russia.* Stanford, Calif.: Stanford University Press, 1969.

2279 Anweiler, Oskar. *Geschichte der Schule und Pädagogik in Russland vom Ende des Zarenreiches bis zum Beginn der Stalin-Ära.* Wiesbaden, West Germany: Verlag Otto Harrassowitz, 1978.

2280 Anweiler, Oskar, Fredrich Kuebart, and Klaus Meyer. *Die sowjetische Bildungspolitik von 1958-1973.* Wiesbaden: Verlag Otto Harrassowitz, 1976.

2281 Apanasewicz, Nellie. *Education in the U.S.S.R.: An Annotated Bibliography of English-Language Materials, 1965-1973.* Washington, D.C.: U.S. Office of Education, 1974.

2282 Apanasewicz, Nellie. *Soviet Education; A Bibliography of English-Language Materials.* Washington, D.C.: U.S. Office of Education, 1964.

2283 Benton, William. *The Teachers and the Taught in the U.S.S.R.* New York: Atheneum, 1966.

2284 Bereday, George Z. F., William Brickman, and Gerald Read, eds. *The Changing Soviet School.* Boston: Houghton Mifflin, 1960.

2285 Bereday, George Z. F., and Jaan Pennar, eds. *The Politics of Soviet Education.* New York: Praeger, 1960.

2286 Bereday, George Z. F., Jaan Pennar, and Ivan Bakalo. *Modernization and Diversity in Soviet Education.* New York: Praeger, 1970.

2287 Bowen, James. *Soviet Education: Anton Makarenko and the Years of Experiment.* Madison: University of Wisconsin Press, 1962.

2288 Bronfenbrenner, Urie. *Two Worlds of Childhood: U.S. and U.S.S.R.* New York: Pocket Books, 1973.

2289 DeWitt, Nicholas. *Education and Professional Employment in the U.S.S.R.* Washington, D.C.: National Science Foundation, 1961.

2290 Dunstan, John. *Paths to Excellence and the Soviet School.* Windsor, England: National Foundation for Educational Research, 1978.

2291 *Educational Planning in the U.S.S.R.* Paris: UNESCO, International Institute for Educational Planning, 1968.

2292 Grant, Douglas, ed. *The Humanities in Soviet Higher Education.* Toronto: University of Toronto Press, 1960.

2293 Grant, Nigel. *Soviet Education.* Harmondsworth, England: Penguin, 1979.

2294 Hans, Nicholas A. *History of Russian Educational Policy 1701-1917.* New York: Russell and Russell, 1964.

2295 Hans, Nicholas A. *The Russian Tradition in Education.* London: Routledge and Kegan Paul, 1963.

2296 Hechinger, Fred M. *The Big Red Schoolhouse.* Garden City, N.Y.: Doubleday, 1962.

2297 Jacoby, Susan. *Inside Soviet Schools.* New York: Hill and Wang, 1974.

2298 Johnson, William Herman Eckart. *Russia's Educational Heritage.* New York: Octagon Books, 1969.

2299 King, Edmund, ed. *Communist Education.* London: Methuen, 1963.

2300 Korol, Alexander. *Soviet Research and Development: Its Organization, Personnel and Funds.* Cambridge, Mass.: M.I.T. Press, 1965.

2301 Korol, Alexander G. *Soviet Education for Science and Technology.* Cambridge, Mass.: Technology Press of M.I.T., 1957.

2302 McClelland, James. *Autocrats and Academics: Education, Culture and Society in Tsarist Russia.* Chicago: University of Chicago Press, 1979.

2303 Medlin, William K., and N. J. Rokitiansky. *Bibliography of Published Materials on Russian and Soviet Education: A Research and Reference Tool.* Washington, D.C.: U.S. Office of Education, 1960.

2304 Mickiewicz, Ellen Propper. *Soviet Political Schools: The Community Party Adult Instruction System*. New Haven, Conn.: Yale University Press, 1967.

2305 Noah, H. J. *Financing Soviet Schools*. New York: Teacher's College Press, 1966.

2306 Noah, Harold J., ed. *The Economics of Education in the U.S.S.R.* New York: Praeger, 1969.

2307 Nozhko, K., C. Momoszon, V. Zhamin, and V. Severtsev. *Educational Planning in the USSR*. Paris: UNESCO, 1968.

2308 Pennar, Jaan, Ivan Bakalo, and George Bereday. *Modernization and Diversity in Soviet Education with Special Reference to Nationality Groups*. New York: Praeger, 1971.

2309 Rosen, Seymour Michael. *Education and Modernization in the U.S.S.R.* Reading, Mass.: Addison-Wesley, 1971.

2310 Rosen, Seymour M. *Education in the U.S.S.R.: Current Status of Higher Education*. Washington, D.C.: U.S. Office of Education, 1980.

2311 Rudman, Herbert C. *The School and State in the USSR*. New York: Macmillan, 1967.

2312 Shneidman, N. N. *Literature and Ideology in Soviet Education*. Lexington, Mass.: D. C. Heath, 1973.

2313 Simon, Brian, ed. *Educational Psychology in the USSR*. Stanford, Calif.: Stanford University Press, 1963.

2314 Tomiak, J. *The Soviet Union*. Hamden, Conn.: Archon Books, 1972.

2315 Weaver, Kitty D. *Lenin's Grandchildren: Preschool Education in the Soviet Union*. New York: Simon and Schuster, 1971.

Articles

2316 Anderson, C. Arnold. "Educational Dilemmas in the USSR." *School Review* 67 (Spring 1959): 26-44.

2317 Azrael, Jeremy. "Soviet Union." In *Education and Political Develop-*

ment, edited by J. S. Coleman, pp. 233-71. Princeton: Princeton University Press, 1964.

2318 Bilinsky, Yaroslav. "Education of the Non-Russian Peoples in the Soviet Union." *Comparative Education Review* 8 (June 1964): 78-90.

2319 Brickman, William W. "Selected Bibliography on the History of Education in Russia to 1917." *Paedagogica Historica* 14 (1974): 164-70.

2320 Burn, Barbara. "Higher Education in the Soviet Union." In B. Burn, *Higher Education in Nine Countries*, pp. 277-316. New York: McGraw-Hill, 1971.

2321 Cary, Charles D. "Patterns of Emphasis Upon Marxist-Leninist Ideology: A Computer Content Analysis of Soviet School History, Geography and Social Science Textbooks." *Comparative Education Review* 20 (February 1976): 11-29.

2322 Central Statistical Administration of the USSR, 1965. "Soviet Education in Statistics." *Soviet Education* 9 (October 1967): 5-44.

2323 Dobson, Richard. "Social Status and Inequality of Access to Higher Education in the USSR." In *Power and Ideology in Education*, edited by J. Karabel and A. H. Halsey, pp. 254-74. New York: Oxford University Press, 1977.

2324 Dobson, Richard, and Michael Swafford. "The Educational Attainment Process in the Soviet Union: A Case Study." *Comparative Education Review* 24 (June 1980): 252-69.

2325 "Economics of Higher Education; Symposium." *Soviet Education* 18 (November 1975): 3-113.

2326 Egorov, N. S. "Main Trends in the Development of Higher Education." *Soviet Education* 20 (April 1978): 18-29.

2327 Filippova, Liliya. "Union of Soviet Socialist Republics." In *International Encyclopedia of Higher Education*, edited by A. Knowles, pp. 4185-94. San Francisco: Jossey-Bass, 1977.

2328 Kashin, Mikhail. "Reform of Contents and Teaching Methods in the U.S.S.R." *Prospects* 8, no. 1 (1978): 19-32.

2329 Kostanian, S. L. "Education and Soviet Economic Growth." *International Review of Education* 18, no. 2 (1972): 155-71.

2330 Kotliarov, V. F., D. S. Leshchinskii, and N. K. Sokolovskii. "The Organization and Planning of Public Education in the Belorussian S.S.R." *Soviet Education* 15 (September 1973): 4-86.

2331 Kravetz, Nathan. "Education of Ethnic and National Minorities in the USSR: A Report on Current Developments." *Comparative Education* 16 (March 1980): 13-25.

2332 Kreusler, Abraham. "Modernization of the Russian Secondary School System." *Slavic and East European Journal* 16 (Summer 1958): 130-44.

2333 Kreusler, Abraham. "U.S.S.R." In *Perspectives on World Education*, edited by C. Beck, pp. 113-32. Dubuque, Iowa: Brown, 1970.

2334 Lilge, Frederic. "Lenin and the Politics of Education." In *Power and Ideology in Education*, edited by J. Karabel and A. H. Halsey, pp. 556-72. New York: Oxford University Press, 1977.

2335 Medlin, W. K., and W. M. Cave. "Social Change and Education in Developing Areas: Uzbekistan." *Comparative Education Review* 8 (October 1964): 166-76.

2336 Mitter, Wolfgang. "On the Efficiency of the Soviet School System." *Comparative Education* 9 (March 1973): 34-47.

2337 Obraztsov, Ivan. "Higher Education in the Union of Soviet Socialist Republics: Development Problems and Concepts." In *Educational Reforms: Experiences and Prospects*, pp. 170-76. Paris: UNESCO, 1979.

2338 Panachin, F. G. "Teacher Education in the USSR, Historical Development and Current Trends." *Soviet Education* 19 (July-August 1977): 3-246.

2339 Piskunov, A. I., and E. D. Dneprov. "A Short History of the Soviet School and Soviet Pedagogy over Sixty Years." *Soviet Education* 20 (February-March 1978): whole issue.

2340 Price, R. F. "Labor and Education in Russia and China." *Comparative Education* 10 (March 1974): 13-23.

2341 Shorish, M. Mobin. "The Pedagogical, Linguistic, and Logistical Problems of Teaching Russian to the Central Asians." *Slavic Review* 35 (September 1976): 443-62.

2342 "Statistics on Soviet Higher Education." *Soviet Education* 9 (August 1967): 5-51.

2343 Strumilin, Stanislav. "The Economics of Education in the U.S.S.R." *International Social Science Journal* 14, no. 4 (1962): 633-46.

2344 Whyte, Martin K. "Educational Reform: China in the 1970's and Russia in the 1920's." *Comparative Education Review* 18 (February 1974): 112-28.

2345 Zajda, Joseph. "Education and Social Stratification in the Soviet Union." *Comparative Education Review* 16 (March 1980): 1-13.

2346 Zhamin, V. A., and S. L. Kostanian. "Education and Soviet Economic Growth." *International Review of Education* 18, no. 2 (1972): 155-72.

Spain

Books

2347 Brickman, William W. *Educational Reform and Renewal in Contemporary Spain*. Washington, D.C.: U.S. Office of Education, 1972.

2348 Horowitz, Morris A. *Manpower and Education in Franco Spain*. Hamden, Conn.: The Shoestring Press, 1974.

2349 Kagan, L. Richard. *Students and Society in Early Modern Spain*. Baltimore, Md.: Johns Hopkins University Press, 1975.

Articles

2350 Estarellas, Juan. "The Education of Don Quixote." *Comparative Education Review* 6 (June 1962): 25-33.

2351 Giner de San Julian, Salvador. "Freedom and Political Power in the Spanish University: The Democratic Movement Under Francoism." *Western European Education* 10 (Fall 1978): 51-65.

2352 Horowitz, Morris A. "The University System in Spain: An Analysis of Structure." *Higher Education* 3 (August 1974): 341-52.

2353 McNair, John. "The Contribution of the Schools to the Restoration of Regional Autonomy in Spain." *Comparative Education* 16 (March 1980): 33-45.

2354 "Reform in Spanish Education." *Western European Education* 4 (Fall 1972): 196-212.

2355 Tasquets, J., and J. A. Benavent. "Linguistic and Cultural Unity in Spanish Education." *Compare* 8 (April 1978).

2356 Tena Artigas, J. "Zero Growth in Higher Education?: The Case of Spain." *Paedagogica Europaea* 12, no. 2 (1977): 31-48.

Sweden

Books

2357 Boalt, Gunnar, and Herman Lantz. *Universities and Research: Observations on the United States and Sweden.* New York: Wiley Interscience, 1970.

2358 Dixon, C. W. *Society, Schools and Progress in Scandinavia.* Elmsford, N.Y.: Pergamon Press, 1976.

2359 Edstrom, L. O. *Struktur und Reform schwedischer Erwachsenbildung.* Braunschweig: Westermann, 1973.

2360 *Higher Education: Proposals by the Swedish 1968 Educational Commission* Stockholm: Almanna Forlaget, 1973.

2361 Husén, Torsten. *Problems of Differentiation in Swedish Compulsory Schooling.* Stockholm: Svenska Bokforlaget, 1962.

2362 Marklund, Sixten, and Gunnar Bergendal. *Trends in Swedish Educational Policy.* Stockholm: Swedish Institute, 1979.

2363 Marklund, Sixten, and Pär Söderberg. *The Swedish Comprehensive School.* New York: Humanities Press, 1968.

2364 Organization for Economic Cooperation and Development. *National Background Reports: Sweden*. Paris: OECD, 1980.

2365 Organization for Economic Cooperation and Development. *Reviews of National Policies for Education: Sweden*. Paris: OECD, 1969.

2366 Orring, Jonas. *School in Sweden*. Stockholm: So-Förlaget, 1968.

2367 Paulston, Rolland G. *Educational Change in Sweden: Planning and Accepting the Comprehensive School Reforms*. New York: Teacher's College Press, 1968.

Articles

2368 Ackin, M. C. "Analysis of National Curriculum and Instructional Reform: Application to Sweden." *International Review of Education* 19, no. 2 (1973): 208-18.

2369 Anderson, C. Arnold. "Sweden Re-examines Higher Education—A Critique of the U68 Report." *Comparative Education* 10 (October 1974): 167-80.

2370 Bergendal, Gunnar. "U68—A Reform Proposal for Swedish Higher Education." *Higher Education* 3 (August 1974): 353-64.

2371 Bjerstedt, A. "Educational Research in Sweden: Some Areas of Current and Potential Development." *International Review of Education* 14 (1968): 259-76.

2372 Burn, Barbara. "Higher Education in Sweden." In B. Burn, *Higher Education in Nine Countries*, pp. 197-227. New York: McGraw-Hill, 1971.

2373 Canfield, Alvah T. "Folk High Schools in Denmark and Sweden: A Comparative Analysis." *Comparative Education Review* 9 (February 1965): 18-24.

2374 Dahllöf, U. "The Curriculum Development System in Sweden." *International Review of Education* 19, no. 2 (1973): 219-31.

2375 Dahllöf, Urban. "Recent Reforms of Secondary Education in Sweden." *Comparative Education* 2 (March 1966): 71-93.

2376 Heidenheimer, Arnold J. "The Politics of Educational Reform: Explaining

Different Outcomes of School Comprehensivization Attempts in Sweden and West Germany." *Comparative Education Review* 18 (October 1974): 388-410.

2377 Husén, Torsten. "Curriculum Research in Sweden." *International Review of Education* 11, no. 2 (1965): 189-208.

2378 Husén, Torsten. "Educational Change in Sweden." *Comparative Education* 1 (June 1965): 181-92.

2379 Husén, Torsten. "Loss of Talent in Selective School Systems: The Case of Sweden." *Comparative Education Review* 4 (October 1960): 70-75.

2380 Husén, Torsten. "Swedish University Research at the Crossroads." *Minerva* 14 (Winter 1976-77): 419-46.

2381 Magnusson, L. "Cost-Benefit Analysis of Investment in Higher Education: Some Swedish Results." *Swedish Journal of Economics* 75 (June 1973): 119-27.

2382 Mallea, John R. "The Implementation of Swedish Educational Policy and Planning." *Comparative Education* 6 (June 1970): 99-115.

2383 Marklund, S. "Comparative School Research and the Swedish School Reform." *International Review of Education* 17, no. 1 (1971): 39-49.

2384 Norinder, Yngve. "The Evolving Comprehensive School in Sweden." *International Review of Education* 3, no. 3 (1957): 257-76.

2385 Paulston, Rolland G. "The Swedish Comprehensive School Reform: A Selected Annotated Bibliography." *Comparative Education Review* 10 (February 1966): 87-94.

2386 "The Reorganization of Higher Education in Sweden." *Minerva* 12 (January 1974): 83-114.

2387 Sjostrand, Wilhelm. "Sweden." In *Perspectives on World Education*, edited by C. Beck, pp. 99-112. Dubuque, Iowa: Brown, 1970.

2388 Sjostrand, W. "Recent Trends and Developments in Primary and Secondary Education in Scandinavia." *International Review of Education* 13, no. 2 (1967): 180-97.

2389 "Sweden." In *International Encyclopedia of Higher Education*, edited by A. Knowles, pp. 4023-34. San Francisco: Jossey-Bass, 1977.

2390 Tomasson, R. F. "From Elitism to Egalitarianism in Swedish Education." *Sociology of Education* 38 (Spring 1965): 203-23.

2391 Willmann, Bodo. "Economic Change, Educational Needs, and Secondary School Reform in Sweden." *Western European Education* 9 (Summer 1977): 5-109.

Switzerland

Books

2392 Bodenman, Paul S. *The Educational System of Switzerland*. Washington, D.C.: U.S. Office of Education, 1979.

2393 Egger, F., and E. Blanc. *Education in Switzerland*. Geneva: Swiss Educational Documentation Center, 1974.

2394 UNESCO. *Innovations in Switzerland: Traits and Trends*. Paris: UNESCO, 1978.

2395 Rickover, Hyman G. *Swiss Schools and Ours: Why Theirs are Better*. Boston: Little, Brown, 1962.

Articles

2396 Cravsaz, Roselyne. "Higher Education in Switzerland." *European Journal of Education* 14 (March 1979): 37-58.

2397 "Education in Switzerland." *Western European Education* 7 (Spring-Summer 1975): 5-204.

2398 Jolly, Robert. "Elementary Schools in Geneva, Switzerland and Oakland, California." *Comparative Education Review* 5 (June 1961): 67-68.

2399 Panchaud, Georges. "School Reform in Switzerland." *Comparative Education Review* 11 (October 1967): 374-86.

2400 Santini, Bruno. "Attitudes of Swiss Teachers Towards the Study and Planning of the Curriculum." *Journal of Curriculum Studies* 5 (November 1973): 156-65.

Yugoslavia

Books

2401 Apanasewicz, Nellie, and Seymour Rosen. *Selected Bibliography of Materials on Education in Yugoslavia*. Washington, D.C.: U. S. Office of Education, 1961.

2402 Bach, Uwe. *Bildungspolitik in Jugoslawien, 1945-1974*. Wiesbaden: Verlag Otto Harrassowitz, 1977.

2403 David, M. *Adult Education in Yugoslavia*. Paris: UNESCO, 1962.

2404 Filipovic, Marijan. *Higher Education in Yugoslavia*. Belgrade: Federal Council for Education and Culture, 1971.

2405 Juhas, M. *Education and Its Reform in Yugoslavia*. Belgrade: Institute for Studies in Education, 1975.

2406 Organization for Economic Cooperation and Development. *Country Reports: Yugoslavia*. Paris: OECD, 1965.

2407 Tomich, Vera. *Education in Yugoslavia and the New Reform*. Washington, D.C.: U.S. Office of Education, 1963.

2408 Zagreb Univerzitet Institut za Drastvenaistrazivanja. *Reforms in Yugoslavia*. Paris: OECD, 1970.

Articles

2409 Anderson, Arnold C. "The Spectrum of Social Status Selection Across an Entire School System: Serbia 1884/85." *Comparative Education* 8 (December 1972): 105-9.

2410 Bertsch, Gary K., and Karen L. Persons. "Workers' Education in Socialist Yugoslavia." *Comparative Education Review* 24 (February 1980): 87-97.

2411 Crvenkovski, Krste. "Ability and Educational Opportunity in Present-day Yugoslavia." *International Review of Education* 7, no. 4 (1961): 394-401.

2412 Dorotich, Daniel A. "Ethnic Diversity and National Unity in Yugoslav Education." *Compare* 8 (April 1978): 81-92.

2413 Filipovic, Dragomir. "Permanent Education and Reform of the Educational System in Yugoslavia." *Convergence* 1 (December 1968): 42-47.

2414 Georgeoff, John. "Nationalism in the History Textbooks of Yugoslavia and Bulgaria." *Comparative Education Review* 10 (October 1966): 442-48.

2415 Georgeoff, John. "Yugoslav Youth and Student Organizations." *Comparative Education Review* 8 (June 1964): 104-11.

2416 Kintzer, F. C. "Educational Reforms in Yugoslavia." *Educational Record* 59 (Winter 1978): 87-104.

2417 Pervan, R. "Problems of University Development: The Yugoslav Experience." *Australian University* 14 (September 1976): 38-61.

LATIN AMERICA

General

Books

2418 Albornoz, Orlando. *Ideología y Política en la Universidad Latinoamericana*. Caracas: Instituto Societas, 1972.

2419 Benjamin, Harold. *Higher Education in the American Republics*. New York: McGraw-Hill, 1965.

2420 Benveniste, Guy. *The Politics of Expertise*. Berkeley, Calif.: Glendessary Press, 1972.

2421 Centro de Estudios Educativos. *Educación y Realidad Socio Económica*. Mexico City: 1979.

2422 Centro de Estudios Educativos. *Prospectiva de la Educación en América Latina*. Mexico City: 1979.

2423 Cummings, Richard L., and Donald A. Lemke. *Educational Innovations in Latin America*. Metuchen, N. J.: Scarecrow Press, 1973.

2424 Freire, Paulo. *Pedagogy of the Oppressed*. New York: Herder and Herder, 1972.

2425 Gale, Laurence. *Education and Development in Latin America*. New York: Praeger, 1969.

2426 Garcia Huidobro, J. E., and Jorge Ochoa. *Tendencias de la Investigación en Educación en América Latina*. Santiago: Centro de Investigación y Desarrollo de la Educación, 1978.

2427 García Laguardia, J. M. *La Autonomía Universitaria en América Latina*. Mexico City: Universidad Nacional Autónoma de Mexico, 1977.

2428 Garcia Laguardia, J. M. *Legislación Universiaria de America Latina*. Mexico City: Universidad Nacional Autónoma de Mexico, 1973.

2429 Havighurst, Robert J. *La Sociedad y la Educación en América Latina*. Buenos Aires: Editorial Universiaria de Buenos Aires, 1973.

2430 LaBelle, Thomas, ed. *Education and Development: Latin America and the Caribbean*. Los Angeles: University of California, Latin American Center Publications, 1973.

2431 LaBelle, Thomas. *Nonformal Education and Social Change in Latin America*. Los Angeles: Latin American Center, University of California, 1976.

2432 LaBelle, Thomas J., ed. *Educational Alternatives in Latin America: Social Change and Social Stratification*. Los Angeles: UCLA Latin American Center Publications, 1975.

2433 Liebman, Arthur, Kenneth Walker, and Myron Glazer. *Latin American Students, A Six Nation Study*. Cambridge, Mass.: Harvard University Press, 1972.

2434 Lyons, R. F. *Problems and Strategies of Educational Planning: Lessons from Latin America*. Paris: International Institute for Educational Planning, 1965.

2435 Maier, Joseph, and Richard Weatherhead, eds. *The Latin American University*. Albuquerque: University of New Mexico Press, 1979.

2436 Morales-Gomez, Daniel, ed. *La Educación y Desarrollo Dependiente en América Latina*. Mexico City: Ediciones Gernika, 1979.

2437 Poston, Susan. *Nonformal Education in Latin America: An Annotated*

Bibliography. Los Angeles: Latin American Center, University of California at Los Angeles, 1976.

2438 Vasconi, Tomás Amadeo. *Ideología, Lucha de Clases, y Apartos Educativos en el Desarrollo de América Latina*. Bogotá: Editorial Latina, 1975.

2439 Waggoner, George R., and Barbara Ashton Waggoner. *Education in Central America*. Lawrence: University of Kansas Press, 1971.

Articles

2440 Albornoz, Orlando. "Academic Freedom and Higher Education in Latin America." *Comparative Education Review* 10 (June 1966): 250-56.

2441 Albornoz, Orlando. "Excellence or Equality at the University: The Latin American Case." *Latin American Research Review* 11 (1976): 125-36.

2442 Arnove, Robert F. "Education and Political Participation in Rural Areas of Latin America." *Comparative Education Review* 17 (June 1973): 198-215.

2443 Arnove, Robert F. "A Survey of Literature and Research on Latin American Universities." *Latin American Research Review* 3 (Fall 1967): 45-62.

2444 Barkin, David. "Educación: Una Barrera al Desarrollo Económico." *El Trimestre Económico* 39 (October-December 1972): 151-213.

2445 Beltran, Gonzalo Aguirre. "Teoría y Práctica de la Educación Indígena." *Revista Mexicana de Sociología* 16 (May-August 1954): 225-35.

2446 Bernheim, Carlos Tunnermann. "Central America." In *International Encyclopedia of Higher Education*, edited by A. Knowles, pp. 838-47. San Francisco: Jossey-Bass, 1977.

2447 Bruck, Nicholas. "Higher Education and Economic Development in Central America." *Review of Social Economy* 27 (September 1969): 160-80.

2448 Bueno, Miguel. "Educación y Sociedad." *Revista Mexicana de Sociologia* 23 (September-December 1961): 887-97.

2449 Burnett, Jacquetta Hill. "Recent Social Science Research Appraisals of

Latin American Education." *Latin American Research Review* 3 (Fall 1967): 11-31.

2450 Carrington, Lawrence D. "Education in Four Caribbean States." *Prospects* 8, no. 4 (1978): 523-30.

2451 Davis, Russell G. "Prototypes and Stereotypes in Latin American Universities." *Comparative Education Review* 9 (October 1965): 275-81.

2452 de Moura Castro, Claudio. "Planeación Educacional: Concepto y Praxis." *Revista del Centro de Estudios Educativos* 7, no. 1 (1977): 51-66.

2453 Duncan, Raymond W. "Education and Political Development: The Latin American Case." *Journal of Developing Areas* 2 (January 1968): 187-210.

2454 Epstein, Erwin H. "A Truce Between Two Cultures: Educational Transfer in the Americas." In *Schools in Transition*, edited by A. Kazamias and E. Epstein, pp. 32-44. Boston: Allyn and Bacon, 1968.

2455 Epstein, Erwin H. "Educación, Nacionalismo y Revolución en Comunidades Campesinos." In *Proceedings of the 42nd International Congress of Americanists* 3 (1978), pp. 53-68.

2456 Farrell, Joseph P. "Educational Differentiation and National Development: A Statistical Study (Latin American Data)." *Interchange* 1, no. 2 (1970): 62-76.

2457 Farrell, Joseph P. "National Planning Systems in Latin America: Their Environment and Their Impact." *Educational Planning* 1 (May 1974): 20-33.

2458 Farrell, Joseph P. "The Structural Differentiation of Developing Educational Systems: A Latin American Comparison." *Comparative Education Review* 13 (October 1969): 294-311.

2459 Freire, Paulo. "The Adult Literacy Process as Cultural Action for Freedom." *Harvard Educational Review* 40 (May 1970): 205-25.

2460 Goodman, Margaret Ann. "The Political Role of the University in Latin America." *Comparative Politics* 5 (January 1973): 279-92.

2461 Hennessy, Alistair. "University Students in National Politics." In *The

Politics of Conformity in Latin America, edited by Claudio Veliz, pp. 119-57. New York: Oxford University Press, 1967.

2462 Jacob, Jeffrey C. "The Role of the School in Latin American Rural to Urban Migration." *Canadian and International Education* 5 (June 1976): 71-94.

2463 Jordan, John E. "Latin American Education." *Latin American Research Review* 3 (Fall 1967): 63-76.

2464 LaBelle, Thomas J. "Goals and Strategies of Non-formal Education in Latin America." *Comparative Education Review* 20 (October 1976): 328-45.

2465 LaBelle, Thomas J., and Robert E. Verhine. "Non Formal Education and Occupational Stratification: Implications for Latin America." *Harvard Education Review* 45 (May 1975): 160-90.

2466 McCleary, Lloyd. "Status of Research on Education in Latin America." *Latin American Research Review* 3 (Fall 1967): 5-11.

2467 Marquardt, William F., and Richard Cortright. "Reviews of Contemporary Research on Literacy and Adult Education in Latin America." *Latin American Research Review* 3 (Summer 1968): 47-69.

2468 Mena Soto, J. "La Universidad Latinoamericana." *International Review of Education* 12, no. 4 (1966): 432-49.

2469 Oxtoby, Robert. "Vocational Education and Development Planning: Emerging Issues in the Commonwealth Caribbean." *Comparative Education* 13 (October 1977): 223-42.

2470 Paulson, R. G. "Problems of Educational Development and Rural Transformation in Latin America: Some Lessons from Cuba and Peru." In *Rural Reform and Transformation*, edited by R. Lonsdale and W. Avery, pp. 271-96. Oxford: Pergamon Press, 1978.

2471 Pelczar, Richard. "The Latin American Professoriate: Progress and Prospects." *Higher Education* 6 (May 1977): 235-54.

2472 Pescador, José Angel. "Nota Bibliográphica sobre Dos Enfoques Alternativos en la Economía de la Educación." *Revista del Centro de Estudios Educativos* 7, no. 2 (1977): 97-104.

2473 Petersen, John H. "Recent Research on Latin American University Students." *Latin American Research Review* 5 (Spring 1970): 37-58.

2474 Schiefelbein, Ernesto. "La Subestimación del Problema de la Repetición en América Latina." *Revista del Centro de Estudios Educativos* 7, no. 2 (1977): 79-96.

2475 Schiefelbein, Ernesto. "Repeating: An Overlooked Problem of Latin American Education." *Comparative Education Review* 19 (October 1975): 468-87.

2476 Solari, Aldo. "Secondary Education and the Development of Elites." In *Elites in Latin America*, edited by S. M. Lipset and A. Solari, pp. 457-83. New York: Oxford University Press, 1967.

2477 Suchlicki, Jaime. "Sources of Student Violence in Latin America: An Analysis of the Literature." *Latin American Research Review* 7 (Fall 1972): 31-46.

2478 Walker, Kenneth N. "Political Socialization in Universities." In *Elites in Latin America*, edited by S. M. Lipset and A. Solari, pp. 408-30. New York: Oxford University Press, 1967.

2479 Winn, Ira J. "Paradox and Perspective in Technical Assistance to Latin America." *International Review of Education* 15, no. 1 (1969): 27-41.

Argentina

Books

2480 Iglesias, E. *Administración de la Escuelas Agrotécnicas de la República Argentina*. Santiago de Chile: UNESCO, 1978.

2481 Organization for Economic Cooperation and Development. *Education, Human Resources and Development in Argentina*. Paris: OECD, 1967.

2482 Walter, Richard J. *Student Politics in Argentina: The University Reform and Its Effects 1918-1964*. New York: Basic Books, 1968.

Articles

2483 "The Anniversary of the Cordoba Declaration and its Ramifications in the Argentine." *Minerva* 7 (Autumn-Winter 1968-69): 95-112.

2484 DiTella, Torcuato S. "La Controversia Sobre la Educación en Argentina: Sus Raíces." *Revista Mexicana de Sociologia* 28 (October-December 1966): 855-89.

2485 Inglese, Juan Osvaldo. "El Poder Socializador de la Instituciones Educativas Argentinas." *Aportes* 5 (July 1967): 80-100.

2486 Nasatir, David. "Education and Social Change: The Argentine Case." *Sociology of Education* 39 (Spring 1966): 167-82.

2487 Nasatir, David. "University Experience and Political Unrest of Students in Buenos Aires." *Comparative Education Review* 10 (June 1966): 273-81.

2488 Portes, Alejandro, and Adréan Ross. "Modernization for Emigration: The Medical Brain Drain from Argentina." *Journal of Inter-American Studies and World Affairs* 18 (November 1976): 395-422.

2489 Socolow, Daniel J. "The Argentine Professorate: Occupational Insecurity and Political Interference." *Comparative Education Review* 17 (October 1973): 375-88.

2490 Walker, Kenneth N. "A Comparison of the University Reform Movements in Argentina and Colombia." *Comparative Education Review* 10 (June 1966): 251-72.

2491 Walter, Richard J. "Intellectual Background of the 1918 University Reform in Argentina." *Hispano-American Historical Review* 49 (May 1969): 233-53.

Belize

Articles

2492 Ashcraft, Norman, and Cedric Grant. "The Development and Organization of Education in British Honduras." *Comparative Education Review* 12 (June 1968): 171-79.

Bolivia

Books

2493 Suarez Arnez, Faustino. *Historia de la Educación en Bolivia*. La Paz: Editorial Trabajo, 1963.

Articles

2494 Quevedo, P. M. "Bolivia." In *International Encyclopedia of Higher Education*, edited by A. Knowles, pp. 644-52. San Francisco: Jossey-Bass, 1977.

Brazil

Books

2495 Faust, Augustus F. *Brazil: Education in an Expanding Economy*. Washington, D.C.: U.S. Government Printing Office, 1959.

2496 Haar, Jerry. *The Politics of Higher Education in Brazil.* New York: Praeger, 1977.

2497 Harrell, William A. *Educational Reform in Brazil: The Law of 1961.* Washington, D.C.: U.S. Office of Education, 1968.

2498 Haussman, Fay, and Jerry Haar. *Education in Brazil*. Hamden, Conn.: Archon, 1978.

2499 Havighurst, Robert J., and Aparecida J. Gouveia. *Brazilian Secondary Education and Socio-Economic Development*. New York: Praeger, 1969.

2500 Havighurst, Robert J., and J. Roberto Moreira. *Society and Education in Brazil*. Pittsburgh: University of Pittsburgh Press, 1965.

2501 McNeill, Malvina Rosat. *Guidelines to Problems of Education in Brazil: A Review and Selected Bibliography*. New York: Teacher's College Press, 1970.

Articles

2502 Abu-Merhy, Nair Fortes. "Emerging National Policies for Higher Education in Brazil." In *Higher Education in a Changing World*, edited by B. Holmes and D. Scanlon, pp. 334-48. New York: Harcourt Brace Jovanovich, 1971.

2503 Bonilla, Frank. "Brazil." In *Education and Political Development*, edited by J. S. Coleman, pp. 195-223. Princeton: Princeton University Press, 1964.

2504 Cummings, Richard L. "Education in Brazil." In *Perspectives on World Education*, edited by C. Beck, pp. 320-25. Dubuque, Iowa: Brown, 1970.

2505 DeSouza, H. G. "Brazil." In *International Encyclopedia of Higher Education*, edited by A. Knowles, pp. 669-76. San Francisco: Jossey-Bass, 1977.

2506 Elias, John L. "Adult Literacy Education in Brazil 1961-1964: Método Paulo Freire." *Canadian and International Education* 2 (June 1973): 67-84.

2507 Foracchi, Marialice M. "El Movimiento Estudiantil en la Sociedad Brasileña." *Revista Mexicana de Sociología* 31 (July-September 1969): 609-21.

2508 Goertzel, Ted. "American Imperialism and the Brazilian Student Movement." *Youth and Society* 6 (December 1974): 123-50.

2509 Havighurst, R. J., and P. J. Gouveia. "Socioeconomic Development and Secondary Education in Brazil." *International Review of Education* 12 (1966): 397-415.

2510 Heimer, Franz-Wilhelm. "Education and Politics in Brazil." *Comparative Education Review* 19 (February 1975): 51-67.

2511 Holsinger, Donald B. "Education and the Occupational Attainment Process in Brazil." *Comparative Education Review* 19 (June 1975): 267-75.

2512 Kimball, Solon T. "Primary Education in Brazil." *Comparative Education Review* 4 (June 1960): 49-55.

2513 Moreira, J. Roberto. "Some Social Aspects of Brazilian Education." *Comparative Education Review* 4 (October 1960): 93-97.

2514 Myhr, Robert O. "Nationalism in the Brazilian University Student Movement." *Inter-American Economic Affairs* 22 (Spring 1969): 81-94.

2515 Myhr, Robert O. "The University Student Tradition in Brazil." *Journal of Inter-American Studies and World Affairs* 12 (January 1970): 126-40.

2516 Nascimento e Silva, L. G. D. "Fundamentos para una Política Educacional Brasileña." *Journal of Inter-American Studies* 11 (April 1969): 173-85.

2517 O'Neil, Charles. "Problems of Innovation in Higher Education: The University of Brasília, 1961-1964." *Journal of Latin American Studies and World Affairs* 15 (November 1973): 415-31.

2518 Saunders, John V. D. "Education and Modernization in Brazil." In *The Shaping of Modern Brazil*, edited by Eric N. Baklanoff, pp. 109-41. Baton Rouge: Louisiana State University Press, 1969.

2519 Teiyeira, Anisio. "The Changing Role of Education in Brazilian Society." In *Modern Brazil: New Patterns and Development*, edited by John Saunders, pp. 71-95. Gainesville: University of Florida Press, 1970.

2520 Vasque de Miranda, Glaura. "Women's Labor Force Participation in a Developing Society: The Case of Brazil." *Signs* (Autumn 1977): 261-74.

Chile

Books

2521 Bonilla, Frank, and Myron Glazer. *Student Politics in Chile*. New York: Basic Books, 1970.

2522 Fischer, Kathleen B. *Political Ideology and Educational Reform in Chile, 1964-1976*. Los Angeles: Latin American Studies Center, University of California at Los Angeles, 1979.

2523 Gill, Clark C. *Education and Social Change in Chile*. Washington, D.C.: Department of Health, Education, and Welfare, 1966.

2524 Silvert, Kalman M., and Leonard Riessman. *Education, Class and Nation: The Experience of Chile and Venezuela*. New York: Elsevier, 1976.

Articles

2525 Barrera, Manuel. "Estructura Educativa de la Fuerza de Trabajo Chilena." *Revista del Centro de Estudios Educativos* 7, no. 4 (1977): 1-20.

2526 Barrera, Manuel. "La Mujer Chilena en la Educación y el Trabajo." *Revista del Centro de Estudios Educativos* 7, no. 4 (1977): 1-20.

2527 Barrera, M. "Las Universidades Chilenas y la Educación de los Trabajadores." In *Universidad Contemporánea: Un Intento de Analysis Empirico*, edited by E. Schiefelbein and N. McGinn. Santiago, Chile: Corporación de Promoción Universitaria, 1944.

2528 Campbell, Margaret V. "Education in Chile." *Journal of Inter-American Studies* 1 (July 1959): 353-76.

2529 Glazer, Myron. "The Professional and Political Attitudes of Chilean University Students." *Comparative Education Review* 10 (June 1966): 282-95.

2530 Glazer, Myron, and Penina M. Glazer. "Estudiantes y Profesores en la Reforma Universitaria de Chile." *Aportes* 23 (January 1972): 101-19.

2531 Platt, William J. "Chile's Search for Educational-Economic Consistency." In *The Social Sciences and the Comparative Study of Educational Systems*, edited by J. Fischer, pp. 472-96. Scranton, Pa.: International Textbook, 1970.

2532 Schiefelbein, Ernesto. "Educational Planning Trends in Chile, 1950-1970." *Educational Planning* 2 (March 1976): 4-12.

2533 Schiefelbein, Ernesto. "The Politics of National Planning: The Chilean Case." *Educational Planning* 1 (January 1975): 27-34.

2534 Schiefelbein, Ernesto, and Joseph P. Farrell. "Social and Pedagogical Factors Influencing Survival in the Schools of Chile." *Canadian and International Education* 7 (June 1978): 59-88.

Colombia

Books

2535 Benoit, Andre. *Changing the Educational System: A Colombian Case Study*. Munich, West Germany: Weltforum Verlag, 1974.

2536 Jallade, Jean Pierre. *Public Expenditures on Education and Income Distribution in Colombia*. Baltimore, Md.: Johns Hopkins University Press, 1974.

2537 Renner, Richard R. *Education for a New Colombia*. Washington, D.C.: U.S. Office of Education, 1971.

Articles

2538 Adams, Dale W. "Leadership, Education and Agricultural Development Programs in Colombia." *Inter-American Economic Affairs* 22 (Summer 1968): 87-96.

2539 Cohen, Lucy M. "Woman's Entry into the Professions in Colombia: Selected Characteristics." *Journal of Marriage and the Family* 35 (May 1973): 322-30.

2540 Hanson, Mark. "Reform and Governance in the Ministry of Education: The Case of Colombia." *International Review of Education* 20 (1974): 155-77.

2541 Jallade, Jean Pierre. "Préstamos a Estudiantes en los Países en Desarrollo (Evaluación del Caso Colombiano)." *Revista del Centro de Estudios Educativos* 7, no. 2 (1977): 39-78.

2542 Piñango, Ramon, and John Sudarsky. "Estructura Social, Orientaciones Motivacionales y Educación en Bogotá." *Revista del Centro de Estudios Educativos* 6 (1976): 9-37.

2543 Stern, Larry N., and Monte Palmer. "Political Socialization, Student Attitudes and Political Participation: A Sample of Colombian University Students." *Journal of Developing Areas* 6 (October 1971): 63-76.

2544 Ucrós, Jorge. "El Revolucionarismo en la Universidad Colombiana." *Revista Mexicana de Sociologia* 30 (January-March 1968): 103-15.

2545 Walker, Kenneth N. "A Comparison of University Reform Movements in Argentina and Colombia." *Comparative Education Review* 10 (June 1966): 257-72.

Costa Rica

Books

2546 Gill, Clark C. *The Educational System of Costa Rica*. Washington, D.C.: U.S. Office of Education, 1980.

Articles

2547 Fry, Gerald. "Educational Problems Related to the Economic Development of Costa Rica." *Public and International Affairs* 4 (Spring 1966): 66–87.

Cuba

Books

2548 Carnoy, Martin, and Jorge Werthein. *Cuba: Economic Change and Educational Reform, 1955–1974.* Washington, D.C.: World Bank, 1975.

2549 Fagen, Richard R. *The Transformation of Political Culture in Cuba.* Stanford, Calif.: Stanford University Press, 1969.

2550 Figueroa, Max, et al. *The Basic Secondary School in the Country: An Educational Innovation in Cuba.* Paris: UNESCO Press, 1974.

2551 Gallo, Garcia, Fidel Castro, Oscar Rego, Elio Enriques, et al. *La Educación en Cuba.* Buenos Aires: Editorial Convergencia, 1975.

2552 Gillette, Arthur. *Cuba's Educational Revolution.* London: Fabian Society, 1972.

2553 Kozol, Jonathan. *Children of the Revolution.* New York: Delacourte, 1978.

2554 Leiner, Marvin. *Children Are the Revolution: Day Care in Cuba.* New York: Viking Press, 1974.

2555 Paulston, Rolland. *Preconditions for System-Wide Educational Reform: Learning from the Cuban Experience.* Pittsburgh: University of Pittsburgh International and Development Education Program, 1976.

2556 Paulston, Rolland. *The Educational System of Cuba.* Washington, D.C.: U.S. Office of Education, 1976.

2557 Suchlicki, Jaime. *University Students and Revolution in Cuba, 1920–1968.* Coral Gables, Fla.: University of Miami Press, 1969.

Articles

2558 Bowles, Samuel. "Cuban Education and the Revolutionary Ideology." *Harvard Educational Review* 41 (November 1971): 472–500.

2559 Carnoy, Martin, and Jorge Werthein. "Cambio Económico y Reforma Educativa en Cuba." *Revista del Centro de Estudios Educativos* 7, no. 1 (1977): 9-32.

2560 Carnoy, Martin, and J. Werthein. "Socialist Ideology and the Transformation of Cuban Education." In *Power and Ideology in Education*, edited by J. Karabel and A. H. Halsey, pp. 273-88. New York: Oxford University Press, 1977.

2561 Franco, Zoila. "Women in the Transformation of Cuban Education." *Prospects* 5, no. 3 (1975): 387-90.

2562 Gillette, Arthur. "Cuba: Au-delà de l'éducation rurale integrée." *International Review of Education* 24, no. 2 (1978): 187-96.

2563 Jolly, Richard. "Education: The Pre-Revolutionary Background." In *Cuba: The Economic and Social Revolution*, edited by Dudley Seers, pp. 161-280. Chapel Hill: University of North Carolina Press, 1964.

2564 Ministry of Education. "Recent Developments in Cuban Education." *School and Society* 97 (Summer 1969): 289-93.

2565 Morton, Lawrence, and Beverly Lindsay. "An Overview of Cuban Education." *International Education* 7 (Spring 1978): 24-42.

2566 Paulston, Rolland G. "Cuba." In *International Encyclopedia of Higher Education*, edited by A. Knowles, pp. 1175-84. San Francisco: Jossey-Bass, 1977.

2567 Paulston, Rolland G. "Cultural Revitalization and Educational Change in Cuba." *Comparative Education Review* 16 (October 1972): 474-85.

2568 Paulston, Rolland G. "Education." In *Revolutionary Change in Cuba: Economy, Polity, and Society*, edited by Carmelo Mesa-Lago, pp. 375-98. Pittsburgh: University of Pittsburgh Press, 1971.

2569 Paulston, Rolland G. "Reforma de la educación Latinoamericana: ¿Cuba como Modelo?" *Educación Hoy* 6 (May-August 1976): 106-21.

2570 Periú, María de los Angeles. "Experiencas de la Educación Obrera y Campesina en Cuba." *Cuba Socialista* 5 (February 1965): 18-38.

2571 Read, Gerald H. "The Cuban Revolutionary Offensive in Education." *Comparative Education Review* 14 (June 1970): 131-43.

2572 Read, G. H. "Persisting Problems in Cuban Education." *Phi Delta Kappan* 53 (February 1972): 352-57.

2573 Roucek, Joseph S. "Pro-Communist Revolution in Cuban Education." *Journal of Inter-American Studies* 6 (July 1964): 323-36.

2574 Suchlicki, Jaime. "Stirrings of Cuban Nationalism: The Student Generation of 1930." *Journal of Inter-American Studies* 10 (July 1968): 350-68.

Ecuador

Books

2575 Nemeth, Edward. *The Educational System of Ecuador*. Washington, D.C.: U.S. Office of Education, 1976.

2576 Wilson, Jacques M. P. *The Development of Education in Ecuador*. Coral Gables, Fla.: University of Miami Press, 1971.

Articles

2577 Hurtado, O. "Visión Histórica de la Universidad Ecuateriana." *Estudios Sociales* 11 (1974): 30-45.

2578 Mena Soto, Joaquín. "El Movimiento Educativo en el Ecuador y Sus Problemas." *International Review of Education* 6 (1960): 188-206.

2579 Trujillo, Julio Cesar. "Universidad y Sistemas Sociopolíticos: el Caso de Ecuador." In *La Universidad Latinoamericana: Enfoques Tipológicos*, pp. 182-208. Santiago, Chile: Corporación Promoción Universitaria, 1972.

El Salvador

Books

2580 Mayo, John K., Robert C. Hornik, and Emile G. McAnany. *Educational Reform with Television: The El Salvador Experience*. Stanford, Calif.: Stanford University Press, 1976.

Articles

2581 Pineda, Hernandez, and Leonel Hugo. "Relaciones entre la Educación y el Desarrollo Económico, el Caso Salvadoreño." *Economía Salvadoreña* 15 (January-December 1966): 7-52.

Guatemala

Books

2582 Moore, G. Alexander. *Life Cycles in Atehalan; The Diverse Careers of Certain Guatemalans*. New York: Teacher's College Press, 1973.

2583 Sexton, James D. *Education and Innovation in a Guatemalan Community: San Juan la Laguna*. Los Angeles: Latin American Center, University of California, 1972.

Articles

2584 Benjamin, George K. "Community Goes to School in Guatemala." *Educational Outlook* 26 (March 1952): 91-101.

2585 Escobar, A., and C. Tunnermann Bernheim. "Guatemala." In *International Encyclopedia of Higher Education*, edited by A. Knowles, pp. 1936-40. San Francisco: Jossey-Bass, 1977.

2586 Horst, Oscar H., and Avril McLelland. "The Development of an Educational System in a Rural Guatemalan Community." *Journal of Inter-American Studies* 10 (July 1968): 474-97.

2587 MacVean, Robert B., and F. Nieves O. "Educational Reorganization in Guatemala." *Comparative Education Review* 1 (February 1958): 18-24.

2588 Peterson, John H. "Student Political Activism in Guatemala." *Journal of Inter-American Studies and World Affairs* 13 (January 1971): 78-88.

2589 Williams, David T. "Discrepancy Between Goal and Function in Educational Planning: The Guatemalan Experience." *Comparative Education Review* 13 (June 1969): 196-208.

2590 Williams, David T. "Educational Development in Ghana and Guatemala: Some Problems in Estimating 'Levels of Educational Growth.'" *Comparative Education Review* 10 (October 1966): 462-69.

2591 Williams, David T. "Wastage Rates and Teacher Quality in Guatemalan Primary Schools." *Comparative Education Review* 9 (February 1965): 46-52.

Guyana

Books

2592 Bacchus, M. K. *Education and Socio Cultural Integration in a Plural Society.* Montreal: McGill University, Center for Developing Areas Studies, 1970.

Articles

2593 Bacchus, M. K. "Education, Social Change and Cultural Pluralism: Guyana." *Sociology of Education* 42 (Fall 1969): 368-85.

2594 Baksh, Ahamad. "The Mobility of Degree Level Graduates of the University of Guyana." *Comparative Education Review* 10 (March 1974): 65-86.

2595 Craig, Dennis R. "English in Secondary Education in a Former British Colony: A Case Study of Guyana." *Caribbean Studies* 10 (January 1971): 113-51.

Haiti

Books

2596 Dale, G. *Education in the Republic of Haiti.* Washington, D.C.: U.S. Office of Education, 1959.

Articles

2597 Clark, G. P., and D. Purcell. "Tangled Roots of Haiti's Educational System." *International Educational and Cultural Exchange* 6 (Summer 1970): 48-56.

2598 Clark, George P., and Donald Purcell. "The Dynamic Conservatism of Haitian Education." *Phylon* 36 (Spring 1975): 46-54.

2599 Ronceray, Hubert de. "Algunos Aspectos de la Ideología Educacional en Haiti." *América Latina* 11 (August-December 1968): 49-84.

Honduras

Articles

2600 "Honduras." In *International Encyclopedia of Higher Education*, edited by A. Knowles, pp. 2047-52. San Francisco: Jossey-Bass, 1977.

Mexico

Books

2601 Barranco, Manuel. *Mexico: Its Educational Problems—Suggestions for Their Solution*. New York: A.M.S. Press, 1972.

2602 Booth, George C. *Mexico's School-made Society*. New York: Greenwood Press, 1969.

2603 Camp, Roderic A. *Mexico's Leaders: Their Education and Recruitment*. Tucson: University of Arizona Press, 1980.

2604 de Ibarrola N., María. *Pobreza y Aspiraciones Escolares*. Mexico City: Centro de Estudios Educativos, 1970.

2605 Gill, Clark C. *Education in a Changing Mexico*. Washington, D.C.: U.S. Office of Education, 1969.

2606 Heath, Shirley B. *Telling Tongues: Language Policy in Mexico, Colony to Nation*. New York: Teacher's College Press, 1972.

2607 King, Richard, et al. *The Provincial Universities of Mexico: An Analysis of Growth and Development*. New York: Praeger, 1971.

2608 Levy, Daniel C. *University and Government in Mexico: Autonomy in an Authoritarian System*. New York: Praeger, 1980.

2609 McGinn, Noel F. *The Technology of Instruction in Mexican Universities*. New York: Education and World Affairs, 1968.

2610 Myers, Charles Nash. *Education and National Development in Mexico*. Princeton: Industrial Relations Section, Princeton University, 1965.

2611 Myers, Charles Nash. *U.S. University Activity Abroad: Implications of the Mexican Case*. New York: Education and World Affairs, 1968.

2612 Osborn, T. N., II. *Higher Education in Mexico.* El Paso: Texas Western Press, 1976.

2613 Sanchez, G. I. *The Development of Higher Education in Mexico.* Westport, Conn.: Greenwood Press, 1970.

2614 Vázquez de Knauth, Josefina. *Nacionalism y Educacion en Mexico.* Mexico City: El Colegio de México, 1970.

Articles

2615 Britton, John A. "Urban Education and Social Change in the Mexican Revolution, 1931-1940." *Journal of Latin American Studies* 5 (November 1973): 233-45.

2616 Camp, Roderic. "Education and Political Recruitment in Mexico: The Alemán Generation." *Journal of Inter-American Studies and World Affairs* 18 (August 1976): 295-322.

2617 Carnoy, Martin. "Earnings and Schooling in Mexico." *Economic Development and Cultural Change* 15 (July 1967): 408-19.

2618 Elu de Lenero, Carmen. "Educación y Participación de la Mujer en la P. T. A. de México." *Revista del Centro de Estudios Educativos* 7, no. 1 (1977): 71-83.

2619 Glaván de Terrazas, Luz Elena. "Bibliographía Comentado sobre la Educación Mexicana en la Etapa Revolucionaria: 1910-1930." *Revista del Centro de Estudios Educativos* 7, no. 2 (1977): 135-62.

2620 Munoz Izquierdo, Carlos Rodriguez, and P. Gerardo Rodriquez. "Origen, Distribución y Eficiencia del Gasto Educativo en Mexico." *Revista del Centro de Estudios Educativos* 7, no. 3 (1977): 1-54.

2621 Pescador, J. Angel. "El Efecto Redistributivo del Gasto en Educación Superior en México: Una Estimación Preliminar." *Revista del Centro de Estudios Educativos* 7, no. 3 (1977): 55-78.

2622 Rodriguez, Pedro Gerardo, and Andres Sotelo Marban. "La Enseñanza Superior en Mexico, 1975-1976." *Revista del Centro de Estudios Educativos* 7, no. 3 (1977): 157-77.

2623 Schoijet, Mauricio. "The Condition of Mexican Science." *Minerva* 17 (Autumn 1979): 381-412.

2624 Suárez, Enrique Contreras. "La Adecuación Educación-ocupación. Un Estudio sobre la Educación Técnica Mecánica a Nivel Medio en el Distrito Federal." *Revista Mexicana de Sociología* 31 (January-March 1969): 93-109.

2625 Treviño, Victor L., and Rafael González Montemayor. "La Educación del Obrero Manual en Mexico." *Revista Mexicana de Sociología* 16 (January-April 1954): 83-92.

2626 Van Patten, James. "Mexico." In *World Perspectives on Education*, edited by C. Beck, pp. 365-74. Dubuque, Iowa: Brown, 1970.

2627 Vaughan, Mary K. "Women, Class and Education in Mexico, 1880-1928." *Latin American Perspectives* 4 (Winter-Spring 1977): 135-52.

Panama

Books

2628 Goldrich, Daniel. *Sons of the Establishment: Elite Youth in Panama and Costa Rica*. Chicago, Ill.: Rand McNally, 1966.

2629 Guiraud, H. H. *Educación y Empleo en Panama*. Paris: UNESCO, 1976.

2630 Harper, Alda Alexander. *Tracing the Course of Growth and Development in Educational Policy for the Canal Zone Colored Schools, 1905-1955*. Ann Arbor: University of Michigan, 1974.

Articles

2631 Goldrich, D. "Peasant Sons in City Schools: an Inquiry into the Politics of Urbanization in Panama and Costa Rica." *Human Organization* 23 (Winter 1964): 328-33.

2632 Perez-Venero, Mirna M. "The Education of Women on the Isthmus of Panama." *Journal of the West* 12 (April 1973): 325-34.

Paraguay

Articles

2633 Apmann, Robert P. "Engineering Education in Paraguay." *Journal of Developing Areas* 8 (January 1974): 257-70.

2634 Poletti Liuzzi, D. A. "Paraguay." In *International Encyclopedia of Higher Education*, edited by A. Knowles, pp. 3149-58. San Francisco: Jossey-Bass, 1977.

2635 Rivarola, D. M. "Universidad y Estudiantes en una Sociedad Tradicional." *Aportes* No. 12 (April 1969): 47-84.

2636 Sarubbi, Mario S. "La Educación de Adultos en Paraguay." *Revista Interamericana Educación de Adultos* 1, no. 3 (1978): 359-91.

2637 Winkler, Donald R. "The Distribution of Educational Resources in Paraguay: Implications for Equality of Opportunity." *Comparative Education Review* 24 (February 1980): 73-86.

Peru

Books

2638 Alberti, Georgio, and Julio Cotler. *Aspectos Sociales de la Educación Rural en el Perú*. Lima: Instituto de Estudios Perunas, 1972.

2639 Bizot, Judith. *Educational Reform in Peru*. Paris: UNESCO, 1975.

2640 Churchill, Stacy. *The Peruvian Model of Innovation: The Reform of Basic Education*. Paris: UNESCO, 1976.

2641 Kay, George Andrews. *Educational Finance and Educational Reform in Peru*. Paris: UNESCO, 1976.

2642 Organization for Economic Cooperation and Development. *Human Resources, Education and Economic Development in Peru; Forecasts of Manpower Requirements in 1980 and of Educational Development Prospects*. Paris: UNESCO: 1970.

2643 Paulston, R. G. *Society, Schools and Progress in Peru*. Elmsford, N.Y.: Pergamon Press, 1971.

Articles

2644 Cornehls, James V. "Forecasting Manpower and Educational Requirements for Economic and Social Development in Peru." *Comparative Education Review* 12 (February 1968): 1-27.

2645 Drysdale, Robert. "Education for Rural Society in Transition: The Case of Peru." *Canadian and International Education* 3 (December 1974): 74-98.

2646 Drysdale, Robert, and Robert Myers. "Continuity and Change: Peruvian Education." In *The Peruvian Experiment*, edited by Abraham Lowenthal, pp. 254-301. Princeton: Princeton University Press, 1975.

2647 Epstein, Erwin H. "Education and Peruanidad: Internal Colonialism in the Peruvian Highlands." *Comparative Education Review* 15 (June 1971): 188-201.

2648 Hazen, Dan C. "The Politics of Schooling in the Nonliterate Third World: The Case of Highland Peru." *History of Education Quarterly* 18 (Winter 1978): 419-44.

2649 Myers, Robert G. "International Education, Emigration, and National Policy (A Longitudinal Case Study of Peruvians Trained in the United States)." *Comparative Education Review* 17 (February 1973): 71-90.

2650 Paulston, Rolland. "Educational Stratification and Cultural Hegemony in Peru." In *Power and Ideology in Education*, edited by J. Karabel and A. H. Halsey, pp. 412-22. New York: Oxford University Press, 1977.

2651 Paulston, Rolland G. "Sociocultural Constraints on Educational Development in Peru." *Journal of Developing Areas* 5 (April 1971): 410-16.

2652 Paulston, Rolland G. "United States Educational Intervention in Peru." *Paedagogica Historica* 11 (1971): 426-54.

2653 Picón-Espinoza, César. "Education Reform in Peru." In *Educational Reform: Experiences and Prospects*, pp. 177-87. Paris: UNESCO, 1979.

2654 Primov, George. "The School as an Obstacle to Structural Integration Among Peruvian Indians." *Education and Urban Society* 10 (February 1978): 209-22.

2655 Salazar, Juana Consuelo Ibáñez. "Non-formal Education Programs for Children and Parents in Peru." *Prospects* 7, no. 4 (1977): 549-56.

2656 Salazar Bondy, Augusto. "On Educational Reform in Peru." *Prospects* 2 (Winter 1972): 383-91.

2657 Wallace, James M. "Progress Without Development: Rural Education at the Cultural Interface in Highland Peru." *Anthropology and Education Quarterly* 8 (May 1976): 14-18.

2658 Van den Berghe, Pierre. "Education, Class and Ethnicity in Southern Peru: Revolutionary Colonialism." In *Education and Colonialism*, edited by P. G. Altbach and G. P. Kelly, pp. 270-300. New York: Longmans, 1978.

Puerto Rico

Books

2659 Beirne, Charles J. *The Problem of Americanization in the Catholic Schools of Puerto Rico*. Rio Piedras: Universidad de Puerto Rico, 1975.

2660 Brameld, Theodore. *The Remaking of a Culture: Life and Education in Puerto Rico*. New York: Harper and Row, 1959.

2661 Cebollero, Pedro Angel. *A School Language Policy for Puerto Rico*. New York: Arno Press, 1975.

2662 Epstein, Erwin H., ed. *Politics and Education in Puerto Rico: A Documentary Survey of the Language Issue*. Metuchen, N.J.: Scarecrow Press, 1970.

2663 Fernandez Vanga, Epifanio. *El Idioma de Puerto Rico y el Idioma Escolar de Puerto Rico*. New York: Arno Press, 1975.

2664 Leibman, Arthur. *The Politics of Puerto Rican University Students*. Austin: University of Texas Press, 1970.

2665 Mellado Parsons, Ramón. *La Educación en Puerto Rico*. Hato Rey, Puerto Rico: Romallo, 1976.

2666 Negrón de Montilla, Aida. *Americanization in Puerto Rico and the Public-school System, 1900-1930*. Rio Piedras, Puerto Rico: Editorial Edil, 1970.

2667 Osuna, Juan José. *A History of Education in Puerto Rico*. Rio Piedras: Editorial de la Universidad de Puerto Rico, 1949.

2668 Parker, Franklin, and June Parker, eds. *Education in Puerto Rico and of Puerto Ricans in the USA: Abstracts of American Doctoral Dissertations*. San Juan, Puerto Rico: Inter American University Press, 1978.

2669 Quintero Alfaro, Angel A. *Educación y Cambio Social en Puerto Rico*. Rio Piedras, Puerto Rico: Editorial Edil, 1972.

Articles

2670 Carnoy, Martin. "The Quality of Education, Examination Performance and Urban-Rural Income Differentials in Puerto Rico." *Comparative Education Review* 14 (October 1970): 335-49.

2671 Carnoy, Martin. "The Rate of Return to Schooling and the Increase in Human Resources in Puerto Rico." *Comparative Education Review* 16 (February 1972): 68-86.

2672 Cunningham, Ineke. "The Relationship between Modernity of Students in a Puerto-Rican High School and Their Academic Performance, Peers and Parents." *International Journal of Comparative Sociology* 14 (September-December 1973): 203-21.

2673 Epstein, Erwin H. "English and Politics in Puerto Rican Schools." *Educational Forum* 33 (January 1969): 325-30.

2674 Epstein, Erwin H. "La Enseñanza del Idioma y el Status Político de Puerto Rico." *Revista de Ciencias Sociales* 11 (September 1967): 293-314.

2675 Epstein, Erwin H. "Linguistic Orientation and Changing Values in Puerto Rico." *International Journal of Comparative Sociology* 9 (March 1968): 61-76;

2676 Epstein, Erwin H. "National Identity and the Language Issue in Puerto Rico." *Comparative Education Review* 11 (June 1967): 133-44.

2677 Epstein, Erwin H. "Social Change and Learning English in Puerto Rico." In *Schools in Transition*, edited by A. Kazamias and E. H. Epstein, pp. 356-69. Boston: Allyn and Bacon, 1968.

2678 Heifetz, Robert. "Manpower Planning: A Case Study from Puerto Rico." *Comparative Education Review* 8 (June 1964): 28-36.

2679 Liebman, Arthur. "The Student Left in Puerto Rico." *Journal of Social Issues* 27, no. 1 (1971): 167–81.

2680 Sussman, Leila. "Democratization and Class Segregation in Puerto Rican Schooling: The U.S. Model Transplanted." *Sociology of Education* 41 (Fall 1968): 321–41.

Uruguay

Articles

2681 Pelaez, Leon Cortiñas. "Autonomy and Student Co-government in the University of Uruguay." *Comparative Education Review* 7 (October 1963): 166–72.

Venezuela

Books

2682 Albornoz, Orlando. *Teoría y Praxis de la Educación Superior Venezolana.* Caracas: Universidad Central de Venezuela, 1979.

2683 Arnove, Robert F. *Student Alienation: A Venezuelan Study.* New York: Praeger, 1971.

2684 Burroughs, G. E. R. *Education in Venezuela.* London: David and Charles, 1974.

2685 Centro de Estudios Sociales con la Cooperación AITEC. *La Participación Feminina en el Sistema Educacional Venezolano.* Documento Técnico No. 2. Caracas, 1975.

2686 McGinn, Noel F., and Russell G. Davis. *Build a Mill, Build a City, Build a School: Industrialization, Urbanization, and Education in Ciudad Guayana.* Cambridge, Mass.: M.I.T. Press, 1969.

2687 Nemeth, Edward J. *The Educational System of Venezuela.* Washington, D.C.: U.S. Office of Education, 1976.

Articles

2688 Albornoz, Orlando. "Higher Education and the Politics of Development in

Venezuela." *Journal of Inter-American Studies and World Affairs* 19 (August 1977): 291–315.

2689 Arnove, Robert. "Students in Venezuelan Politics, 1958-1974." In *Venezuela: Is Democracy Institutionalized?*, edited by David J. Myers and John D. Martz, pp. 197-214. New York: Praeger, 1977.

2690 Echevarría-Salvat, Oscar A. "Educación y Desarrollo—el Caso de Venezuela." *Journal of Inter-American Studies* 10 (October 1968): 587-96.

2691 Hanson, Mark. "Characteristics of Centralized Education in Latin America: The Case of Venezuela." *Comparative Education Review* 6 (March 1970): 49-60.

2692 Hanson, Mark. "A Social Systems Analysis of Educational Subsystems in Venezuela." *International Review of Education* 18, no. 2 (1972): 373-90.

2693 Hanson, Mark. "Decentralization and Regionalization in the Ministry of Education: The Case of Venezuela." *International Review of Education* 22 (1976): 155-77.

West Indies

Books

2694 Figueroa, John F. *Society, Schools and Progress in the West Indies*. New York: Pergamon Press, 1971.

2695 Figueroa, Peter, and Ganga Persaud, eds. *Sociology of Education: A Caribbean Reader*. London: Oxford University Press, 1977.

2696 Gordon, S. C. *Century of West Indian Education: A Source Book*. Essex, England: Longmans, 1963.

2697 Gordon, S. C. *Reports and Repercussions in West Indian Education*. Aylesbury, England: Ginn, 1968.

2698 Irvine, J. C. *Report of the West Indies Committee of the Commission on Higher Education in the Colonies*. London: H.M.S.O., 1945.

2699 Rubin, Vera, and Marisa Zavalloni. *We Wish to Be Looked Upon: A Study of the Aspirations of Youth in a Developing Society.* New York: Teacher's College Press, 1969.

2700 Thomas, L. *Proposed Network of Educational Innovation for Development in the Caribbean: Report of Mission.* Paris: UNESCO, 1977.

2701 Wilgus, A. C., ed. *The Caribbean Contemporary Education.* Gainesville: University of Florida Press, 1960.

2702 Williams, E. *Education in the British West Indies.* New York: University Place Book Shop, 1968.

Articles

2703 Bacchus, M. K. "The Development of Educational Planning with Special Reference to the West Indies." *Teacher Education* (February 1967): 221-30, and (May 1967): 36-62.

2704 Bird, Edris. "Adult Education and the Development of Women in the Caribbean." *Convergence* 8 (1975): 57-68.

2705 Connell-Smith, Gordon. "The United States and the Caribbean: Colonial Patterns, Old and New." *Journal of Latin American Studies* 4 (1972): 113-22.

2706 Epstein, Erwin H. "Ecological Factors in Comparative Analysis: Effects on School Achievement in St. Lucia." *Comparative Education Review* 14 (October 1970): 312-21.

2707 Epstein, Erwin H., and Burton A. Weisbrod. "Parasitic Disease and Academic Performance of School Children." *Social and Economic Studies* 23 (December 1974): 551-70.

2708 Fergus, Howard A. "Restructuring Education in Montserrat and St. Kitts." *Caribbean Journal of Education* 5 (January-April 1978): 32-46.

2709 Maraj, James A. "A Caribbean Plan for Primary Education." *Caribbean Quarterly* 13 (June 1967): 27-32.

2710 Rooke, Patricia T. "The Pedagogy of Conversion, Missionary Education to Slaves in the British West-Indies, 1800-1833." *Paedagogica Historica* 18 (1978): 356-74.

2711 Sherlock, Philip. "Caribbean, Regional Analysis." In *International Encyclopedia of Higher Education*, edited by A. Knowles, pp. 811-15. San Francisco: Jossey-Bass, 1977.

2712 Verner, Joel Gordon. "The Recruitment of Cabinet Ministers in the Former British Caribbean: A Five-Country Study." *Journal of Developing Areas* 7 (July 1973): 635-52.

BARBADOS

Articles

2713 Clarke, Desmond. "Barbados." In *International Encyclopedia of Higher Education*, edited by A. Knowles, pp. 600-7. San Francisco: Jossey-Bass, 1977.

DOMINICAN REPUBLIC

Articles

2714 Duryea, E. D. "University Reform in the Dominican Republic." *Teachers College Record* 67 (November 1965): 129-33.

2715 Schiefelbein, Ernesto. "Educación y Empleo en Santo Domingo." *Educación Hoy* 5 (May-June 1975): 3-20.

2716 Schiefelbein, Ernesto. "Las Relaciones entre Educacíon y Empleo en la República Dominican." *Revista del Centro de Estudios Educativos* 7, no. 3 (1977): 126-34.

JAMAICA

Books

2717 Foner, Nancy. *Status and Power in Rural Jamaica: A Study of Educational and Political Change*. New York: Teacher's College Press, 1973.

Articles

2718 Campbell, Carl. "Denominationalism and the Mico Charity Schools in Jamaica, 1835-1842." *Caribbean Studies* 10 (January 1971): 152-72.

2719 Foner, Nancy. "Competition, Conflict and Education in Rural Jamaica." *Human Organization* 31 (Winter 1972): 395-402.

2720 Girling, Robert. "Technology and the Dependent State: Reflections on the Jamaican Case." *Latin-American Perspectives* 3 (Fall 1976): 54-64.

2721 Howells, C. A. "Authoritarianism in Jamaican Education." *Caribbean Journal of Education* 5 (January-April 1978): 71-80.

2722 Manley, D. R. "The School Certificate Examination, Jamaica 1962." *Social and Economic Studies* 18 (March 1969): 54-71.

2723 Miller, Errol. "Ambitions of Jamaican Adolescents and the School System." *Caribbean Quarterly* 13 (March 1967): 29-33.

2724 Smith, M. G. "Education and Occupational Choice in Rural Jamaica." *Social and Economic Studies* 9 (September 1960): 332-54.

2725 Turner, Trevor A. "The Socialization Intent in Colonial Jamaican Education, 1867-1911." *Caribbean Journal of Education* 4 (January-April 1977): 50-84.

TRINIDAD AND TOBAGO

Books

2726 Oxall, Ivar. *Black Intellectuals Come to Power: The Rise of Creole Nationalism in Trinidad and Tobago*. Cambridge, Mass.: Schenkman, 1968.

Articles

2727 Cross, Malcolm, and Allan M. Schwartzbaum. "Social Mobility and Secondary School Selection in Trinidad and Tobago." *Social and Economic Studies* 18 (June 1969): 189-207.

2728 Newton, E., and R. H. E. Braithwaite. "New Directions in Education in Trinidad and Tobago—Challenge and Response." *Comparative Education* 11 (October 1975): 237-46.

2729 Roberts, G. W. "A Note on School Enrollment in Trinidad and Tobago: 1960." *Social and Economic Studies* 16 (June 1967): 113-26.

2730 Schwartzbaum, Allan H., and Malcolm Cross. "Secondary School Environment and Development: The Case of Trinidad and Tobago." *Social and Economic Studies* 19 (September 1970): 368-88.

MIDDLE EAST AND NORTH AFRICA
General

Books

2731 Al-Attas, S. N., ed. *Aims and Objectives of Islamic Education*. London: Hodder and Stoughton, 1979.

2732 Arab Information Center. *Education in the Arab States*. New York: Arab Information Center, 1966.

2733 *Comparative Statistical Data on Education in the Arab States: An Analysis 1960/61–1967/68*. Beirut: Regional Center for Educational Planning and Administration, 1961-68.

2734 Dodge, Bayard. *History of Education in the Arab World*. New York: Arab Information Center, 1963.

2735 El-Ghannam, Mohd. A. *Education in the Arab Region Viewed from the 1970 Marrakesh Conference*. Paris: UNESCO, 1971.

2736 El-Koussy, Abdul Aziz H. *A Survey of Educational Progress in the Arab States*. Beirut: Regional Center for the Advanced Training of Educational Personnel in the Arab States, 1966.

2737 Harby, Mohammed K., Mohammed El-Hadj Affifi, and M. A. El-Ghannam. *Technical Education in the Arab States*. Paris: UNESCO, 1965.

2738 Husain, S. S., and S. A. Ashraf. *Crisis in Muslim Education*. London: Hodder and Stoughton, 1979.

2739 Keddie, Nikki R. *Scholars, Saints and Sufis: Muslim Religious Institutions in the Middle East Since 1500*. Berkeley: University of California Press, 1972.

2740 Lerner, Daniel. *The Passing of Traditional Society: Modernizing the Middle East*. Glencoe, Ill.: Free Press, 1958.

2741 Mathews, Roderick D., and Matta Akrawi. *Education in Arab Countries of the Near East*. Washington, D.C.: American Council on Education, 1949.

2742 Mertz, R. A. *Education and Manpower in the Arabian Gulf*. Washington, D.C.: American Friends of the Middle East, 1972.

2743 Nakosteen, Mehdi. *History of Islamic Origins of Western Education*. Boulder: University of Colorado Press, 1964.

2744 Quabain, Fahim I. *Education and Science in the Arab World*. Baltimore, Md.: Johns Hopkins University Press, 1969.

2745 Shalaby, Ahmad. *History of Muslim Education*. Beirut: Dar-el-Kashaf, 1954.

2746 Szyliowicz, Joseph S. *Education and Modernization in the Middle East*. Ithaca, N.Y.: Cornell University Press, 1973.

2747 Tibawi, A. L. *Arabic and Islamic Themes: Historical, Educational and Literary Studies*. London: Luzac, 1976.

2748 Tibawi, A. L. *Islamic Education: Its Traditions and Modernization into the Arab National Systems*. London: Luzac, 1972.

2749 Totah, K. *The Contributions of the Arabs to Education*. New York: Columbia University Teacher's College, 1926.

2750 Tritton, A. S. *Materials on Muslim Education in the Middle Ages*. London: Luzac, 1957.

2751 Waardenburg, Jean-Jacques. *Les universités dans le monde arabe actuel*, 2 vols. Paris: Mouton, 1966.

2752 Werdelin, Ingvar, et al. *A Statistical Panorama of Education in the Arab Countries*. Beirut: Regional Center for Educational Planning and Administration in the Arab Countries, 1972.

Articles

2753 Abdul-Hadi, Mohammed. "The New Trends in Arab Education." *Comparative Education Review* 1 (February 1958): 24–31.

2754 Abu-Laban, Baha, and Sharon McIrvin Abu-Laban. "Education and Development in the Arab World." *Journal of Developing Areas* 10 (April 1976): 285–304.

2755 Akrawi, Matta. "Arab World." In *International Encyclopedia of Higher Education*, edited by A. Knowles, pp. 361–79. San Francisco: Jossey-Bass, 1977.

2756 Akrawi, M., and A. A. El-Koussy. "Recent Trends in Arab Education." *International Review of Education* 17, no. 2 (1971): 181-96.

2757 Clift, Virgil A. "Social and Cultural Factors Relating to Education in the Middle East." *Journal of Educational Sociology* 35 (September 1961): 18-26.

2758 Dorozynski, Alexandre. "Science, Technology and Education on the Arabian Peninsula." *Impact of Science on Society* 26 (May-September 1976): 193-97.

2759 El-Ghannam, Mohammed A. "The Administrative Crisis in Education in the Arab Countries." *Prospects* 7, no. 1 (1977): 104-12.

2760 El-Koussy, Abdul Aziz Hamid. "For a Self-Criticism of Education in the Arab Countries." *Prospects* 3 (Spring 1973): 57-66.

2761 El-Koussy, A. A. H. "Recent Trends and Developments in Primary and Secondary Education in the Arab World." *International Review of Education* 13 (1967): 198-211.

2762 Goldziher, Ignaz. "Muslim Education." In *Encyclopedia of Religion and Ethics*, pp. 198-212. Edinburgh: Clark, 1912.

2763 Haddad, F. S. "Early Arab Theory of Instruction." *International Journal of Middle East Studies* 5 (June 1974): 240-59.

2764 Halloway, Owen. "University Students of the Middle East." *Journal of the Royal Central Asian Society* 38 (January 1951): 10-20.

2765 Kettani, M. Ali. "Engineering Education in the Arab World." *Middle East Journal* 28 (Autumn 1974): 441-51.

2766 Kinany, A. K. H. "Problèmes d'éducation dans le monde arabe." *International Review of Education* 8 (1963): 276-91.

2767 Lengyel, Emil. "Educational Revolution in the Middle East." *Teachers College Record* 64 (1962): 99-105.

2768 Mustaffa-Kedah, Omar. "The Education of Women in the Arab States." *Literacy Discussion* 6 (Winter 1975-76): 119-39.

2769 Szyliowicz, Joseph S. "Education and Political Development in Turkey,

Egypt, and Iran." *Comparative Education Review* 13 (June 1969): 150-66.

2770 Waardenburg, Jean-Jacques. "Some Historical Aspects of Muslim Higher Education and Their Relationship to Islam." *Numen* 12 (January 1965): 96-138.

2771 Wheeler, D. K. "Educational Problems in Arab Countries." *International Review of Education* 12 (1966): 300-16.

Algeria

Books

2772 Baghli, Sid-Ahmed. *Aspects of Algerian Cultural Policy*. Paris: UNESCO, 1978.

2773 Forrester, Anne N., and Charles C. Haunch. *Educational Data: Algeria*. Washington, D.C.: U.S. Office of Education, 1964.

2774 Zerdoumi, N. *Enfants d'hier: L'éducation de l'enfant de milieu traditionnel algérien*. Paris: Maspero, 1970.

Articles

2775 Belguedj, M. "Algeria." In *International Encyclopedia of Higher Education*, edited by A. Knowles, pp. 311-19. San Francisco: Jossey-Bass, 1977.

2776 Colonna, F. "Le système d'enseignement en Algérie coloniale." *Archives Européenes de Sociologie* 13 (1972): 195-220.

2777 Colonna, F. "Verdict scolaire et position de classe dans l'Afrique coloniale." *Revue Française de Sociologie* 14 (April-June 1973): 180-201.

2778 Gillespie, Joan, and Manfred Halpern. "Algeria." In *The Educated African*, edited by Helen Kitchen, pp. 11-22. New York: Praeger, 1962.

2779 Heggoy, Alf A. "Arab Education in Colonial Algeria." *Journal of African Studies* 2 (Summer 1975): 149-60.

2780 Heggoy, Alf A. "Education in French Algeria: An Essay on Cultural Conflict." *Comparative Education Review* 17 (June 1973): 180-97.

2781 Knight, Eleanor J. "Education in French North Africa." *Islamic Quarterly* 2 (December 1955): 294-308.

2782 Peroncel-Hugoz, J. P. "L'enseignement en Algérie." *Revue Française des Etudes Politiques Africaines* 52 (April 1970): 21-76.

2783 Samaan, Wahib I. "Algeria." In *Encyclopedia of Education*, edited by Lee C. Deighton, vol. 1, pp. 169-71. New York: Macmillan, 1971.

2784 Schliesendinger, Odile. "Politique de l'éducation en Algérie." *Etudes* 339 (October 1973): 371-82.

2785 Remli, Abderrahmane. "Educational Reform: Constraints and Obstacles: The Algerian Experience." In *Educational Reform: Experiences and Prospects*, pp. 212-28. Paris: UNESCO.

Bahrain

Articles

2786 "Bahrain, State of." In *International Encyclopedia of Higher Education*, edited by A. Knowles, pp. 594-95. San Francisco: Jossey-Bass, 1977.

2787 Winder, R. Bayly. "Education in Al-Bahrayn." In *The World of Islam*, edited by James Kritzeck and R. Bayly Winder, pp. 283-335. New York: St. Martin's Press, 1960.

Egypt

Books

2788 Boktor, Amir. *The Development and Expansion of Education in the United Arab Republic*. Cairo: American University in Cairo Press, 1963.

2789 Dodge, Bayard. *Al-Azhar: A Millenium of Muslim Learning*. Washington, D.C.: Middle East Institute Press, 1961.

2790 el-Sa'id, S. M. *The Expansion of Higher Education in the United Arab Republic*. Cairo: Cairo University Press, 1960.

2791 Galt, Russel. *The Effects of Centralization of Education in Modern*

Egypt. Cairo: Department of Education, American University of Cairo, 1936.

2792 Heyworth, Dunne J. *An Introduction to the History of Education in Modern Egypt.* London: Luzac, 1938.

2793 Hyde, Georgie D. M. *Education in Modern Egypt: Ideals and Realities.* London: Routledge and Kegan Paul, 1978.

2794 Korb, Yusuf S. *Science and Science Education in Egyptian Society.* New York: Teacher's College Press, 1958.

2795 Matveyev, A., et al. *Arab Republic of Egypt: The Feasibility of Establishing Technical Universities in the Arab Republic of Egypt.* Paris: UNESCO, 1972.

2796 Radwan, Abu Al-Futouh Ahmed. *Old and New Forces in Egyptian Education.* New York: Teacher's College Press, 1951.

2797 Tignor, Robert L. *Modernization and British Rule in Egypt: 1882-1914.* Princeton: Princeton University Press, 1966.

Articles

2798 Crecelius, Daniel. "Al-Azhar in the Revolution." *Middle East Journal* 20 (Winter 1966): 31-49.

2799 Efrat, Moshe. "Educational Progress in the U. A. R." *New Outlook* 11 (October 1968): 24-31.

2800 El-Sayed, Afaf Lutzi. "The Role of the Ulama in Egypt During the Early Nineteenth Century." In P. M. Holt, *Political and Social Change in Modern Egypt.* London: Oxford University Press, 1968.

2801 Faksh, Mahmud A. "Education and Elite Recruitment: An Analysis of Egypt's Post 1952 Political Elite." *Comparative Education Review* 20 (June 1976): 140-50.

2802 Faksh, Mahmud A. "An Historical Survey of the Educational System in Egypt." *International Review of Education* 22, no. 2 (1976): 234-45.

2803 Ghobrial, G. B. "Egypt: UAR." In *World Perspectives on Education*, edited by C. Beck, pp. 393-406. Dubuque, Iowa: Brown, 1970.

2804 Haim, Sylvia G. "State and University in Egypt." In *Universität und Modern Gesellschaft*, edited by Chauncy D. Harris and Max Horkheimer, pp. 99-118. Frankfurt am Main: Ludwig Oehms, 1959.

2805 Howard-Merriam, Kathleen. "Women, Education and the Professions in Egypt." *Comparative Education Review* 23 (June 1979): 256-70.

2806 Kerr, Malcolm. "Egypt." In *Education and Political Development*, edited by J. S. Coleman, pp. 169-94. Princeton: Princeton University Press, 1964.

2807 Kimsey, David. "Efforts for Educational Synthesis Under Colonial Rule: Egypt and Tunisia." *Comparative Education Review* 15 (June 1971): 172-87.

2808 Kraemer, J. "Tradition and Reform at al-Azhar University." *Middle Eastern Affairs* 7 (March 1956): 89-94.

2809 Najjar, F. M. "State and University in Egypt During the Period of Socialist Transformation, 1961-1967." *Review of Politics* 38 (January 1976): 57-87.

2810 Reid, Donald M. "Educational and Career Choices of Egyptian Students." *International Journal of Middle East Studies* 8 (July 1977): 349-78.

2811 Samaan, Sodek. "Some Aspects of Education in Egypt." *Teachers College Record* 58 (December 1956): 175-81.

2812 Smock, A. C., and N. H. Youssef. "Egypt: From Seclusion to Limited Participation." In *Women: Roles and Status in Eight Countries*, edited by J. Z. Giele and A. C. Smock. New York: Wiley, 1977.

2813 Sorour, A. H. "Egypt." In *International Encyclopedia of Higher Education*, edited by A. Knowles, pp. 1408-16. San Francisco: Jossey-Bass, 1977.

2814 Steppat, Fritz. "National Education Projects in Egypt Before the British Occupation." In *Beginnings of Modernization in the Middle East*, edited by W. R. Polk and R. C. Chambers, pp. 281-98. Chicago: University of Chicago Press, 1966.

Israel

Books

2815 Apanasewicz, Nellie, and Seymour M. Rosen. *The Educational System of Israel*. Washington, D.C.: U.S. Office of Education, 1971.

2816 Bentwick, J. S. *Education in Israel*. London: Routledge and Kegan Paul, 1965.

2817 Adler, C. *The Education of the Disadvantaged in Israel*. Jerusalem: Hebrew University, School of Education, NCJW Research Institute for Innovation in Education, 1975.

2818 Cohen, J., et al. *Research in Action*. Jerusalem: Hebrew University, School of Education, NCJW Research Institute for Innovation in Education, 1979.

2819 Eisenstadt, S. N. *Some Problems of Educating a National Minority: A Study of Israeli Education of Arabs*. Jerusalem: Hebrew University, 1971.

2820 Kleinberger, A. E. *Society, Schools and Progress in Israel*. London: Pergamon Press, 1969.

2821 Lewis, Arnold. *Power, Poverty and Education: An Ethnography of Schooling in an Israeli Town*. Ramat Gan, Israel: Turtledove, 1979.

2822 Nakhleh, Khalil. *Palestinian Dilemma: University Education and Radical Change Among Palestinians in Israel*. Detroit: Association of Arab-American University Graduates, 1979.

2823 Rabin, A. I., and B. Hazan. *Collective Education in the Kibbutz*. New York: Springer, 1973.

2824 Zahlan, Antoine. *Science and Higher Education in Israel*. Beirut: Institute for Palestine Studies, 1970.

Articles

2825 Adler, C. "The Israeli School System as a Selective Institution." In *Schools in Transition: Essays in Comparative Education*, edited by Andreas Kazamias and Erwin Epstein, pp. 209-21. Boston: Allyn and Bacon, 1965.

2826 Adler, Chaim. "Social Stratification and Education in Israel." *Comparative Education Review* 18 (February 1974): 10-23.

2827 Belsky, Florence. "Religion and Education in Israel." *Comparative Education Review* 2 (June 1958): 22-28.

2828 Bendor, S. "Israel." In *International Encyclopedia of Higher Education*, edited by A. Knowles, pp. 2330-41. San Francisco: Jossey-Bass, 1977.

2829 Borus, Michael E. "A Cost-Effectiveness Comparison of Vocational Training for Youth in Developing Countries: A Case Study of Four Training Modes in Israel." *Comparative Education Review* 21 (February 1977): 1-13.

2830 Dror-Elboim, Rachel. "Educational Normative Standards in Israel—A Comparative Analysis." *International Review of Education* 4 (1958): 389-408.

2831 Iram, Yaacov. "Higher Education in Transition—The Case of Israel—A Comparative Study." *Higher Education* 9 (January 1980): 81-96.

2832 Kahane, Reuven, and Laura Starr. "The Impact of Rapid Social Change on Technological Education: An Israeli Example." *Comparative Education Review* 20 (June 1976): 165-78.

2833 Kashti, Yitzhak. "Stagnation and Change in Israeli Education." *Comparative Education* 14 (June 1978): 151-62.

2834 Lewy, Arieh, and D. Davis. "What Can Students Read? The Level of Reading Mastery in Israeli Schools." *Comparative Education Review* 18 (June 1974): 248-61.

2835 Nachmias, Chava. "Curriculum Tracking: Some of Its Causes and Consequences Under a Meritocracy." *Comparative Education Review* 24 (February 1980): 1-20.

2836 Ortar, Gina R. "Educational Achievements of Primary School Graduates in Israel as Related to Their Socio Cultural Background." *Comparative Education* 4 (November 1967): 23-34.

2837 Peleg, R. "Compensatory Education in Israel: Conceptions, Attitudes and Trends." *American Psychologist* 3 (November 1977): 945-58.

2838 Robinsohn, Saul B. "Problems of Education in Israel." *Comparative Education Review* 7 (October 1963): 125-41.

2839 Schachter, H. "Educational Institutions and Political Coalitions in Israel." *Comparative Education Review* 16 (October 1972): 462-73.

2840 Shapira, R. "Ivory Tower or Social Involvement? University Professors in Israel." *Universities Quarterly* 28 (Autumn 1974): 437-49.

2841 Tadmor, Shlomo. "Problems and Reform in Elementary School Teacher Training in Israel." *International Review of Education* 14, (1968): 445-55.

2842 Wilson, Stephen. "Educational Changes in the Kibbutz." *Comparative Education* 5 (February 1969): 67-72.

Iran

Books

2843 Arasteh, Reza. *Education and Social Awakening in Iran*. Leiden: E. J. Brill, 1962.

2844 Ayman, Iraj. *Educational Innovation in Iran*. Paris: UNESCO, 1974.

2845 UNESCO. *Iran Education Project. Project Findings and Recommendations*. Paris: UNESCO, 1977.

Articles

2846 Afzal, Manuchehr. "Availability of Education to Rural Youth in Iran, and the New Educational Plan." *Comparative Education* 3 (March 1967): 123-33.

2847 Afzal, Manuchehr. "Problems of Secondary Education in Iran." *Comparative Education Review* 6 (October 1962): 86-93.

2848 Arasteh, Reza. "Growth of Modern Education in Iran." *Comparative Education Review* 3 (February 1960): 33-40.

2849 Arasteh, R. "The Role of Intellectuals in Administrative Development and Social Change in Modern Iran." *International Review of Education* 9 (1963-64): 326-35.

2850 Bazargan, Fereydoun. "A Survey of Educational Problems in Iran." *Canadian and International Education* 6 (December 1977): 60-74.

2851 Brammer, Lawrence M. "Iran's Educational Revolution—Military Style." *Comparative Education Review* 10 (October 1966): 493-98.

2852 Doerr, Arthur. "An Assessment of Educational Development: The Case Study of Pahlavi University, Iran." *Middle East Journal* 22 (Summer 1968): 317-23.

2853 Harris, Ben. "Literacy Corps—Iran's Gamble to Conquer Illiteracy." *International Review of Education* 9 (1963-64): 430-37.

2854 Parsa, Mohamad. "Tribal Education in Iran." *Compare* 10, no. 1 (1980): 55-60.

2855 Watson, Keith. "The Shah's White Revolution—Education and Reform in Iran." *Comparative Education* 12 (March 1976): 23-36.

Iraq

Books

2856 Clark, Victor. *Compulsory Education in Iraq.* Paris: UNESCO, 1951.

2857 Parker, Orin D., and Garland C. Parker. *Iraq: A Study of the Educational System of Iraq and Guide to the Academic Placement of Students from Iraq in United States Educational Institutions.* Washington, D.C.: American Association of Collegiate Registrars and Admissions Officers, 1966.

2858 Sassani, Abul H. K. *Educational Data: Iraq.* Washington, D.C.: U.S. Office of Education, 1959.

Articles

2859 Al-Rubaiy, Abdula. "The Failure of Political Integration in Iraq: The Education of the Kurdish Minority." *Intellect* 102 (April 1974): 440-44.

2860 Alzobaie, A. J., and M. A. El-Ghannam. "Iraqi Student Perceptions of Occupations." *Sociology and Social Research* 52 (April 1968): 231-36.

2861 Baali, Fuad. "Educational Aspirations Among College Girls in Iraq." *Sociology and Social Research* 51 (July 1967): 485-93.

2862 Gezi, Khalil I. "Secondary Education in Iraq." *High School Journal* 45 (December 1961): 92-97.

2863 "Iraq, Republic of." In *International Encyclopedia of Higher Education*, edited by A. Knowles, pp. 2318-23. San Francisco: Jossey-Bass, 1977.

2864 Mannello, M. "Impressions of Iraqi Education." *Phi Delta Kappan* 36 (June 1955): 345-50.

2865 Mertz, Robert Anton. "Iraq." In *The Encyclopedia of Education*, edited by Lee C. Deighton, vol. 5, pp. 216-19. New York: Macmillan, 1971.

Jordan

Books

2866 al-Bukhari, Najah. *Education in Jordan*. Amman: The Hashemite Kingdom of Jordan, Ministry of Culture and Information, 1972.

2867 al-Bukhari, Najah. *Issues in Occupational Education and Training: A Case Study in Jordan*. Stanford, Calif.: Stanford International Development Education Center, Stanford University, 1968.

2868 Ayesh, Husori. *Educational Planning and Educational Administration in the Hashemite Kingdom of Jordan*. Amman: Ministry of Education, 1972.

2869 Parker, Garland, ed. *Jordan: A Study of the Educational System of Jordan and Guide to the Academic Placement of Students from Jordan in the United States Educational Institutions*. Washington, D.C.: American Association of Collegiate Registrars and Admissions Offices, 1969.

Articles

2870 Gilliam, John. "Junior Colleges in Jordan." *Junior College Journal* 40 (October 1969): 12-16.

2871 "Jordan." In *International Encyclopedia of Higher Education*, edited by A. Knowles, pp. 2375-82. San Francisco: Jossey-Bass, 1977.

2872 Nasir, Huda J. "Jordan." In *World Perspectives on Education*, edited by C. Beck, pp. 247-51. Dubuque, Iowa: Brown, 1970.

2873 Shafiq, M. Muri. "Jordan." In *Encyclopedia of Education*, vol. 5, edited by Lee C. Deighton, pp. 264-67. New York: Macmillan, 1971.

Kuwait

Articles

2874 Al-Ebraheem, H. A., and Richard P. Stevens. "Organization, Management and Academic Problems in the Arab University: The Kuwait University Experience." *Higher Education* 9 (March 1980): 203-18.

2875 Al-Nouri, Anwar. "Kuwait, State of." In *International Encyclopedia of Higher Education*, edited by A. Knowles, pp. 2409-13. San Francisco: Jossey-Bass, 1977.

2876 El-Araby, Salah A. "The Arab States Educational Media Center." In *International Yearbook of International and Instructional Technology 1978-79*, edited by Ann Howe and A. J. Romiszowski, pp. 312-20. London: Kogan Page and Nichols, 1978.

2877 Cornell, M. Louise. "The Development of Education for Women in Kuwait." *Canadian and International Education* 5 (December 1976): 73-84.

2878 Farah, T., and F. S. A. Al-Salem. "Political Efficacy, Political Trust and the Orientations of University Students in Kuwait." *International Journal of Middle East Studies* 8 (July 1977): 317-28.

2879 Graves, William. "Kuwait." In *Perspectives on World Education*, edited by C. Beck, pp. 252-56. Dubuque, Iowa: Brown, 1970.

2880 Meleis, Afaf Ibraham, Nagat El-Sanabary, and Diane Beeson. "Women, Modernization, and Education in Kuwait." *Comparative Education Review* 23 (February 1979): 115-24.

Lebanon

Books

2881 Abou, Selim. *Le bilinguisme arabe français au Liban*. Paris: Presses Universitaires de France, 1962.

2882 Barakat, Halim. *Lebanon in Strife: Student Preludes to the Civil War*. Austin: University of Texas Press, 1976.

2883 Brun, Jean. *L'école catholique au Liban et ses contradictions*. Beirut: Dar-al-Machriq, 1973.

2884 Chapman, Eunice. *Lebanon: A Study of the Educational System of Lebanon and Guide to the Academic Placement of Students from Lebanon in Educational Institutions in the U.S.A*. Washington, D.C.: American Association of Collegiate Registrars and Admissions Officers, 1964.

2885 Dodge, Bayard. *The American University of Beirut*. Beirut, Khayats, 1958.

2886 Hanf, Theodor. *Erziehungswesen in Gesellschaft und Politik des Liban*. Bielefeld, West Germany: Bertelsmann Universitäts Verlag, 1969.

2887 Khalaf, Nadim G. *The Economics of the American University of Beirut*. Beirut: Khayats, 1958.

2888 Lindsay, Rao H. *Nineteenth Century American Schools in the Levant: A Study of Purpose*. Ann Arbor: University of Michigan Press, 1965.

2889 Monro, John M. *A Mutual Concern: The Story of the American University of Beirut*. Delmar, N.Y.: Caravan Books, 1977.

2890 Valin, E. J-P. *Le pluralism socio-scolaire au Liban*. Beirut: Dar-Al-Machriq, 1969.

Articles

2891 Abu-Laban, Baha. "Sources of College Aspirations of Lebanese Youth." *Journal of Developing Areas* 2 (January 1968): 225-40.

2892 Barakat, Halim. "University Students in Lebanon and the Palestinian Resistance Movement: Social Forces Influencing Their Attitudes." *Journal of Palestine Studies* 1 (Autumn 1971): 87-112.

2893 Bashshur, Munir R. "Higher Education and Political Development in Syria and Lebanon." *Comparative Education Review* 10 (October 1966): 451-61.

2894 Bashshur, Munir. "Lebanon." In *International Encyclopedia of Higher Education*, edited by A. Knowles, pp. 2459-68. San Francisco: Jossey-Bass, 1977.

2895 Bashshur, Munir. "Political Recruitment and Integration in Lebanon: The American University of Beirut." In *Schools in Transition*, edited by A. Kazamias and E. Epstein, pp. 111-25. Boston: Allyn and Bacon, 1968.

2896 Dodge, Bayard. "American University of Beirut." *Journal of World History* 10 (1967): 780-800.

2897 Kurani, Halib A. "Lebanon." In *The Encyclopedia of Education*, edited by Lee C. Deighton, vol. 5, pp. 476-82. New York: Macmillan, 1971.

2898 Kurani, Halib. "Lebanon Educational Reform." In *Yearbook of Education*, pp. 448-61. London: Evans, 1949.

2899 Mourad, Farouk. "Lebanon." In *Perspectives on World Education*, edited by C. Beck, pp. 257-61. Dubuque, Iowa: Brown, 1970.

2900 Nasr, Nafhat, and Monte Palmer. "Family, Peers, Social Control, and Political Activism Among Lebanese College Students." *Journal of Developing Areas* 9 (April 1975): 377-94.

2901 Weightman, George H., and Siham F. Adam. "Occupational Choices and Mobility Orientation Among Lebanese College Students." *Asian Studies* 5 (August 1967): 345-57.

2902 Weightman, George H., and Zahi Rihani. "Social Stratification and Adolescent Academic Performance in a Lebanese Town." *Comparative Education Review* 11 (June 1967): 208-16.

Libya

Books

2903 Sassani, Abul H. K. *Educational Data: Libya.* Washington, D.C.: U.S. Office of Education, 1971.

Articles

2904 Ghanem, S. "Libyan Arab Republic." In *International Encyclopedia of Higher Education*, edited by A. Knowles, pp. 2636-41. San Francisco: Jossey-Bass, 1977.

2905 Gulick, B. F. "Libya." In *The Educated African*, edited by Helen Kitchen, pp. 54-66. New York: Praeger, 1962.

2906 Samaan, Wahib I. "Libya." In *The Encyclopedia of Education*, edited by Lee C. Deighton, vol. 6, pp. 1-3. New York: Macmillan, 1971.

Morocco

Books

2907 UNESCO. *Développement planification de l'éducation: MAROC*. Paris: UNESCO, 1977.

2908 UNESCO. *Education in Morocco: Priority, Problems and Projects*. Paris: UNESCO, 1974.

Articles

2909 Berry, William. "Morocco." In *The Educated African*, edited by Helen Kitchen, pp. 23-43. New York: Praeger, 1962.

2910 Farsi-Fihri, Mohamed. "Mohamed V University." In *Creating the African University*, edited by T. M. Yesufu, pp. 131-36. Ibadan, Nigeria: Oxford University Press, 1973.

2911 Le Veugle, Jean. "Problèmes de l'éducation ouvrière au Maroc." *International Review of Education* 5 (1959): 46-59.

2912 "Morocco." In *International Encyclopedia of Higher Education*, edited by A. Knowles, pp. 2895-2903. San Francisco: Jossey-Bass, 1977.

2913 Rivet, D. "Ecole et colonisation au Maroc: La politique de Lyantey au début des années." *Cahiers Histoire* 21 (1976): 173-98.

2914 Samaan, Wahib I. "Morocco." In *The Encyclopedia of Education*, edited by Lee C. Deighton, vol. 6, pp. 406-8. New York: Macmillan, 1971.

2915 Wagner, Daniel, and Abdelhamid Lotfi. "Traditional Islamic Education in

Morocco: Sociohistorical and Psychological Perspectives." *Comparative Education Review* 24 (June 1980): 238-51.

2916 Zartman, I. William. "Problems of Arabization in Moroccan Education." In *The Contemporary Middle East*, edited by B. Rivlin and J. Szyliowicz, pp. 328-37. New York: Random House, 1965.

Oman

Articles

2917 "Oman, Sultanate of." In *International Encyclopedia of Higher Education*, edited by A. Knowles, pp. 3098-99. San Francisco: Jossey-Bass, 1977.

Palestine

Books

2918 Badr, Ahmed. *Education of the Palestinians: An Annotated Bibliography.* Detroit, Mich.: Association of Arab-American University Graduates, 1977.

Articles

2919 Dickerson, George. "Education for the Palestine Refugees: The UNRWA/ UNESCO Programme." *Journal of Palestine Studies* 3 (Spring 1974): 122-30.

2920 Larsen, C. A. Hoeg. "Introducing Objective Tests in Palestine Refugee Schools." *International Review of Education* 7 (1961): 63-72.

Qatar

Articles

2921 "Qatar, State of." In *International Encyclopedia of Higher Education*, edited by A. Knowles, pp. 3445-46. San Francisco: Jossey-Bass, 1977.

Saudi Arabia

Books

2922 Molek, Frank J., ed. *The Admission and Academic Placement of Students from Selected Arab Countries.* Washington, D.C.: Association for Foreign Student Affairs, 1975.

2923 Sassani, Abul H. K. *Educational Data: Saudi Arabia.* Washington, D.C.: U.S. Department of Health, Education, and Welfare, Office of Education, 1959.

2924 Saudi Arabia Ministry of Education. *The Educational Policy of Saudi Arabian Kingdom.* Riyadh: Saudi Arabia Ministry of Education, 1970.

2925 Saudi Arabia Ministry of Information. *Education in Saudi Arabia.* Riyadh: Saudi Arabia Ministry of Information 1963.

2926 Thomas, A. *The Educational Renaissance of the Kingdom of Saudi Arabia,* 2 vols. Tempe, Ariz.: 1965.

2927 Thomas, Alfred. *Saudi Arabia: A Study of the Educational System of the Kingdom of Saudi Arabia and Guide to the Academic Placement of Students from the Kingdom of Saudi Arabia in United States Educational Institutions.* Washington, D.C.: American Association of Collegiate Registrars and Admissions Officers, 1967.

2928 Wassie, Abd-el Wahab. *Education in Saudi Arabia.* Basingstoke, England: Macmillan, 1979.

Articles

2929 Mertz, Robert Anton. "Saudi Arabia." In *The Encyclopedia of Education,* edited by Lee C. Deighton, vol. 8, pp. 10-13. New York: Macmillan, 1971.

2930 "Saudi Arabia." In *International Encyclopedia of Higher Education,* edited by A. Knowles, pp. 3673-80. San Francisco: Jossey-Bass, 1977.

Syria

Books

2931 Parker, Garland G. *Syrian Arab Republic: A Study of the Educational System of the Syrian Arab Republic and a Guide to the Academic Placement of Students in Educational Institutions of the United States.* Washington, D.C.: American Association of Collegiate Registrars and Admissions Officers, 1978.

2932 Tibawi, A. C. *American Interests in Syria 1800-1901. A Study of Educational Literacy and Religious Work*. Oxford: Clarendon Press, 1966.

Articles

2933 Methven, Lily Steward. "Syria—U.A.R." In *Perspectives on World Education*, edited by C. Beck, pp. 273-76. Dubuque, Iowa: Brown, 1970.

2934 Mertz, Robert Anton. "Syria." In *The Encyclopedia of Education*, edited by Lee C. Deighton, vol. 8, pp. 580-83. New York: Macmillan 1971.

2935 Potter, Willis N. "Modern Education in Syria." *Comparative Education Review* 5 (June 1961): 35-38.

2936 Saliba, Djemil. "Syria." In *Yearbook of Education*, pp. 445-51. London: Evan Bros., 1953.

2937 Sharabi, H. B. "The Syrian University." *Middle Eastern Affairs* 6 (May 1955): 152-59.

2938 "Syria, Arab Republic of." In *International Encyclopedia of Higher Education*, edited by A. Knowles, pp. 4043-49. San Francisco: Jossey-Bass, 1977.

2939 Tibawi, A. L. "The Genesis and Early History of the Syrian Protestant College (Part I)." *Middle East Journal* 21 (Winter 1967): 1-15.

Tunisia

Books

2940 Al-Bukhari, Najati. *Issues in Occupational Education and Training: A Case Study of Tunisia*. Stanford, Calif.: School of Education, Stanford University, 1968.

2941 American Friends of the Middle East. *Education in Tunisia*. Washington, D.C.: American Friends of the Middle East, 1963.

2942 Sassani, Abul H. K. *Educational Data: Republic of Tunisia*. Washington, D.C.: U.S. Office of Education, 1960.

2943 Sraieb, N. *Colonisation, décolonisation et enseignement, l'exemple tunisien*. Tunis: Institut National des Sciences de l'Education de Tunis, 1974.

2944 Wenk, Karen L. *The Educational System of Tunisia*. Washington, D.C.: U.S. Government Printing Office, 1974.

Articles

2945 Brown, L. C. "Tunisia." In *Education and Political Development*, edited by James S. Coleman, pp. 144-68. Princeton: Princeton University Press, 1965.

2946 Carnoy, M., R. Sack, and H. H. Thias. "Middle Level Manpower in Tunisia: Socio-economic Origins, Schooling and Economic Success." In *Change in Tunisia: Essays in the Social Sciences*, edited by R. Stone and J. Simmons, pp. 263-87. Albany, N.Y.: State University of New York Press, 1976.

2947 Damis, John. "The Free School Phenomenon: The Cases of Tunisia and Algeria." *International Journal of Middle Eastern Studies* 5 (1974): 434-49.

2948 Hochschild, Arlie. "Women at Work in Modernizing Tunisia: Attitudes of Urban Adolescent Schoolgirls." *Berkeley Journal of Sociology* 11 (1966): 32-53.

2949 Kerr, Malcolm H. "Tunisian Education: Seeds of Revolution?" *Middle East Forum* 47 (Autumn-Winter 1971): 83-91.

2950 Kinsey, D. C. "L'éducation de masse et ses implications socio-économiques en Tunisie." *Revue Tunisienne de Sciences Sociales* 24 (1971): 163-83.

2951 Kinsey, D. C. "Efforts for Educational Synthesis Under Colonial Rule: Egypt and Tunisia." *Comparative Education Review* 15 (June 1971): 172-87.

2952 Klineberg, Stephen L. "Parents, Schooling and Modernity: An Exploratory Investigation of Sex Differences in the Attitudinal Development of Tunisian Adolescents." *International Journal of Comparative Sociology* 14 (1976): 221-43.

2953 Ostle, Robin. "Tunisia." In *Educational and National Development*, edited by Nancy Parkinson, pp. 165-94. London: Macmillan, 1976.

2954 Sack, Richard. "The Impact of Education on Individual Modernity in Tunisia." *International Journal of Comparative Sociology* 14 (September-December 1973): 245-72.

2955 Samaan, Wahib I. "Tunisia." In *The Encyclopedia of Education*, edited by Lee C. Deighton, vol. 9, pp. 279-80. New York: Macmillan, 1971.

2956 Simmons, John. "The Determinants of Earnings: Towards an Improved Model." In *Change in Tunisia: Essays in the Social Sciences*, edited by R. Stone and J. Simmons, pp. 249-62. Albany, N.Y.: State University of New York Press, 1976.

2957 Tibi, Claude. "Tunisia: A Case Study." In *Population Growth and Costs of Education in Developing Countries*, edited by Ta Ngoe Châu, pp. 227-73. Paris: UNESCO, 1972.

2958 Toumi, Mohsen. "La scolarisation et le tissu en Tunisie." *Revue Française d'Etudes Politiques Africaines* 109 (January 1975): 32-61.

2959 "Tunisia." In *International Encyclopedia of Higher Education*, edited by A. Knowles, pp. 4157-64. San Francisco: Jossey-Bass, 1977.

Turkey

Books

2960 Kazamias, Andreas J. *Education and the Quest for Modernity in Turkey*. Chicago: University of Chicago Press, 1966.

2961 Szyliowicz, Joseph S. *A Political Analysis of Student Activism: The Turkish Case*. Beverly Hills, Calif.: Sage, 1972.

Articles

2962 Davison, Roderic H. "Westernized Education in Ottoman Turkey." *Middle East Journal* 15 (Summer 1961): 289-301.

2963 Dodd, C. H. "The Social and Educational Background of Turkish Officials." *Middle Eastern Studies* 1 (April 1965): 268-76.

2964 Hyman, H. H. "Values of Turkish College Youth." *Public Opinion Quarterly* 22 (Fall 1958): 275-91.

2965 Kazamias, Andreas M. "Potential Elites in Turkey: The Social Origins of Lise Youth." *Comparative Education Review* 10 (October 1966): 470-81.

2966 Kazamias, Andreas M. "Potential Elites in Turkey: Exploring the Values and Attitudes of Lise Youth." *Comparative Education Review* 11 (February 1967): 22-37.

2967 Krueger, A. O. "Rates of Return to Turkish Higher Education." *Journal of Human Resources* 7 (November 1972): 482-99.

2968 Le Compte, William, and Guney Le Compte. "Effects of Education and Intercultural Contact on Traditional Attitudes in Turkey." *Journal of Social Psychology* 80 (February 1970): 11-21.

2969 Okyar, Osman. "Universities in Turkey." *Minerva* 6 (Winter 1968): 213-43.

2970 Ozelli, M. T. "The Evolution of the Formal Educational System and its Relation to Economic Growth Policies in the First Turkish Republic." *International Journal of Middle East Studies* 5 (January 1974): 77-92.

2971 Reed, Howard A. "Turkey." In *International Encyclopedia of Higher Education*, edited by A. Knowles, pp. 4165-75. San Francisco: Jossey-Bass, 1977.

2972 Roos, Leslie L., and Noralou Roos. "Students and Politics in Turkey." *Daedalus* 97 (Winter 1968): 184-203.

2973 Roos, Leslie L., Jr., and George W. Angell, Jr. "New Teachers for Turkish Villages: A Military-Sponsored Educational Program." *Journal of Developing Areas* 2 (July 1968): 519-32.

2974 Stone, Frank A. "The Evolution of Contemporary Turkish Educational Thought." *History of Education Quarterly* 13 (Summer 1973): 145-62.

2975 Stone, Frank. "Rural Revitalization and the Village Institutes in Turkey: Sponsors and Critics." *Comparative Education Review* 18 (October 1974): 419-29.

2976 Szyliowicz, Joseph S. "Education and Political Development in Turkey,

Egypt, and Iran." *Comparative Education Review* 13 (June 1969): 150–66.

2977 Tinto, Vincent. "University Productivity and the Organization of Higher Education in Turkey." *Higher Education* 3, no. 3 (1974): 285–301.

2978 Vdovichenko, D. I. "The Present Situation in Education in Turkey." *Soviet Education* 1 (January 1959): 67–73.

2979 Weiker, Walter F. "Academic Freedom and Problems of Higher Education in Turkey." *Middle East Journal* 16 (Summer 1962): 279–95.

United Arab Emirates

Articles

2980 "United Arab Emirates." In *International Encyclopedia of Education*, edited by A. Knowles, pp. 4195–96. San Francisco: Jossey-Bass, 1977.

Yemen

Articles

2981 Weinstein, Stanley. "Yemen." In *Perspectives on World Education*, edited by C. Beck, pp. 277–81. Dubuque, Iowa: Brown, 1970.

2982 "Yemen, Arab Republic of." In *International Encyclopedia of Higher Education*, edited by A. Knowles, pp. 4451–53. San Francisco: Jossey-Bass, 1977.

Yemen, People's Democratic Republic

Articles

2983 "Yemen, People's Democratic Republic of." In *International Encyclopedia of Higher Education*, edited by A. Knowles, p. 4453. San Francisco: Jossey-Bass, 1977.

NORTH AMERICA

Canada

Books

2984 Adams, H. *The Education of Canadians 1800-1867: The Roots of Separatism.* Montreal: Harvest Books, 1968.

2985 Audet, Louis-Philippe. *Histoire de l'enseignement au Québec, 1608-1971,* 2 vols. Monreal: Holt, Rinehart and Winston, 1971.

2986 Bélanger, Pierre, and Guy Rocher, eds. *Ecole et société au Québec.* Montreal: Edition HMH, 1970.

2987 Carlton, Richard, et al., eds. *Education, Change and Society: A Sociology of Canadian Education.* Toronto: Gage Educational Publishing, 1977.

2988 Chaiton, A., and N. McDonald. *Canadian Schools and Canadian Identity.* Toronto: Gage, 1977.

2989 D'Oyley, Vincent, ed. *The Impact of Multi-ethnicity on Canadian Education.* Toronto: Urban Alliance on Race Relations, 1977.

2990 Harris, Robin S. *A History of Higher Education in Canada.* Toronto: University of Toronto Press, 1976.

2991 Harris, Robin S. *Quiet Evolution: A Study of the Educational Systems of Ontario.* Toronto: University of Toronto Press, 1967.

2992 Katz, Joseph. *Education in Canada.* Hamden, Conn.: Archon, 1973.

2993 Katz, Joseph. *Society, Schools and Progress in Canada.* Elmsford, N.Y.: Pergamon Press, 1969.

2994 Johnson, F. H. *A Brief History of Canadian Education.* Toronto: McGraw-Hill, 1968.

2995 Martel, George, ed. *The Politics of the Canadian Public School.* Toronto: James Lewis and Samuel, 1974.

2996 Martin, Wilfred B. W. *Canadian Education: A Sociological Analysis.* Scarborough, Ont.: Prentice-Hall of Canada, 1978.

2997 Mattingly, Paul, and Michal Katz, eds. *Education and Social Change: Themes from Ontario's Past*. New York: New York University Press, 1975.

2998 Munroe, D. *The Organization and Administration of Education in Canada*. Ottawa: Information Canada, 1974.

2999 Nelsen, Randle W., and David A. Nock, eds. *Reading, Writing and Riches: Education and the Socio-Economic Order in North America*. Kitchener, Ont.: Between the Lines, 1978.

3000 Organization for Economic Cooperation and Development. *Reviews of National Policies for Education: Canada*. Paris: OECD, 1976.

3001 Pike, Robert, and Elia Zurek, eds. *Socialization and Values in Canadian Society*. Toronto: McClelland and Stewart, 1975.

3002 Prentice, Alison, and Susan Houston, eds. *Family, School and Society in Nineteenth Century Canada*. Toronto: Oxford University Press, 1975.

3003 Stevenson, Hugh, and J. Donald Wilson, eds. *Precepts, Policy and Process: Perspectives on Contemporary Canadian Education*. London, Ont.: Alexander, Blake Associates, 1977.

3004 Wilson, J. Donald, et al., eds. *Canadian Education: A History*. Scarborough, Ont.: Prentice-Hall of Canada, 1970.

3005 Wolcott, Harry F. *A Kwakiut Village and School*. New York: Holt, Rinehart and Winston, 1967.

Articles

3006 Arricale, Frank C. "Varieties of Church-State Relations in Canadian Education." *Comparative Education Review* 7 (June 1963): 36-42.

3007 Burn, Barbara. "Higher Education in Canada." In B. Burn, *Higher Education in Nine Countries*, pp. 91-124. New York: McGraw-Hill, 1971.

3008 Cuneo, Carl J. "Education, Language and Multidimensional Continentalism." *Canadian Journal of Political Science* 7 (September 1974): 536-50.

3009 Heyman, Richard, R. F. Lawson, and R. M. Stamp. "Urban Industrial Change and Curriculum Reform in Early Twentieth Century Ontario." In R. Heyman et al., *Studies in Educational Change*, pp. 9-88. Toronto: Holt, Rinehart and Winston, 1972.

3010 Houston, Susan E. "Politics, Schools and Social Change in Upper Canada." *Canadian Historical Review* 43 (September 1972): 249-71.

3011 Jaenen, Cornelius J. "Minority Group Schooling and Canadian National Unity." *Journal of Educational Thought* 7 (August 1973): 81-94.

3012 Lawson, Robert F. "A Critical Survey of Education in Western Canada." *Comparative Education Review* 4 (November 1967): 9-23.

3013 Lorimer, James. "Canadian Textbooks and the American 'Knowledge' Industry." *This Magazine is About Schools* 5 (Summer 1971): 47-63.

3014 Munroe, David C. "Canada." In *International Encyclopedia of Higher Education*, edited by A. Knowles, pp. 785-94. San Francisco: Jossey-Bass, 1977.

3015 Nash, Paul. "Quality and Equality in Canadian Education." *Comparative Education Review* 5 (October 1961): 118-29.

3016 Price, John A. "An Ethnographic Approach to U.S. and Canadian Indian Education." *Canadian and International Education* 3 (December 1974): 99-115.

3017 Ray, Douglas W. "Cultural Pluralism and the Reorientation Educational Policy in Canada." *Comparative Education* 14 (March 1978): 19-32.

3018 Ross, Peter N. "The Establishment of the Ph.D. at Toronto: A Case of American Influence." *History of Education Quarterly* 13 (Fall 1972): 358-80.

3019 Scarfe, Janet, and Edward Sheffield. "Notes on the Canadian Professoriate." *Higher Education* 6 (August 1977): 337-58.

3020 Silva, Edward T. "Cultural Autonomy and Ideas in Transit: Notes from the Canadian Case." *Comparative Education Review* 24 (February 1980): 63-72.

OCEANIA

Australia

Books

3021 Austin, A. G. *Australian Education 1788-1900*. Melbourne: Pittman, 1961.

3022 Browne, Ronald K., William S. Simkins, and Lois E. Foster. *A Guide to the Sociology of Australian Education*. South Melbourne: Macmillan of Australia, 1974.

3023 Cowan, R. W. T. *Education for Australians*. Melbourne: Cheshire, 1964.

3024 Findlay, Ian R. *Education in Australia*. Hamden, Conn.: Archon, 1973.

3025 Harman, G. S., et al., eds. *Academia Becalmed: Australian Tertiary Education in the Aftermath of Expansion*. Canberra: Australian National University Press, 1980.

3026 Harman, G. S., and C. Selby Smith, eds. *Readings in the Economics and Politics of Australian Education*. Sydney: Pergamon Press, 1976.

3027 Hore, T., R. D. Linke, and L. T. H. West, eds. *The Future of Higher Education in Australia*. South Melbourne: Macmillan, 1978.

3028 Jones, Phillip E. *Education in Australia*. Newton Abbot, England: David and Charles, 1974.

3029 Maclaine, A. G. *Australian Education: Progress, Problems, and Prospects*. Sydney: Ian Novak, 1975.

3030 Maclaine, A. G., and Selby Smith, eds. *Fundamental Issues in Australian Education*. Sydney: Novak, 1971.

3031 Marjoribanks, Kevin. *Ethnic Families and Children's Achievements*. Sydney: Allen and Unwin, 1980.

3032 Musgrave, P. W. *Society and the Curriculum in Australia*. London: Allen and Unwin, 1977.

3033 Partridge, P. H. *Society, Schools and Progress in Australia*. Rushchutters Bay, N.S.W.: Pergamon Australia, 1973.

3034 Rosier, Malcolm J. *Early School Leavers in Australia*. Stockholm: Almquist and Wiksell, 1978.

Articles

3035 Anderson, D. S. "Education for Adolescents in Australia." *International Review of Education* 21 (1975): 177-95.

3036 Bessant, Bob. "Rural Schooling and the Rural Myth in Australia." *Comparative Education* 14 (June 1978): 121-32.

3037 Burn, Barbara. "Higher Education in Australia." In B. Burn, *Higher Education in Nine Countries*, pp. 125-64. New York: McGraw-Hill, 1971.

3038 Harman, Grant. "Academic Staff and Academic Drift in Australian Colleges of Advanced Education." *Higher Education* 6 (August 1977): 313-36.

3039 Holdaway, E. A. "A Comparison of Staff Utilization in Education in Australia and Canada." *Journal of Educational Administration* (Australia) 13 (May 1975): 5-22.

3040 Lawry, J. R. "The Development of a National System of Education in New South Wales." *History of Education Quarterly* 7 (Fall 1967): 349-56.

3041 O'Bryne, Vera de Rudnyanszky. "L'enseignement des langues des groupes ethniques en Australie." *Canadian and International Education* 7 (June 1978): 37-41.

3042 Partridge, P. H. "Universities in Australia." *Comparative Education* 2 (November 1965): 19-30.

3043 Schonell, F. J., and G. Needham. "Education in Australia since 1945, Part II." *International Review of Education* 4, no. 2 (1958): 220-30.

3044 Sheehan, Barry A. "The Organization and Financing of Education in Australia." *Comparative Education* 8 (December 1972): 133-46.

3045 Wiseman, R. "Secondary School and Family Background—A Review of Some Recent Australian Studies." *Australian Journal of Education* 13 (March 1970): 66-75.

New Zealand

Books

3046 Bates, Richard. *Prospects in New Zealand Education*. Auckland: Hodder and Stoughton, 1970.

3047 Barney, David. *Who Gets to Pre-school*. Wellington: New Zealand Council for Educational Research, 1975.

3048 Cumming, Ian, and Alan Cumming. *The History of State Education in New Zealand 1840–1975*. Wellington: Pitman Pacific Books, 1978.

3049 Dakin, J. C. *Education in New Zealand*. Newton Abbot, England: David and Charles, 1973.

3050 McDonald, Geraldine. *Maori Mothers and Pre-school Education*. Wellington: New Zealand Council for Educational Research, 1973.

3051 McLaren, Ian A. *Education in a Small Democracy: New Zealand*. London: Routledge and Kegan Paul, 1974.

3052 Parkyn, G. W. *Success and Failure at the University*, 2 vols. Wellington: New Zealand Council for Educational Research, 1969.

3053 Parton, Hugh. *The University of New Zealand*. London: Routledge and Kegan Paul, 1974.

3054 Robinson, G. H., and B. T. O'Rourke. *Schools in New Zealand Society: A Book of Readings*. Sydney: Wiley, Australasia, 1973.

3055 Watson, John E. *Intermediate Schooling in New Zealand*. Wellington: New Zealand Council for Educational Research, 1964.

Articles

3056 Barrington, John. "Cultural Adaptations and Maori Educational Policy: The African Connection." *Comparative Education Review* 20 (February 1976): 1–10.

3057 Beeby, C. E. "New Zealand—An Example of Secondary Education Without Selection." *International Review of Education* 2, no. 4 (1956): 396–409.

3058 Boyd, Ellie M. "New Zealand." In *International Encyclopedia of Higher Education*, edited by A. Knowles, pp. 3007-13. San Francisco: Jossey-Bass, 1977.

3059 McKenzie, David. "The Changing Concept of Equality in New Zealand Education." *New Zealand Journal of Educational Studies* 10 (November 1975): 93-110.

3060 Minogue, W. J. D. "Education in a Dependent Culture—New Zealand: Some Problems Relating to the British Influence in New Zealand Education." *Comparative Education* 1 (June 1965): 203-9.

3061 Mitchell, Frank W. "Religious Instruction and Observances in the Public Schools of New Zealand." *Comparative Education Review* 7 (February 1964): 297-300.

3062 Ogilvy, B. J. "A Cost Benefit Study of Education in New Zealand." *New Zealand Journal of Educational Studies* 5 (May 1970): 33-46.

3063 Small, J. J. "Religion in the Schools of New Zealand." *Comparative Education Review* 9 (February 1965): 53-62.

3064 Watson, John. "New Zealand." In *World Perspectives on Education*, edited by C. Beck, pp. 181-90. Dubuque, Iowa: Brown, 1970.

3065 Watson, John E. "The Social Position of Teachers in New Zealand." *Comparative Education Review* 8 (December 1964): 327-33.

Pacific Islands

Books

3066 Brammall, J., and R. J. May, eds. *Education in Melanasia*. Canberra: Australian National University, 1974.

3067 Coletta, N. J. *American Schools for the Natives of Ponapae: A Study of Education and Culture Change in Micronesia*. Honolulu: University of Hawaii Press, 1980.

3068 Howard, Alan. *Learning to be Rotuman: Enculturation in the South Pacific*. New York: Teacher's College Press, 1970.

Articles

3069 Coletta, N. J. "A Case Study of Bureaucratic Organization and Cross-Cultural Conflict in Micronesian High School." *International Review of Education* 20, no. 2 (1974): 178-99.

3070 Thomas, R. Murray. "A Scheme for Assessing Unmet Educational Needs: The American Samoa Example." *International Review of Education* 23, no. 1 (1977): 59-78.

Papua New Guinea

Books

3071 Conroy, J. D. *Education, Employment and Migration in Papua New Guinea.* Canberra: Australian National University, 1976.

3072 Department of Education, Papua, New Guinea. *Educational Plan, 1976-80.* Port Moresby, Papua New Guinea: Government Printer, 1976.

3073 Smith, Geoffrey. *Education in Papua New Guinea.* Melbourne: Oxford University Press, 1975.

3074 Thomas, E. B., ed. *Papua New Guinea Education.* Melbourne: Oxford University Press, 1976.

Articles

3075 Barrington, Thomas. "Problems and Needs of Education in a Developing Country: The Papua New Guinean Experience." *Australian Journal of Education* 18 (June 1974): 124-37.

3076 Cleverly, John. "Planning Educational Change in Papua New Guinea: A Comparative Study of the 1973 and 1974 Five-Year Plans for Education." *Comparative Education* 12 (March 1976): 55-65.

3077 Colebatch, H. "Educational Policy and Political Development in Australian New Guinea." *Melbourne Studies in Education* (1968): 107.

3078 Conroy, J. D., and R. Curtain. "Migrants in the Urban Economy: Rural School Leavers in Port Moresby." *Oceania* 44 (December 1973): 81-95.

3079 Richardson, Penelope. "Papua-New Guinea." In *World Perspectives on Education*, edited by C. Beck, pp. 191–99. Dubuque, Iowa: Brown, 1970.

3080 Roe, E. "Educational Problems in Papua-New Guinea." *Australian Journal of Higher Education* 3 (December 1968): 126–33.

CROSS-REFERENCE INDEX

EDUCATIONAL POLICY

EDUCATIONAL PLANNING

DEVELOPMENT OF EDUCATIONAL SYSTEMS: PROBLEMS AND PERSPECTIVES

EDUCATION AND ECONOMIC DEVELOPMENT

EDUCATION AND SOCIAL DEVELOPMENT

EDUCATION AND POLITICAL DEVELOPMENT
941, 950, 1064, 1082, 1102, 1189, 1197, 1201, 1218, 1386, 1402, 1410, 1451, 1489, 1514, 1521, 1565, 1569, 1612, 1640, 1649, 1677, 1699, 1764, 1801, 1809, 1887, 1889, 2425, 2430, 2442, 2453, 2456, 2503, 2610, 2614, 2746, 2754, 2769, 2839, 2895, 2945, 2960, 2976.

EDUCATION AND INDIVIDUAL MODERNITY
986, 1184, 2672, 2954

COLONIALISM AND EDUCATION
936, 938, 949, 961, 962, 963, 967, 968, 970, 977, 979, 980, 999, 1013, 1018, 1021, 1024, 1031, 1049, 1058, 1059, 1060, 1095, 1097, 1103, 1108, 1166, 1172, 1209, 1210, 1214, 1261, 1265, 1267, 1304, 1325, 1337, 1341, 1342, 1366, 1420, 1524, 1527, 1550, 1562, 1571, 1586, 1614, 1637, 1645, 1654, 1657, 1664, 1667, 1670, 1671, 1681, 1711, 1719, 1724, 1725, 1741, 1750, 1761, 1767, 1793, 1795, 1800, 2454, 2630, 2652, 2659, 2666, 2705, 2710, 2730, 2772, 2776, 2777, 2779, 2781, 2797, 2807, 2809, 2888, 2932, 2943, 2951, 3060, 3067.

EDUCATION AND EMPLOYMENT
964, 1042, 1043, 1078, 1120, 1127, 1292, 1397, 1399, 1515, 1543, 2511, 2582, 2594, 2860, 2901.

EDUCATION AND INCOME
1125, 1668, 1846, 2617, 2956.

EDUCATION AND HUMAN RESOURCE MIGRATION
1398, 1639, 1721, 1855, 2488, 2649, 3071.

POLITICS OF EDUCATION AND POLITICAL SOCIALIZATION
953, 957, 997, 1017, 1048, 1069, 1077, 1111, 1131, 1134, 1223, 1286, 1298, 1303, 1431, 1455, 1464, 1471, 1472, 1478, 1490, 1499, 1500, 1506, 1531, 1540, 1545, 1551, 1585, 1625, 1626, 1628, 1629, 1676, 1712, 1713, 1723, 1798, 1870, 1910, 1981, 2042, 2071, 2103, 2139, 2157, 2172, 2179, 2263, 2285, 2334, 2337, 2478, 2510, 2543, 2616, 2631, 2698, 2723, 2725, 2728, 2784, 2988, 2995, 3001, 3011.

ETHNICITY AND EDUCATION
1015, 1085, 1223, 1224, 1225, 1226, 1227, 1229, 1230, 1231, 1232, 1233, 1234, 1235, 1237, 1241, 1242, 1244, 1245, 1246, 1247, 1248, 1250, 1253, 1254, 1255, 1256, 1390, 1404, 1567, 1652, 1653, 1663, 1672, 1678, 1680, 1746, 1790, 1997, 2013, 2331, 2412, 2658, 2718, 2819, 2859, 2989, 3016, 3041, 3050, 3056.

LANGUAGE AND EDUCATION
966, 993, 1044, 1045, 1051, 1090, 1159, 1186, 1187, 1297, 1387, 1462, 1517, 1708, 1732, 1751, 1921, 2152, 2341, 2355, 2595, 2606, 2661, 2662, 2673, 2675, 2676, 2677, 2881, 3008, 3041.

WOMEN AND EDUCATION
969, 973, 974, 1106, 1188, 1207, 1272, 1273, 1285, 1316, 1528, 1674, 1689, 1730, 1740, 1760, 1871, 2076, 2170, 2520, 2539, 2561, 2627, 2632, 2685, 2704, 2768, 2805, 2812, 2861, 2877, 2880, 2948, 2952.

CURRICULUM
1008, 1093, 1133, 1143, 1458, 1714, 2008, 2051, 2099, 2124, 2125, 2167, 2321, 2367, 2374, 2414, 2835, 2920, 3032.

EDUCATIONAL ACHIEVEMENT
1215, 1222, 1312, 1319, 1320, 1321, 1322, 1350, 1454, 1552, 1620, 1916, 2061, 2244, 2272, 2290, 2324, 2474, 2591, 2670, 2706, 2707, 2729, 2834, 2836, 2902.

TEACHER EDUCATION
981, 1182, 1276, 1308, 1473, 1546, 1593, 1606, 1659, 1685, 1728, 1745, 1780, 1837, 1890, 1985, 2023, 2232, 2251, 2283, 2338, 2400, 2841, 2973, 3059.

NONFORMAL EDUCATION
1032, 1116, 1302, 1414, 1705, 1706, 1707, 1814, 1852, 2431, 2437, 2464, 2465, 2467, 2645, 2655.

REFORM AND INNOVATION
989, 1026, 1027, 1037, 1038, 1047, 1071, 1100, 1101, 1110, 1113, 1130, 1141, 1144, 1150, 1268, 1280, 1281, 1282, 1296, 1300, 1301, 1328, 1330, 1419, 1435, 1446, 1461, 1463, 1477, 1485, 1486, 1495, 1496, 1497, 1498, 1504, 1534, 1577, 1634, 1688, 1729, 1874, 1892, 1904, 1915, 1934, 1952, 1968, 1969, 2003, 2004, 2026, 2041, 2063, 2064, 2065, 2070, 2073, 2078, 2080, 2117, 2136, 2138, 2144, 2153, 2154, 2168, 2218, 2230, 2231, 2232, 2248, 2257, 2328, 2344, 2347, 2375, 2376, 2383, 2391, 2399, 2405, 2407, 2408, 2416, 2433, 2497, 2517, 2522, 2530, 2535, 2540, 2545, 2550, 2555, 2559, 2567, 2580, 2583, 2586, 2639, 2640, 2653, 2656, 2700, 2708, 2785, 2844, 2855, 2898.

EDUCATIONAL FINANCE
1105, 1112, 1115, 1167, 1279, 1655, 1726, 1738, 1769, 1771, 1831, 1872, 2305, 2306, 2325, 2641, 2967, 3044, 3062.

COMPARATIVE HIGHER EDUCATION

933, 958, 985, 990, 992, 1000, 1001, 1006, 1081, 1156, 1170, 1173, 1178, 1181, 1191, 1192, 1196, 1203, 1211, 1236, 1258, 1259, 1262, 1290, 1294, 1310, 1338, 1345, 1352, 1358, 1364, 1365, 1367, 1368, 1376, 1384, 1388, 1391, 1395, 1408, 1421, 1422, 1442, 1465, 1474, 1476, 1481, 1494, 1503, 1510, 1513, 1518, 1523, 1533, 1558, 1560, 1570, 1580, 1591, 1598, 1609, 1617, 1618, 1704, 1734, 1744, 1756, 1773, 1777, 1784, 1804, 1818, 1819, 1821, 1824, 1829, 1842, 1843, 1854, 1856, 1859, 1868, 1875, 1893, 1907, 1909, 1931, 1939, 1961, 1973, 1993, 1998, 2006, 2015, 2024, 2025, 2049, 2052, 2056, 2058, 2062, 2074, 2097, 2105, 2108, 2112, 2114, 2116, 2121, 2126, 2129, 2131, 2137, 2140, 2148, 2155, 2159, 2162, 2171, 2173, 2188, 2193, 2196, 2201, 2202, 2207, 2210, 2211, 2214, 2242, 2243, 2271, 2276, 2292, 2310, 2320, 2323, 2326, 2342, 2351, 2352, 2356, 2369, 2370, 2372, 2380, 2396, 2404, 2417, 2418, 2419, 2427, 2428, 2435, 2441, 2443, 2451, 2460, 2468, 2490, 2496, 2502, 2544, 2579, 2607, 2608, 2612, 2613, 2688, 2698, 2714, 2751, 2770, 2790, 2804, 2831, 2852, 2874, 2885, 2887, 2893, 2910, 2937, 2969, 2979, 2990, 3007, 3025, 3027, 3037, 3042, 3052, 3053.

ACADEMIC PROFESSION

1002, 1066, 1238, 1516, 1541, 1610, 1611, 1978, 2122, 2189, 2198, 2302, 2471, 2489, 2840, 3019, 3038, 3039.

STUDENTS AND STUDENT ACTIVISM

934, 944, 983, 1035, 1067, 1094, 1135, 1228, 1252, 1309, 1328, 1330, 1346, 1356, 1385, 1394, 1396, 1434, 1445, 1479, 1511, 1512, 1564, 1573, 1597, 1621, 1642, 1691, 1755, 1763, 1765, 1782, 1786, 1869, 1888, 1920, 2019, 2028, 2053, 2164, 2197, 2204, 2433, 2461, 2473, 2477, 2482, 2487, 2508, 2514, 2515, 2521, 2529, 2557, 2574, 2577, 2588, 2635, 2664, 2679, 2681, 2683, 2689, 2699, 2730, 2764, 2810, 2852, 2878, 2891, 2900, 2961, 2964, 2972.

BIBLIOGRAPHIES

912, 913, 914, 915, 916, 917, 918, 919, 920, 921, 922, 923, 924, 925, 926, 927, 928, 929, 930, 931, 1361, 1362, 1428, 1438, 1440, 1456, 1457, 1468, 1469, 1482, 1519, 1535, 1561, 1596, 1600, 1605, 1624, 1627, 1679, 1806, 1810, 1811, 1812, 1813, 1878, 1879, 1942, 1963, 2055, 2135, 2178, 2236, 2281, 2282, 2303, 2319, 2385, 2401, 2472, 2501.

ABOUT THE AUTHORS

PHILIP G. ALTBACH is Professor and Chairman, Department of Social Foundations of Education, Professor of Higher Education and Director of the Comparative Education Center, State University of New York at Buffalo. He edits the *Comparative Education Review* and serves as advisory editor to the Praeger Comparative Education Series. He is author of *Comparative Higher Education* (1979), *Publishing in the Third World* (1980), coeditor of *Education and Colonialism* (1978), and other books.

GAIL P. KELLY is Associate Professor of Social Foundations of Education at the State University of New York at Buffalo. She is associate editor of the *Comparative Education Review*. She is coeditor of *Education and Colonialism* (1978) and author of *From Vietnam to America* (1978). She has recently edited a volume on women and education in the Third World.

DAVID H. KELLY teaches at D'Youville College, Buffalo, New York. He is coauthor of *American Students* (1963) and *Higher Education in Developing Nations* (1974).